Lm. Phërö Ngô Minh Nhật

GOD'S HUMAN FACE

CHRISTOPH SCHÖNBORN, O.P.

God's Human Face

The Christ-Icon

Translated by Lothar Krauth

IGNATIUS PRESS   SAN FRANCISCO

Originally published as *L'Icône du Christ. Fondements théologiques élaborés entre le Ier et le IIe Concile de Nicée (325–787 A.D.)*, Editions Universitaires, 2nd ed. (Fribourg, 1976, 1978); Coll. Paradosis XXIV. This translation was made from the German edition, *Die Christus-Ikone. Eine theologische Hinfuhrung* (Schaffhausen, Germany: Novalis Verlag, 1984).

Cover design by Roxanne Mei Lum
Cover illustration: Christ the Pantocrator
Encaustic icon, 6th century (detail)
Photo by J. Galley-Schwitter A. G. (Basel)

ISBN 0–89870–514–2
Library of Congress catalogue number 94–75957
Printed in the United States of America

In memory of

Father Marie-Joseph Le Guillou, O.P.
(1920–1990)

whose help and fraternal guidance
made this work possible

CONTENTS

ABBREVIATIONS

BKV	*Bibliothek der Kirchenväter* (Kempten and Munich, 1913ff.).
CC	Origen, Contra Celsum.
CM	Eusebius of Caesarea, Contra Marcellum, *GCS* Eusebius Werke, vol. 6.
CSCO	Corpus Scriptorum Christianorum Orientalium
DE	Eusebius of Caesarea, Demonstratio evangelica, vol. 6.
DS	Henricus Denzinger and Adolfus Schönmetzer, S.J., *Enchiridion Symbolorum* (Barcelona, Freiburg, Rome: Herder, 1976).
ET	Eusebius of Caesarea, De Ecclesiastica Theologia, vol. 6.
GCS	*Griechische Christliche Schriftsteller der ersten drei Jahrhunderte* (Leipzig and Berlin, 1897ff.).
HE	Eusebius of Caesarea, Historia Ecclesiastica, vol. 2.
JTS	*Journal of Theological Studies,* new series (1949ff.).
LC	Eusebius of Caesarea, Laus Constantini, vol. 1.
Mansi	J. D. Mansi, *Sanctorum conciliorum nova et amplissima collectio* (Florence, 1759ff.).
PA	Origen, Peri Archôn.
PE	Eusebius of Caesarea, Praeparatio Evangelica, vol. 8.
PG	J. P. Migne, ed., *Patrologiae cursus, series graeca* (Paris, 1857ff.).

PL   J. P. Migne, ed., *Patrologiae cursus, series latina* (Paris, 1844ff.).

SC   *Sources chrétiennes* (Paris, 1941ff.).

Thgr   Eusebius of Caesarea, Theophania, Greek fragments, vol. 3.

Ths   Eusebius of Caesarea, Theophania, Syrian translation, vol. 3.

TRE   *Theologische Realenzyklopädie* (Berlin and New York, 1977ff.).

ZKG   *Zeitschrift für Kirchengeschichte*

PREFACE
TO THE 1984 EDITION

Another book on icons? Yes, and No! This book deals from beginning to end with icons, and yet icons as such are given relatively little specific attention. The topic of this book concerns those foundations without which there would be no icons, and without which the entire meaning of icons could not truly be grasped: the theological, and more precisely, the christological foundations.

There exist numerous historical studies on the artistic aspect of the icons. Yet the basic idea on which iconographic art primarily is built has seldom been studied: *the Christian doctrine of the Incarnation of God.* God has taken on a human face, and this face is the privileged venue of his revelation. This conviction nourishes the art of the icon, not only in its subject matter but even in its very own and distinct technique. *This* is the mystery it wants to express. The fascination still surrounding iconic art even in our own day may well be rooted here.

This book, written in French [in 1973] and published [in 1976], now [in 1983] presented in a thoroughly revised German edition, owes its existence to such a fascination. It began with a totally neglected, worm-eaten, not particularly artistic or valuable icon of Christ that was given to the author rather by accident (see illustration no. 1). It might be that the dilapidated condition of the icon contributed to the aura of mystery surrounding it. It was, above all, *this face:* serious and gentle, almost sad, remote and yet appealingly familiar. Always this face, in countless variations, in faithful copies made from copies of ancient icons, multiform and diverse—and yet always the same face.

The history of iconographic art is *primarily* the ever-new story

of the encounter with this face. It is repeated unceasingly and
never fully achieved. It has often been said that iconographic art is
stiff and sterile, because it endlessly repeats the ancient patterns.
This criticism misunderstands the icon. Never is it a mere mechani-
cal copy of its model; it is always a new encounter with the
inexhaustible mystery of this face.

The human face of God: this is the topic of the present book, and
to that extent, it is a book on icons. Artists and theologians have
meditated on the mystery of this face, trying to depict it. The
purpose of this book is to attempt to unseal the wellsprings of this
meditation, as nowadays they are widely forgotten, appear strange,
or are even entirely lost. These sources are first of all the Church
Fathers, those great teachers of the early Church. It is in their
meditations on Christ that we search for the wellsprings of the
iconic art. The reader, not unlike this writer himself, will perhaps
at first be somewhat baffled by the unfamiliar language, terminology,
and mental framework of these ancient masters. The more the
reader dares to enter in, the more he will be fascinated by the
depth and vitality of patristic theology, and the more he will
realize that the word of the Church Fathers is akin to the image
the artists put on the icon. The christological meditation of the
Church Fathers shall lead to a deeper understanding of the icon
and, beyond that, inspire an encounter with him who has inspired
the masters of the theological word and the sacred image.

Compared to the French edition, certain parts have been revised,
even considerably: the footnotes have been thoroughly simplified;
certain overly "technical" expositions have been dropped; a few
chapters have been revised (such as the sections on Origen and
John Damascene); some chapters have been rearranged, and several historical explanations concerning the icon controversy have
been added. New, above all, are the illustrations, which will, we
hope, add clarity to the text. In all this, we were guided by the
principle of producing a book as academic as necessary, and as
readable as possible. We followed in this the rule set down by J. H.
Newman concerning the translation of ancient texts: "A translation ought to render the thought of the original as faithfully as
possible. Where a choice has to be made between precision and

Illustration 1

Illustration no. 1: Christ the Pantocrator; icon of unknown origin (Russian? 18th century?). Private ownership.

Photo: L. Hilber (Fribourg).

(See pages xiii and 96.)

ease of comprehension, the latter should be preferred. For a work addressed to a larger audience gains more when non-experts understand it than when the experts sing its praises."

From among the many to whom this writer is indebted, two shall be named: Jean Moser, the director of the Novalis Publishing House, who was the driving force behind the German edition and who accompanied its preparation with patience and sensitivity; and Iso Baumer, whose friendly help with proofreading contributed to its final success.

Retz, Lower Austria,
Feast of St. Maximus Confessor,
August 13, 1983

PART ONE

THE THEOLOGICAL FOUNDATIONS
OF THE ICON

Chapter One

The Trinitarian Foundations

I. The Eternal Image

Paul says of Christ: "He is the image of the invisible God" (Col 1:15), and Christ himself says to Philip: "Whoever has seen me, has seen the Father" (Jn 14:9). In the Son we see the Father; for "nobody has ever seen God; the Son, the only-begotten One, who is in the Father's bosom, he has made him known" (Jn 1:18).

The Son, therefore, is the image of the Father. What, then, has this statement of the New Testament to do with the image of Christ, the icon of Christ? At first sight, we seem to be dealing here with two entirely different matters. In truth, however, they are intimately connected; this at least was the conviction during the era we are considering here, on the part of proponents and opponents of icons alike. The arguments of the opponents, for instance, ran like this: it is impossible to paint an image of Christ; for this would amount to the attempt of depicting and grasping the divine nature of Christ. To which the proponents of icons replied: If the Word has truly become flesh and has dwelled among us (Jn 1:14), then this Word has become a reality that can be depicted and described; then the Eternal Word of God can be represented in an image.

This dramatic question was to be at the center of the icon controversy of the eighth and ninth centuries (726–843 A.D.) and with it, the question about the meaning and the possibility of representing and actualizing what is divine through the medium of human art. But before we, in Part Two of this book, consider the details of this debate, we shall first identify the theological roots of the problem. Christian theology finds the deepest and ultimate foundation of any such pictorial representation in the Trinity: God, the primal source and wellspring of all, has a most complete and perfect image of himself—the Son, the Eternal Word. Our initial step, therefore, will serve to clarify this intrinsic divine image as the archetype of all representation in image. We shall be guided in this by the Church Fathers of the fourth century, those unsurpassed masters in trinitarian theology. The second stage, then, will reflect on the Incarnation of the Eternal Word, to find out in what sense the Son, as incarnate, is the *perfect* image of the Father, that is, in what sense a human face can be the perfect image of God. Only after we have fathomed as best we can these dimensions of pictorial representation will the question about the "sacred images", about the artistic expression of the inexpressible mystery, show its far-reaching importance.

1. *The Place of Images in the System of Arius*[1]

We begin our investigation into the trinitarian foundations of icon theology with the first serious crisis facing the Catholic Faith (excepting the Gnostic problem of the second century), the Arian crisis. How does Arius (d. 336 A.D.) interpret the Scripture passages quoted above? Fundamental and central to the theory of the Alexandrian presbyter is the word of Scripture, "Hear, O Israel, the Lord, your God, is one."[2] In his "Creed", Arius professes, "one only God, and him alone uncreated, him alone eternal, him alone without beginning, him alone all-true, him alone immortal".[3] God is one, and consequently anything affecting his oneness has to be rejected. Arius' God is alone, a lonely God: "He alone is wisdom, he alone is goodness, he alone is almighty."[4] Nothing can compare to him: "He alone has no equal; nobody

---

[1] Cf. the article "Arianismus", in TRE, vol. 3, 692–719.
[2] Dt 6:4; cf. Hilarius PL 10, 108A, and Athanasius PG 26, 39C.
[3] PG 26, 708D.
[4] PG 26, 798D.

compares to him or is on a par with him in dignity",[5] nobody—not even the one whom Christians worship as his Son! The primary intention of the Arian faith is to safeguard the absolutely solitary God: "Just as God is *monad* and origin of all that is, so he is also *before* all things; he, therefore, is even before the Son."[6]

All the other statements flow from this basic principle. How, then, would Arius understand the word of St. Paul when he speaks of Christ as "the image of the invisible God"? Since God is absolutely one and only, nothing can resemble him. The Son can be his image only in the distortion of utter dissimilarity. Between God and anything that is not God, there always remains an unbridgeable abyss: the absolute difference between uncreated and created reality. God's eternal solitude alone constitutes the realm of the uncreated. The Trinity, therefore, professed by the Christian Faith, is for Arius a triad, "not composed of three equal dignities, for its substances [hypostases] are not intermingled; the one (of the Father) is of infinitely greater dignity than the other (of the Son)."[7]

Arius speaks of three hypostases, yet understands this term, without doubt, in the classical sense of "substance". Thus he declares about the Son that "nothing in his own substance [hypostasis] is inherently of God; for he is not God's equal, nor is he of the same nature."[8] God cannot beget a Son who would be equally eternal and whose nature would be identical to his, lest one should proclaim the presence in God of two equally eternal principles and divide the divine "monad" the way Sabellius did.[9] Arius cannot conceive the begetting of the Eternal Son to be a purely spiritual and immanent generation: "Before he [the Son] was begotten or created . . . he was not; for he was not unbe-

---

[5] PG 26, 705D.
[6] PG 26, 708C; cf. 709A.
[7] PG 26, 705D–708A.
[8] PG 26, 705D–708A.
[9] PG 26, 709A and 709C–712A.

gotten."[10] God became Father only when he generated the Son.[11] The name of "Father", therefore, cannot denote the essential and eternal nature of God, just as the name of "Son" does not proclaim an eternal relationship[12] but merely the attribute of someone who was created and who was adopted by God as Son.[13] Within the context of this radical difference between God and the Word, there is also situated the only known text by Arius that refers to "image":

> Know, then, that there was the *monas;* but the *dyas* [twofold existence] was not until it came into being. As long as the Son is not, God is not Father. At first the Son was not (but then began to exist by the will of the Father); he alone is the God who came into being, and each of the two is dissimilar one to the other. . . . He, then, is known by countless names, such as spirit, power, wisdom, God's radiance, truth, *image,* Logos.[14]

Arius sees the attribute "image of God" as one of the gifts the Son has received from the Father when the latter created him, or "drew him out of the void".[15] The Son can be God's image only within the limiting confines of his own created nature: "It is evident that he who has a beginning and an origin is unable to absorb the true essence of the One who has no origin."[16] Because the Son is unable to "know the Father as to his intrinsic nature (for the Son does not even know his own nature)",[17] he is even less able to make the Father visible, to be his *perfect* image. Therefore, he cannot be the perfect revelation of the Father. He cannot reveal more than what he himself is: a created being. Arius' God remains captive in his impenetrable solitude: he is unable to confer his own

[10] Letter to Eusebius of Nicomedia, in *Athanasius Werke,* ed. H. G. Opitz, vol. 2, 3, 5; cf. PG 26, 57C.

[11] PG 26, 21A.

[12] PG 26, 709BC.

[13] PG 26, 705D.

[14] PG 26, 708AB; trans. A. Grillmeier, *Jesus der Christus im Glauben der Kirche,* vol. 1 (Freiburg, 1979), 373.

[15] Letter to Eusebius, vol. 2, 3, 5.

[16] PG 26, 708C.

[17] PG 26, 708B.

life fully on the Son. To safeguard God's transcendence, Arius fashions the one and supreme God into a prisoner of his own grandeur.

Arius, invoking a radical and complete transcendence, wholly separates God from the world. This God could not be Trinity; for he was seen only through the projection of the human categories of domination and submission, as a God whose glory it is to rule,[18] not to give himself and share his life. Such a conception basically destroys the true transcendence of the "God and Father of our Lord Jesus Christ", a transcendence that is manifested precisely in its sovereign freedom to give itself completely to the Son and the Holy Spirit without calling into question its own sovereignty. This, it seems to us, is the true reason for Arius' heresy: too small a conception of God; a God who jealously watches his divinity for fear of being robbed of this possession.[19]

What does all of this have to do with the problem of Christianity's sacred images? It is decisive! For Arianism not only destroys the Christian conception of God, but the dignity of creation as well. Creation, for Arius, is not the direct work of God but the product of a created "intermediate agent": the work of the Son.[20] In such a conception, can creation still proclaim the Creator? This seems all the more impossible as God fashions his creation through the mediation of a Word that in essence is dissimilar to God.

We shall have to face the question whether a connection exists between the iconoclastic movement and Arianism. This much can be said already: if creation does not make the Creator transparent, then it is impossible for any art to represent, within the realm of created things, what is uncreated and divine. And if the Son cannot be the perfect image and the complete revelation of the Father, then the possibility of a Christian art is cut off at its roots. For all Christian art, in the minds of the defenders of the sacred

---

[18] "God rules over him [Christ]; for he is his God and he is prior to him" (PG 26, 709C).

[19] Cf. PG 26, 709B.

[20] The Arians, according to Athanasius, taught that the Logos was created by God as mediator, because God saw that finite beings were incapable of having direct participation in him (PG 26, 200A; cf. PG 25, 437A).

images, is based on the principle that Christ is "the image of the invisible God".

2. *Athanasius: The Word as Consubstantial Image*[21]

The anti-Arian reaction on the part of the great Alexandrian Athanasius (295–373 A.D.) was energetic and fearless. Four times, Athanasius paid the price of exile for his steadfastness. Arius' doctrine claimed to be reasonable and coherent. It was important, therefore, to show that the Christian Faith, though transcending our power of reason, nevertheless was ultimately more in line with human reason than the speculations of the presbyter Arius. The Council of Nicea, refuting Arius' doctrine in 325 A.D., could not yet produce such evidence. It is the role of a council to *profess* the Faith, not to explain it: this would be the task of theologians and doctors of the Church.

Athanasius is the eminent figure connected with the theological underpinning of the Nicene Creed. With unfailing insight into the existential, salvific content of the Christian creed, he exposed the shortcomings of the Arian speculation. Athanasius is thus able to show that Arius' position flows from a fundamental misconception of God's transcendence. If we want to approach this transcendence, we have to go beyond our purely human categories. Scripture testifies to Christ as "the only-begotten Son" of the Father (Jn 1:14, 18). In order to understand here the meaning of the term "begotten", we have to look at the one to whom it is applied:

> It is evident that God does not beget as men do, but in God's way. For it is not God who imitates man; rather, men are called "fathers" of their children because of God who alone and in the strict sense is truly Father of his Son, for "from him all fatherhood in heaven and on earth takes its title" (Eph 3:15).[22]

To call God "Father" does not denote something accidental in

[21] Regarding Athanasius' Christology, cf. the corresponding chapter in the great work by Grillmeier, *Jesus der Christus,* 460–79.
[22] PG 26, 60BC.

him, the way it is applied to men. God *is* Father; he is the one and only true Father. Arius has it totally different; for him, God *becomes* Father only after having created the Word: for Arius, the title "Father" cannot be of God's essence. Arius' God resides in inaccessible transcendence, which he never leaves. Of him we shall never see anything else but those things that his will, in total sovereignty, has determined and created. His creations never reveal *him, in himself.*

Not so the conception of transcendence as held by Athanasius: if God *is* Father, then he is so eternally, and the Son is in the same way eternal. Yet the divine Fatherhood must indeed be understood "in God's way"; the Son, to be truly *his image,* must possess the divine attributes of the Father:

> And so, let us consider the attributes of the Father, in order to ascertain whether the image truly represents him. Eternal is the Father, immortal, powerful, radiant light, king, almighty God, Lord, creator, and sculptor. All this has to be present in the image as well, so that whoever has seen the Son has in truth seen the Father (cf. Jn 14:9). If, however, this is not the case, but if on the contrary, as the Arians hold, the Son has come into existence and was not from all eternity, then he is not the true image of the Father, unless the Arians shamelessly contend that the attribute of "image" as chosen for the Son does not denote a similar nature but is only [an extrinsic] way of speaking.[23]

The "shameless" contention of the Arians that the designation of Christ as the "image" of God would be proof that Christ is inferior to God, is nothing else but the Greco-Hellenistic conception of the image, according to which the image, of course, is inferior to the original it depicts. The Arian Logos of God is the image of God in the same sense as Greek philosophy understood an image: it is a reflection, a poor imitation of an unreachable original. Since it belongs to the changeable world of visible things, it can never capture the complete fullness of its singular, unchangeable original.

The conception of Athanasius, in contrast, affirms the paradox

---

[23] PG 26, 56A.

of a *perfect image,* an image not lacking anything of the perfection present in its original: God has an image of himself that is equal to him in every respect of dignity and essence. This, for Athanasius, is the very real sense of Christ's words, "I and the Father are one" (Jn 10:30), and, "All that belongs to the Father, belongs to me" (Jn 16:15).

> The Son is indeed in the Father, as is quite obvious, because the total being of the Son inheres in the substance of the Father, just as brightness comes from light and a river from its source; consequently, whoever sees the Son, also sees what is essential to the Father, and understands that the existence of the Son, being from the Father, is also in the Father.
>
> But there is also the Father in the Son, because that which originates from the Father and is essential to him, is the Son, in the same way as the sun is in the brightness, the spirit in the word, and the river in the source. Whoever sees the Son, therefore, also sees what belongs to the substance of the Father, and understands that the Father is in the Son. Since the form and the divinity of the Father constitute the being of the Son, it follows that the Son is in the Father, and the Father in the Son.[24]

There exists between Father and Son a perfect ontological union. The Son is "true God from true God"; he is, in Athanasius' words, "the most perfect offspring of the Father, uniquely Son and immutably the image of the Father".[25] Because the Christian Faith accords the Son divinity, and because it cannot admit "degrees" in divinity, therefore the notion of "image" undergoes a fundamental correction, with important consequences for the concept of the arts: between the divine original and the divine image there is no longer any ontological gradation. Within the context of trinitarian theology, the concept of "image" loses all connotation of inferiority. The Son is the *consubstantial image* of the Father. This paradoxical notion of an image consubstantial with its original logically necessitates that any aspect of participation is excluded:

[24] PG 26, 328AB.
[25] PG 25, 93C.

the Word does not participate in God, he *is* God. The relation between God and the Word is not as Plotinus has it between his "One" and his first emanation. Against such a conception of participation, Athanasius advances an argument based on a theology of salvation: "If the Word were God and the consubstantial image of the Father only through participation and not in himself, he could not confer divine status on others; for he would first have to be made divine himself (through participation)."[26]

For the same reason, then, Athanasius judges insufficient the Arian conception of the Logos being like God through obedience and merit. The Word not only is *like* God, he *is* God. While such likeness would express only a certain *mode* of being, we are in contrast dealing here with an *identity* in essence: the Son is, in Athanasius' words, "the offspring of the Father's essence".[27] The Catholic Faith thus professes these paradoxes: identity between Father and Son without an intermingling taking place; the Son's origin out of the Father without such origin implying inferiority; an image that emanates from God himself and yet possesses everything found in God: God himself has a perfect image of himself.

Through the revelation of the mystery of the Trinity, a new dimension of the meaning of image *has opened up.* The Arian conception of "image" lacks this new dimension. The Church Fathers knew very well that the trinitarian concept of "image" lies beyond anything conceivable on the level of created beings. Gregory of Nazianzus, the great teacher of trinitarian theology, has expressed this in the following clear formulation:

> He is called "image" because he is of the same essence as the Father and springs from him, while the Father does not spring from him. It is true that it is the nature of every image to be a likeness of an original, but here we have more. Normally, there is the lifeless [image] of a living being, but here we have the living [image] of a living being, much more similar than Seth is similar to Adam, or the offspring to his parent. Noncomposite things by their nature do not resemble each other in this but

[26] PG 26, 784B.
[27] PG 26, 756C.

not in that; instead, one thing as a whole is a likeness of another as a whole, or rather: the one is identical to the other; it is not an imitation.[28]

The concept of "image" here is analogous. It cannot be applied to God and the realm of creation in the same way without at the same time emphasizing the difference. In the area of created things, the dissimilarity between image and original is always greater than the similarity. Yet in the absolutely simple, noncomposite essence of God, likeness and original are perfectly one. With this, the main argument of the Arians is turned against them: God's noncomposite essence does not exclude the Word but, on the contrary, includes him. To illustrate this oneness of being between Father and Son, Athanasius employs a comparison that later on, in the iconoclastic controversy, would frequently be quoted:

That "whoever has seen the Son has seen the Father" ... may become more palpable and understandable through the image of the emperor. The image shows the form and features of the emperor, and the emperor shows the form represented in the image. For the image of the emperor shows his complete likeness, so that whoever looks at the image will see in it the emperor, and whoever sees then the emperor, will recognize the one he saw in the image. Since there exists a complete likeness, the image could say to him who, after having gazed on the image, desires in addition to see the emperor himself: "I and the emperor are one; for I am in him, and he is in me; and whatever you see in me, you also see in him, and whatever you have seen in him, you also see in me." He, therefore, who honors the image, also honors the emperor in it; for it contains his form and shows his features.[29]

Athanasius here refers to the ancient custom, continued with certain adaptations in the christianized empire, of honoring the

---

[28] Or. XXX (Theol. IV), 20, PG 36, 129BC; trans. J. Barbel, *Gregor von Nazianz, Die fünf theologischen Reden* (Düsseldorf, 1963), 211–13.

[29] PG 26, 332; quoted at the Second Council of Nicea, Mansi 13, 68DE, and also by Theodore the Studite, PG 99, 360B; cf. also PG 25, 24C.

image of a new emperor as though he himself were present. The point of comparison here is not the obvious essential difference between the living person of the emperor and the inanimate material of his image, but rather the similarity between the two that makes it possible to say, "Whoever has seen the icon of the emperor, has seen the emperor himself." Those who defended the veneration of images would later adapt this comparison in a way suitable to their agenda. Athanasius simply employs the comparison to demonstrate the *unity* of the divine nature in the distinction of the persons.

Our search for the fundamentals of icon theology can hardly overestimate Athanasius' contribution: by countering Arianism with the paradoxical concept of a perfect and consubstantial image of the Father, he defended, against the overwhelming presence of the Greek notion of images, the full reality of revelation. Only if the Son is the Father's *perfect* image, which in no way diminishes the brightness of its original, only then can he reveal the Father without alteration and loss. Only then is the Son the full revelation of the Father, only then is the Son the direct way to the Father. We touch here on the ultimate root of all theology of the icon: God has a perfect icon of himself.

Odo Casel has shown the consequences of this iconology for the development of Christian art:

> Arianism intended to incorporate the separation of God and world, typical of late antiquity, into the Christian dogma. When the Church, in 325 A.D., determined the consubstantiality of Father and Son, in opposition to Arius, it safeguarded the Christian doctrine of salvation against the intrusion of later antiquity's paganism.... The Son not only resembles the Father, but is identical to him; and thus Christ, who remains Son even in his humanity, is the unmediated access to the Father. With this, Christian art finds its justification.[30]

Following the defeat of Arianism, the first depictions of the *Pantocrator* [Christ on his heavenly throne] consequently ap-

---

[30] "Glaube, Gnosis und Mysterium", in *Jahrbuch für Liturgiewissenschaft* (Munster, 1941), 245.

pear:[31] after the divinity of Christ is firmly established in the profession of the Faith, the arts can dare to contemplate his divinity as the perfect image of the Father (see illustrations no. 2 and no. 5, pages 15 and 95).

II. Toward a New Understanding of Personhood

Athanasius is the great teacher of the *homoousios,* the identity in essence between Son and Father. Did not this strong emphasis on the *unity* of essence outweigh the *distinction* of Persons? This criticism, unjustified, was occasionally directed at him.[32] There existed, of course, a real danger of this. As early as the third century, Sabellius and certain other theologians sought to safeguard the oneness of God by envisioning Father, Son, and Holy Spirit not as distinct Persons but as merely different manifestations of the one God (Modalism or Sabellianism). This approach, it is true, avoided the conceptual difficulty of positing in God both the oneness of substance and the distinction of Persons. But it contradicted all too clearly the realities of the actual history of revelation, which shows Christ as Person in relation to God the Father. How, then, could a rational mind account for the real distinction of Divine Persons without at the same time jettisoning the oneness of essence and professing three gods?

The Church Fathers of the fourth century, the great teachers of trinitarian theology, were well aware that the triune God is a mystery, even *the* ineffable mystery of all. Yet this did not lead them to consider themselves absolved from the seeking a rational approach to this mystery. The achievements of theology in the fourth century, leading the human mind in the light of the revealed mystery toward new insights and new dimensions, are among the

---

[31] Cf. A. Stange, *Das frühchristliche Kirchengebäude als Bild des Himmels* (Cologne, 1950), 80–87.

[32] For example, F. Loofs, *Leitfaden zum Studium der Dogmengeschichte,* 4th ed. (Halle, 1906), 241.

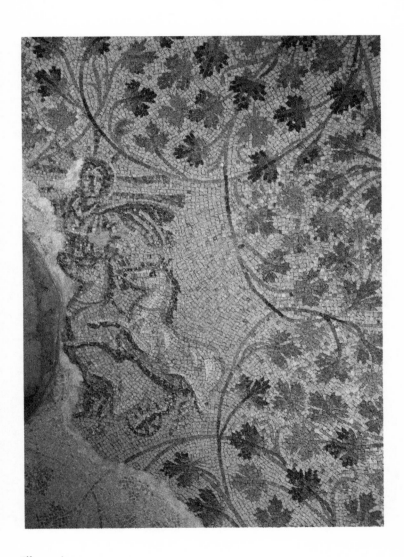

Illustration 2

Illustration number 2: Christus Helios. Ceiling mosaic in the Julian crypt (below St. Peter's Basilica), Vatican City, early 3rd century.

Photo: A. Held (Lausanne).

The iconography of the crypt leaves no doubt about the Christian character of this mosaic. Christ here is depicted as the *Sol Invictus,* the "Invincible Sun", through the image of the Sun God carried by two steeds up to the zenith of the sky.

Othmar Perler devoted a separate study to this mosaic: *Die Mosaiken der Juliergruft im Vatikan* (Freiburg, 1953), 29–32. He interprets its meaning as follows: "It represents *Christ at the moment of his victorious ascension from Hades to the Father on Easter Day, or rather, on Easter Night.* The background of a pale yellow, against which stand out the dazzlingly white Sol and his team of horses, corresponds to the gloomy dungeon whose darkness had given way to a 'pale light' (Prudentius). The impetuously rearing horses, the flapping chlamys [Greek short cloak], the disproportionally large figure of the Lord, his head, erect and turned sideways, the gaze going upward, all are expressions of power and victory, of yearning for the Father, of being immersed in God. The wide halo, the rays flashing upward and sideward, heighten the appearance and splendor of someone triumphant, divine. The globe in his left hand is a symbol of power over the universe: the Risen One, the Exalted One . . . is Lord and King of the world (Ps 24; Acts 2:36). The extended right hand is . . . rather dismissive. Head and eyes are not turned in this direction. The enemy is vanquished. The destination is assured, but heaven itself has not yet been reached. . . . We do not, therefore, behold here a realistic depiction . . . but rather a symbolic-allegorical representation, clothed in the image of the sun, of Christ's ascent from Hades to heaven. . . . We might call this mosaic a visualization of the Easter mystery."

(See page 14.)

greatest feats in the history of human thought. To express what was so utterly new in revelation, a fabric of new concepts had to be developed. Concepts that nowadays have become accepted and common property were created or reinterpreted during that era. The most prominent among these mental, theological progeny is the concept of *person*.

1. The hypostasis *Controversy*

How could the oneness of essence and the distinction of Persons in trinitarian theology be shaped into concepts? The language of Greek philosophy had not provided any conceptual framework for this, as it could not have known the subject matter in question, until, through revelation, it stood before the human mind as a challenge. When the first Christians began to profess Jesus of Nazareth as the Son of God, applied divine attributes to him, and worshipped him as God together with God the Father of Jesus Christ and in the Holy Spirit, they were also urged to explain what they did and believed to those who did not share their Faith. Did they not deny being polytheists, which was the reproach on the part of those Jews who did not accept Jesus as Messiah? How, then, could they reconcile the profession of the *one* God with the worship of Father, Son, and Holy Spirit? Of course, a simple faith found the answer where Athanasius, in the end, would look for it: in the words of Jesus himself, transmitted by the evangelists, "I and the Father are one" (Jn 10:30). Yet when the question arose — why this *oneness* would not eliminate the distinction between Father and Son, and why this *distinction* would not destroy the oneness — then the effort of finding a conceptual answer as well could not be avoided.

The Council of Nicea, with its *homoousios,* intended to profess both, oneness and distinction. In fact, the great controversies began only *after* the Council. Two-thirds of this fourth century would pass in endless disputes, intrigues, and divisions, before the matter was finally clarified and the combatants found peace: it was one of the most painful periods of Church history! One of the elements on which the crisis focused was the vagueness of the concepts employed in the debate. The two key concepts, *ousia* and *hypostasis,* especially triggered unending misunderstandings. Nowadays, we translate these two concepts without hesitation as *essence* and *person.* How vaguely defined they were at the time of the Nicean Council is shown by the fact that the *anathema* attached to the Council's creed condemns those who affirm that the Son would have a hypostasis or *ousia* different from the Father (DS 126). Did both terms mean the same to the Council Fathers at Nicea? The terminology of the Latin Fathers complicated the matter even further. Since the time of Tertullian, they had been wont to distinguish *persona* and *substantia,* and to use *prosôpon* and hypostasis as Greek equivalents. There is no need for us to retrace the labyrinthine course of these disputes that are treated in the history of theology as the "hypostasis controversy".[33] We limit ourselves to what is important for our topic. Recalling Athanasius, we see this focused in the question: how is it possible that a Divine Person (the Son) is the perfect image of another Divine Person precisely in those aspects that are *proper* to him and therefore distinguish one from the other? For a clearer picture, we shall briefly follow the explanations of the Cappadocians (Basil, Gregory of Nazianzus, Gregory of Nyssa), who decisively contributed to the clarification of the trinitarian concept of personhood.

2. *Nature and Person*

Clarifying the terminology of trinitarian theology was one of the most urgent tasks in an era that discussed theological questions with utmost seriousness and impassioned involvement. A decisive document of this clarifying process is the treatise, "On the distinction between *ousia* (essence) and hypostasis (person)", traditionally ascribed as the 38th letter of Basil of Caesarea, but nowadays attributed, for solid reasons, to his younger brother, Gregory of

[33] On this cf. T. de Regnon, *Etudes sur la Sainte Trinité* (Paris, 1892), vol. I, 167–215.

Nyssa.[34] What follows here stays close to the expositions of this treatise; we then shall ask to what extent this treatment of the concept of personhood contributes to a theology of the image.

Gregory sets out stating that the confusion about the meaning of the terms *ousia* and hypostasis demands before anything else a clarification of these concepts. The first approach, therefore, will be of a philological kind, and only then will follow the theological application. The first approach relies on reason, the second flows from faith. Gregory again and again emphasizes that "it is the *doctrine of faith* that teaches the unmixed and undivided difference of the persons" (7, 34f.). The task at hand is to "grasp the glory of the three Persons in the Trinity, professed by faith" (4, 51). This, then, for Gregory, does not simply concern some idle speculation, but the problem that our Faith professes three Divine Persons and our mind desires to find an explanation, to the extent that is possible. Faith, however, is for him the secure medium of cognition: "Just as with regard to things perceived through the senses we obviously gain more by experience than by theorizing about causes, so also with regard to the unfathomable dogmas of faith we profit more through faith than through any understanding based on reasoning" (5, 55–59).

a. *The philological approach to* ousia *and hypostasis*

Gregory, at the beginning of his treatise, leads the reader to a simple linguistic observation. There are two kinds of concepts. One kind denotes many things collectively by meaning what is common to them, such as, for example, the term "man". The other kind denotes something specific, something that is unique and particular and not common to the other individuals of the same nature. Personal names (Peter, Paul) are of this type. They do

---

[34] This was convincingly presented by R. Hübner, "Gregor von Nyssa als Verfasser der sog. Ep. 38 des Basilius", in *Epektasis* (honoring Cardinal Daniélou), ed. J. Fontaine and C. Kannengiesser (Paris, 1972), 463–90. We follow A. Stegmann's translation; "Basilius", BKV vol. 1 (Munich, 1925), 69–80; the numbers refer to paragraph and line of the annotated edition by Y. Courtonne (Paris, 1957), vol. 1, 81–92.

not refer to human nature in general, in which all men share in identical fashion (*homoousioi*), but to those things that make one man different from the other, to a person's specific features. This observation now serves Gregory for his explanation: "The term *hypostasis* describes a thing as individual" (3, 1). Here is sketched out a clear conceptual differentiation: a general concept such as "man" indeed designates the nature (*physis*) of an entity, "but not this entity as existing in and for itself; only a proper name can do this. If, in contrast, you say, 'Paul', you denote the actual subsistence of this nature in the entity so named" (3, 5–8). Twice here, Gregory emphasizes the term *hyphistêmi,* from which the term *hypostasis* is derived and which in Latin is rendered as *subsistere.* "Hypostasis", then, is used by Gregory for that which subsists, which possesses subsistence, that is, independence and individuality: that which gives a general nature its actual concretization. Gregory continues accordingly: this, then, is hypostasis—not the indefinite concept of "essence" (*ousia*), which has not yet a specific standing (*stasis*) and only denotes what is general; but the concept that delineates and circumscribes, based on an entity's peculiar features, what otherwise is general and unspecific in it (3, 8–12).

The choice of "hypostasis" for the actual individual entity, and also for the person, rests first of all on philological reasons. The general concept of "essence" does not yet denote the specific standing (*stasis*) that pertains to a particular entity based on its individual features. To this end, the general concept has to be "circumscribed" in more specific terms. The word *perigraphein,* used by Gregory here, has a very concrete meaning. It literally means "to draw the contours", "to sketch". The words *graphein* and *graphê* still preserve the echo of the artisan's craft that forms the common root of writing and painting: to etch, to carve, to engrave. This determination of "person" as *perigraphê,* as the "circumscribing" and "contouring" of an unspecific, general essence, was to assume again major importance in the icon controversy, when the question arose whether the mystery of Christ's Person could be depicted or not, whether it could be "circumscribed" or not. The direction for the eventual answer was already determined by Gregory of Nyssa: what is captured by the *graphê* of the artist constitutes what is particular, individually distinctive, and specific, so that the one depicted is circumscribed (*perigraphê*) as *this* individual human being; the image is a record of the *person,* not of the general essence, as the theologians would later say when defending the veneration of icons.

Gregory then introduces another concept that eventually would assume major importance. He poses the question as to the particular attributes that circumscribe, within the general essence, the specific hypostasis. For this he uses, as an example, the beginning of the Book of Job. There, Job is presented first as "man", then immediately more precisely as "a man" (*tis*). Following this, according to Gregory, "Scripture characterizes [*charaktêrizei*] him by use of certain particulars", such as name, place, features, and so on. Whatever "circumscribes" the person of Job, therefore, is that which *characterizes* him as *this* man. This new concept is very close to the concept of *perigraphê*. Yet *perigraphein* means the general activity of drawing and sketching certain contours, while *charakterizein* is more specific: it means to engrave and impress in some material the precise features; in a larger sense, it also means to render an exact likeness. The word *charaktêr* not only means "distinguishing feature" but also denotes an engraved, painted, or carved portrait. We shall encounter this concept here repeatedly in just such an application. Because of their double meaning, both abstract and concrete, these two concepts, *perigraphê* and *charaktêr,* would later, in the icon controversy, play a very important role. Gregory of Nyssa uses them to distinguish the person as actual and circumscribed, as "characterized",[35] from the general and unspecific reality of the essence. With this definition of personhood, there is initiated a transition that becomes understandable only against the background of the Christian conception of man: the particular individual, and the unique reality of this singular human being, moves to the center of interest. No longer is the generality of the essence deemed the higher reality, but rather the individual

---

[35] Does this mean only the external features, or also those of the soul? This question is not inconsequential for the image controversy. Gregory seems to have both in mind; cf. 3, 11–12, 21, 25.

personality. The uniqueness of the individual no longer is seen so much as a restriction, always inadequate because limited, of a necessarily general essence—a basic tendency of Greek philosophy—but rather as the more important and significant reality.[36] This gradual growth in emphasis centered on the individual person is a profound process of transformation involving all cultural areas, changing the conception of the arts as well as of history (see illustration no. 3). What triggered and motivated this process was without doubt the awareness, gained within the context of Judeo-Christian revelation, that each man is unique.

b. A theological approach to personhood

But let us continue with Gregory of Nyssa's exposition, which now considers the theological dimension of the topic in question. After having defined the notion of "person" through the pertaining individual characteristics, Gregory now faces the question of how to distinguish the Divine Persons through each one's proper personal attributes. The task requires a search for the distinguishing marks of the Divine Persons without ceasing to see them in their oneness (3, 47).

Athanasius had chiefly discussed the consubstantiality of the Divine Persons. The controversy with the Arians would have made it dangerous to speak too emphatically about the distinctions between the Persons, since the Arians used this to conclude the subordination of the Son under the Father. Gregory is not afraid to tackle the question anew and especially from this angle.

He, too, begins "from the bottom", with the differentiation of

---

[36] We emphasize this aspect, because time and again there appears the assertion that Gregory's approach to the notion of "person" is all too strongly limited by the categories of the "general" and the "particular"; that he defines "person" too one-sidedly by external properties and not sufficiently by the subject of these properties: the person as independent self, as subsistence. We think this critique is justified only in part. It overlooks the fact that for Gregory, contrary to the thrust of Greek philosophy, the *idion*, the particular, is of higher value than the *koinon*, the general. We have seen, too, that Gregory does not at all fail to include the aspect of "subsistence" into his analysis of the person.

Illustration 3

Illustration number 3: Mummy portrait from El Faiyûm, Egypt, 3rd century A.D. (now in Munich, Antique Collection).

Photo: Praun (Munich).

The mummy portraits of El Faiyûm in Egypt, now scattered all over the world, are among the most impressive examples of antique paintings. The encaustic technique (using paint mixed with hot beeswax) succeeds in preserving the incomparable radiance of the colors through the centuries.

The mummy portraits are indicative of a change in the conception of art, a change influenced also by the Jewish-Christian view of man. The interest nowadays would focus on what is individual and personal, rather than what is general and typical. The portrait, it is true, emphasizes certain spiritual qualities, but the image clearly remains a portrait, true-to-life. The "slightly transparent, velvety soft, deeply glowing complexion" (H. Schmid) is an expression of the living vitality of the deceased, in the same way as also the large, shining eyes, which seem to be filled with the splendor of eternal life they now behold. (Is this the first time in art history that the luminous dot is used in the eyes?) Cf. H. Schmid, *Enkaustik und Fresko auf antiker Grundlage* (Munich, 1926), 72f.

We classify the mummy portraits of El Faiyûm as the artistic manifestation of a trend toward a more personalistic attitude, equally found in the philosophy and theology of this era. A comparison with illustrations number 7 and number 8 will show how much the early icons are akin to these portraits.

(See page 22.)

the Persons as they are revealed to us: all the good that God bestows on us is the effect of grace, which works all in all (4, 2–3). Yet this work of the all-effecting grace is not anonymous. Scripture tells us that all this is done "by one and the same Spirit, who gifts each one individually, according to his will and pleasure" (1 Cor 12:11). But the Spirit in turn is not the ultimate source of these salvific gifts: "Scripture leads us to our faith, according to which it is God the only-begotten Son who is the author and source of every good thing prompted in us by the Holy Spirit. For 'all things came to be through him' (Jn 1:3) and 'in him hold together' (Col 1:17)" (4, 8–13). Still, even the Son is not the ultimate source of God's gifts; for Scripture teaches, Gregory continues, that all that exists is created, through the Son, out of nothing; but not as if the Son were the unoriginated origin of it all. This origin is rather the power that exists by itself (*hyphestôsa*), unbegotten and unoriginated; the power that is the causative cause of all that is (4, 14–19).

This unoriginated origin is the Father. It is to him that revelation leads as being the ultimate source, the first cause, the unoriginated origin. The ascent to this origin is the path onto which revelation itself guides us: from the Spirit as the giver of God's gifts, through the Son as the mediator of these gifts, to the Father as the ultimate origin. Gregory contemplates the order of this revelation by looking, once again, at its source: "For from the Father originates the Son, through whom everything is created, and in whom the Holy Spirit is always and inseparably recognized. One cannot think of the Son without having been enlightened by the Holy Spirit" (4, 19–22). The order of revelation corresponds to the order of being. God's actions are revealed to us in a certain order, an order that originates from the Father, is mediated through the Son, and finds fulfillment in the Spirit.

Gregory has chosen this path so that he can lead us to discover what it is that defines the Divine Persons in their mutual relations. One may ask, of course, whether the outward and historical revelation of God through his gifts would be sufficient to understand what defines the Divine Persons within the innermost life of God. Arius sensed this question and tried to answer it by radically separating God's transcendence from his revelation. On one side of the chasm is the one and absolute God, on the other side is God's creation, with the Word as the first of all created beings, the Spirit the second. The activity of this Word and this Spirit, of course, can in no way at all reveal God himself. A *Logos* that is created can reveal only created things, and the chasm between God and the world remains unbridgeable. The order determining the history of revelation and salvation, for which Scripture provides the testimony, could be, in Arius' conception, only the subordination of the Spirit under the Son, and of the Son under the Father. Neither the *Logos* nor the Spirit subordinated under it could reveal God completely and make known God's inner life. Yet this, from the beginning, was the faith and the experience of the Church: that the gift of the Holy Spirit, bestowed on the believer, is the gift of God himself, that communion with Christ is communion with God. The Church Fathers of the fourth century express this in their own language when they say: the gift of salvation, coming to us from Christ in the Holy Spirit, makes us *godlike.* Yet Son and Spirit can make us godlike only if they themselves are God.[37]

The importance of this "fundamental Christian experience" can hardly be overestimated. At the center of this dispute about the trinitarian faith is not some oriental passion to speculate, but the vital reality of this Christian experience. *Herein* lies the absolute significance of the Nicene *homoousios:* because Son and Holy Spirit are consubstantial with the Father—and only under this condition—they can make known and reveal God. The reverse, then, also applies: the salvific activity of the Son and the Holy Spirit reveals this consubstantiality. Then it is true, in short, that God *acts* in the way that he *is,* and since his activity is trinitarian, he *is* Trinity. It further follows that the specific activity of each Divine Person corresponds to each one's specific *being* as Person. For *this* reason are we able to make the step from God's revelation

---

[37] Cf. Athanasius PG 26, 296AB; Gregory of Nazianzus, Or. 31, 28 SC 250, 335; and many others; cf. J. Gross, *La divinisation du chrétien d'après les Pères Grecs* (Paris, 1938).

to his essence.[38] The importance of all this for the theology of the icon will become, we trust, ever more obvious as we continue. This much can be said already here: without these fundamentals, we are unable to comprehend why the icon is conceived as a medium of God's self-revelation and God's presence.

What are, according to Gregory, the properties of the Divine Persons? The Holy Spirit has as his defining property that "he is known after and with the Son, and that he subsists in procession from the Father [*hyphestanai*]" (4, 27–29). The specific property of the Son is that "he, through and in himself, reveals the Holy Spirit who proceeds from the Father, and that he, the only-begotten one, shines as light from the unbegotten light [from the Father]" (4, 29–32). "Regarding God the Almighty, it is the unique property of his hypostasis that he is Father, and that his being is entirely uncaused [*hypostênai*]" (4, 35–38).

These Person-specific properties are the absolutely immediate and unique particularities possessed individually by each of the three Divine Persons (cf. 4, 38–43). The question arises whether this strong emphasis on complete distinction might not endanger the divine oneness. This, however, would be a serious misunderstanding. Let us consider more closely in what the properties of the Divine Persons consist: it is *proper* to the Holy Spirit to proceed from the Father (4, 30) and to be known with the Son; it is *proper* to the Son to be begotten by the Father and to reveal the Spirit. Each Person's own *property,* therefore, is nothing else but the specific way in which this Person relates to the *other* Persons. True, the properties are unmediated and unique, but at the same time, they are also the most perfect manifestation of the ineffable unity that is God: Father, Son, and Holy Spirit—"a new and paradoxical unified differentiation and differentiated unity" (4, 89f.). Gregory illustrates this unity with the image of a chain, in which, as soon as one link is moved, all the links move. The oneness of the Divine Persons, then, is built on the fact that each

---

[38] The roles of the Divine Persons in the economy of salvation reveal their intrinsic and original divine correlations: cf. Athanasius PG 26, 36BC; PG 28, 117C.

Person's property consists precisely in that Person's absolute relatedness to the other two (4, 70–76). *What makes them distinct, also makes them one.* It is easy to foresee the consequences this conception would have for the definition of personhood: the intensive emphasis on the uniqueness of each person is the opposite of a particularizing individualism; for the innermost core of the personal uniqueness already lays the foundation for true community.

c. The Person of the Son as the icon of the Father

We now may once again face the question: How is it possible for the Person of the Son, precisely in his particular property, to be the image of the Father? We have received a preliminary answer: it is the particular property of each of the Divine Persons to reveal each other, since each one's most particular property consists in expressing the other two. For the particular property of each Divine Person is nothing else but each one's particular way of relating to the others, or else, of proceeding from them. When, in the order of revelation, they reveal their specific individual properties, their "ultimate personality", then this becomes the revelation also of the other Divine Persons, especially of the Father who is the "uncaused cause" of the other Divine Persons. Faith teaches that the Son alone knows and reveals the Father (Mt 11:27; Jn 1:18), and that the Spirit alone confers the knowledge of Christ. It is, therefore, the specific property of the Son to reveal the Person of the Father, to be his image. In order to understand the Person of the Son according to his innermost characteristic, we have to investigate in what sense, and how, he is *the image of the Father.*

For this purpose, Gregory engages in an extensive discussion of the well-known and puzzling text in the Letter to the Hebrews (1:3): Christ "is the reflection of (God's) glory and the imprint [*charaktêr*] of his person [*hypostaseôs*]". Because this scriptural passage introduces the concept of hypostasis, it assumes a special importance for Gregory's reasoning, as it obviously constitutes a confirmation by the highest authority, which is Scripture.

At first sight, though, this passage seems to contradict Gregory's purpose. He himself is aware of this difficulty: "Since we have taught that a hypostasis is the sum total of a person's individual properties . . . why, then, does this text apply the concept of hypostasis to the Father alone, and why does Scripture say that the Son is the imprint of (the Father's) hypostasis marked, not by his own properties, but by those of the Father?" (6, 4–12). To put it differently: does this passage not take away the separate existence of the Son? Gregory's response is of particular interest for our inquiry here, because we have already mentioned that the concept of *charaktêr*, employed in the Letter to the Hebrews, has the connotation of "image", "engraving", and "imprint". Gregory, in fact, interpreting the text, starts with this direct meaning of the term *charaktêr*.

We may, so says Gregory, liken the concept of "character" to that of "form": every physical body has a specific form and can be observed only in and with this form. In the same sense, we should also understand the expression, "imprint [*charaktêr*] of his person [*hypostaseôs*]": as the form is inseparable yet distinct from the body, so also is the Son inseparable from the Father whose "imprint" he is. "If we contemplate, with the eyes of the soul, the character of the Son, then we will in the end understand the hypostasis of the Father" (7, 39–42). The principal intention of the text, therefore, aims at emphasizing the intimate and immediate unity between Father and Son. Consequently, Gregory concludes: "He who has seen the Son, has also seen the Father, according to the Lord's word in the Gospel; for this reason the apostle states that the Son is the imprint of the Father's hypostasis" (8, 1–4). Gregory, up to this point, has employed the direct meaning of the term "character" in his interpretation of the Scripture passage in question. Now he analyzes the other concept in this text, the term *hypostasis*. If the term *charaktêr* means the Son, and the term *hypostasis* means the Father, then we might ask whether this formulation is not denying the Son his own hypostasis. In order to show that the Son, on the contrary, can be character or imprint of the Father only if he is a separate hypostasis, Gregory refers to the familiar text in the Letter to the Colossians (1:15): "He is the image of the invisible

God." Here, in the analysis of the concept of "image", we now find the answer to the question considered in this chapter: How can the Person of the Son be the image of the Person of the Father? Gregory begins with a quite surprising definition of "image": "The image is the same as the original [*prôtotypos*], even though it differs from it" (8, 9). And he explains his definition:

> For the concept of "image" could not be sustained at all if it would not imply imprinted and unchangeable characteristics. He who contemplates the beauty of the image will also arrive at the knowledge of the original. And he who has seen, as it were, the form of the Son in the Spirit, has also grasped the imprint of the Person of the Father: we see, after a fashion, the one in the other (8, 10–15).

Thus, then, is the Son the image and the imprint of the hypostasis of the Father. *The beauty of the Son is also the beauty of the Father: it is the only beauty of God.* Yet in the Father it resides in an ungenerated, "fatherlike" way, while in the Son in a communicated, "sonlike" way. This is the meaning of the surprising definition of "image": "It is the same as the original, even though it differs from it." The Son, therefore, is really the image *of the Father,* even though he is "different" from him in being his own hypostasis. Since he is an individual hypostasis, he is able to be the imprint, the character, of the Father's hypostasis. The character of the image would not be preserved if the image were simply identical with the original. Still, he is the same as the original, that is, beauty from beauty, God from God, light from light, even though he "differs", being "begotten" and not ungenerated. If one would use the expression, "He is the imprint of [the Father's] hypostasis", to conclude that the Father alone is a hypostasis, then one would deny that the Son is truly "the image of the invisible God". It is precisely the *proper hypostasis* of the Son that makes us see the hypostasis of the Father. Gregory concludes his skillful but also demanding exposition by summarizing, once again, everything that is important to him, employing the image of the mirror, which he likes to use and which once more brings out the connection to the theology of the image:

Just as he who beholds in a mirror the appearing form gains cognition of the imaged countenance [*prosôpon*], so also does he who knows the Son receive *into his heart,* together with the knowledge of the Son, the imprint of the Person of the Father. For everything that the Father is, is also seen in the Son, and everything that is of the Son is also proper to the Father, because the Son remains completely in the Father, and on his part completely contains the Father. For this reason the Person [hypostasis] of the Son is, as it were, the form and countenance [*prosôpon*] of the perfect cognition of the Father, and the Person of the Father is seen in the form of the Son, while there yet remain the established proprieties of each to allow the distinction of the Persons (8, 19–30).

Gregory, with these words, concludes his famous tract on Essence and Person, which we may characterize, without exaggeration, as some kind of *charter for the theology of the icon: the contemplation of the countenance of the Son imprints in our heart the seal of the Person of the Father.* Because he is the Son of the Father, the Father becomes visible in him. *As Son,* the Word is image and countenance of the Father.

d. *Person and countenance* (hypostasis *and* prosôpon)

Let us try now to summarize the specific results of the debate regarding the terminology used in trinitarian theology. In the first place, we should mention the distinction between essence and person. This distinction between *ousia* and *hypostasis* is a new development in the awareness of the Christian theologians of the fourth century.[39] It was unknown to the pre-Christian philosophers. To them, both concepts had the same meaning.[40] It was a "stroke of genius" on the part of the Cappadocians to differentiate these synonymous concepts and to apply them to those two aspects of the trinitarian mystery that our limited reasoning can never behold in one: the oneness of essence, and yet at the same time the distinction of Persons.

[39] Cf. Theodoret PG 83, 33AB.
[40] Hieronymus points this out: ep. 15,4 PL 22, 357.

The differentiation alone of essence and hypostasis does not suffice, however. One other concept had to be more accurately defined as it relates to these two concepts here: the notion of *prosôpon,* which in common linguistic usage was more closely tied to the Latin concept of *persona* than to the philosophical concept of hypostasis. How does Gregory of Nyssa determine the difference in meaning between *hypostasis* and *prosôpon?* At the conclusion of his exposition on Essence and Person, as we have seen, Gregory states: "The hypostasis of the Son is the form and countenance [*prosôpon*] of the perfect cognition of the Father." Gregory, in this sentence, approves of using the term *prosôpon* for "person", but implicitly also shows its ambiguity, especially when used in isolation. *Prosôpon* here has the meaning of "countenance (in the sense as commonly used in the Greek Bible), yet the term itself, comparable to the Latin *persona,* can also denote "mask" or "role-playing",[41] and it is for this reason that Basil and Gregory hesitate to employ it too freely. For Sabellius had taught this: "God is one according to his hypostasis, but Scripture depicts him through different faces [or masks], depending on specific circumstances, so that he speaks now as Father, now as Son, now as Holy Spirit."[42]

Sabellius took these different *prosôpa* simply as "metamorphoses", different manifestations of a God whom he conceived as one and unique, real subsistence (*hypostasis*). In opposition to this conception, Basil pointed out repeatedly that a *prosôpon,* understood as "countenance" in a concrete sense, is no countenance at all if it is without its own subsistence, its own selfhood, if it is, in Basil's words, *anhypostaton,* without hypostasis.[43] This term, *anhypostaton,* so very important in the subsequent history of theology, shows by its negative form "that it does not suffice to point to the 'faces' [*prosôpa*], as Sabellius did; no, in addition we have to assume that each 'face' has its selfhood in a real hypostasis".[44] Once again we

[41] Cf. Grillmeier, *Jesus der Christus,* 250f.
[42] According to Basilius, Letter 214, 3; Courtonne ed., vol. 2, 204.
[43] Courtonne ed., vol. 2, 205.
[44] Letter 210, 5; Courtonne ed., vol. 2, 196.

can easily surmise what great importance this discussion would assume for a theology of the image!

In order to employ the term *prosôpon* to the full extent of its meaning, that is, in the sense of "proper face" and "personal countenance", we must make sure that any restricted use only as "mask" or "role" is avoided, and that this *prosôpon* is indeed supported by its proper existence, by a subsistence, in short: by a hypostasis, so that this countenance (*prosôpon*) is the expression of a particular person (hypostasis) and not merely a mask hiding this person. The defenders of images were able, based on this theological foundation, to declare that the human countenance of the Word is—paradoxically—the complete expression of the Person (hypostasis) of the Word. But here we are not yet at this point of the development. We still are within the context of trinitarian theology; the christological perspective has not yet come to the fore. Gregory, on his part—by pointing out that every *prosôpon* must be supported by a hypostasis, every "countenance" by a person, in order to be the imprint of that person—has already opened a path for Christology. For if every *prosôpon* expresses the person sustaining it and giving it existence, then this will also be true of the *prosôpon,* the human face, of Christ. Of course, the question arises immediately—and this is the central *theological* question of the icon controversy—in what way a human face could be at all the expression of a divine hypostasis. But let us not get too much ahead of ourselves. Gregory, in relevance to our topic, has above all shown, within a trinitarian perspective, in what way "the Person of the Son is the form and countenance of the perfect cognition of the Father, and the Person of the Father is seen perfectly in the form of the Son" (8, 26–29).

Building on the premises provided us by Athanasius and Gregory of Nyssa, we are now left, as the closing segment of this *trinitarian foundation,* with the questions of *how,* and *in what way and manner,* the Person of the Son is the image of the Father. Gregory of Nyssa, here too, and once again, will be our main guide in this.

III. The Work of the Son as the Image of the Father

In their fight against the Arians, the orthodox found their strongest support in the numerous Scripture texts, especially in John, which speak of the unity of the Son with the Father. There are also passages, however, that seem to present the Son as subordinate to the Father, and the Arians did not hesitate to emphasize those texts. The controversy focused mainly on the famous passage in John 14:28, "The Father is greater than I", and further on passages that show Jesus' humiliation, obedience, and service. Who would deny that here we are often dealing with core texts of revelation? The Arians, consequently, took as their starting point the obedient *work* of the Son within the plan of creation and of salvation, and from there reasoned their way to the essential and ontological subordination of the Son to the Father. Yet it is precisely in his work that the Word is revealed as "the image of the invisible God". We therefore have to ask here in what way the *work* of the Son can be the revelation of the Father.

Within the context of the divine *work,* the danger of misinterpretation was more subtle than the consideration of the divine *nature.* To reject the Son's equality to the Father with regard to the divine nature would contradict the apostolic tradition too bluntly. The problem with regard to the obedient works of the Son presented itself somewhat differently. The Church Fathers before the Council of Nicea had often employed expressions that would seem to imply the inferiority of the Son (Subordinationism). There is but a small step from obedience to subordination, and the Arians made this step. For them it was clear: since the Son is obedient to the Father, he could only be a passive instrument that was moved by the greater power of the Divinity. But if the Word was a mere instrument, what at all could he reveal? How could the hammer, swung by the blacksmith, ever be the image of that blacksmith? How could the passive obedience of an instrument be the living image of him who gave the orders? Once again we are confronted with the insight found in Athanasius: a Word not consubstantial with the Father cannot be his perfect image. It is, therefore, necessary to expand into the realm of the divine work the insights gained relative to the divine nature.

1. *Generation and Subordination*

For the Arians, the fundamental reason for the Word's instrumentality and subordination lies in his being *generated.* Scripture indeed calls Christ the "only-*begotten* Son" (Jn 1:18). The Arians take this as clear proof that the Word is ontologically subordinated to God. It is only logical that they refused to accept the Son as the perfect image of the Father's essence.[45] If, in contrast, we wish to gain some insight as to how the Word, in his work, can be the perfect image of the Father, we have to try, as much as is possible in light of revelation, to ascend to his origin in the Father. The Arians recognized, entirely correctly, namely, that there is a connection between origin and work. This was obvious to them: if the Logos' origins are created, then his work can only be that of a created instrument. In this, they employed an intriguing fallacy: the Son exists either by the will of the Father, or without the will of the Father. If the former, then the Son could also be nonexisting; if the latter, then it would be affirmed that the Father is subject to necessity and thus not free. The "technology"[46] of Eunomius especially uses this kind of argumentation. Let us here retrace the comprehensive refutation by Gregory of Nyssa. It will provide us with valuable insights regarding our topic, the image.

Gregory first unmasks the false dichotomy between will and necessity in God:

> The direct unity of Father and Son does not exclude the will of the Father, as though the Son would have been forced on the unwilling Father by some kind of natural necessity. The will of the Father [to generate the Son], on the other hand, does not

[45] Philostorgius PG 65, 477B.

[46] This seems to be the name Eunomius used for his theology; cf. Theodoret PG 83, 420B.

result in a separation of the two, as though this act of the will would create a separating distance between them.[47]

The Father *wills* to "generate" the Son, yet this willing is everlasting and not bound by the dialectic of desire and fulfillment that marks the human will: "One day we desire something we do not have, on another day we happen to have something we did not want", Gregory remarks ironically.[48] To posit in God a difference between will and being amounts to subjecting him to human limitations. True, the Son is the "only-begotten", therefore willed by the Father; but what God wills is never absent in him.

Athanasius used to confront the Arians with this argument: If God would not always possess his wisdom and his power (Scripture itself applies these terms to the Word), then at one time he would have been without wisdom and power.[49] Following the same line of reasoning, Gregory adds: if the Word exists after the Father, then there would have been a time when God did not possess what he willed—unless one would affirm that God did not will the Son.[50] "The Father alone is origin of everything. Yet in this origin there is also contained the Son, as the Gospel proclaims; in his nature he is what the origin is. For God is the origin, and the Word contained in the origin is God."[51] In these terms, Gregory paraphrases the beginning of John's Gospel.

The generation of the Son, therefore, does not imply subordination; on the contrary, it lies at the heart of that ineffable relationship between Father and Son by which the Son is made the perfect image of the Father. The disrespectful speculations of the Arians on the origin of the Son prompted Gregory of Nazianzus to say words that recommend caution to us as well: "The generation in God is best honored through silence."[52]

If, then, the Son is "begotten" without being inferior in essence

[47] C. Eun. III, VI, 16 PG 45, 773D.
[48] C. Eun. III, IV, 17 PG 45, 776A.
[49] C. Gentes 46 PG 25, 93AC; cf. C. Ar. II, 32 PG 26, 216B.
[50] C. Eun. III, VI, 18 PG 45, 776A.
[51] C. Eun. III, VI, 22 FG 45, 776D–777A.
[52] Or. Theol. III, 8 PG 36, 84C.

to the Father, his work and activity will also be divine. Just as there cannot be a contradiction in God between the free will of the Father and the eternal generation of the Son, so too, there can be no contradiction between the will of the Father and the will of the Son. In a beautiful text in his tract against Eunomius, Gregory meditates on this unity of the divine will. This text has a central importance for our further journey toward a theology of the icon. This exposition was prompted by the Arian contention that the Word is but the passive instrument of God in the creation of the world. For in such a way the Arians interpreted the passage, "through him all things were created" (Col 1:16).

> There is no difference at all between the will of the Son and of the Father. For the Son is the image of the goodness [of God], according to the beauty of the original. When someone gazes into a mirror . . . , his image conforms in every detail to the original that caused the image in the mirror. The mirror-image cannot move unless the movement originates in the original. And when the original moves, the mirror-image, by necessity, moves in the same way.
>
> Just so is the Lord, "the image of the invisible God" (Col 1:15), immediately and inseparably united to the Father whose will he obeys in every movement. The Father wills something. The Son, who is in the Father, wills the same as the Father; or more precisely: he himself becomes the will of the Father. For if he possesses in himself all that the Father possesses, then there is nothing in the Father that he would not possess. And if he has in himself all that belongs to the Father, or rather: the Father himself, and with the Father everything that belongs to the Father, then he also possesses in himself the will of the Father in its entirety.[53]

The illustration of the mirror, favored by Gregory, combines unity and difference: it emphasizes the complete oneness of Father and Son down to the most intimate "movement of the will", and yet preserves the existence of two hypostases. This text constitutes an important step toward a deeper understanding of the christo-

[53] C. Eun. II, 215F. PG 45, 981D–984A; the image of the mirror is found already in Origen, PA I, 2, 12 GCS 22, 45, 10–46, 10.

logical title, "Image of God". For Gregory is showing here that the Son is the image of the Father specifically in his will, which, of course, is not at variance with the Father's will: "The mirror-image, namely, cannot move unless the movement originates in the original." The work of the Son, as a manifestation of his own will, reveals nothing else but the will of the Father; yet not in the manner of a passive instrument, but rather in such a way that the Son makes himself the expression of the Father's will. It is no inconsistency, therefore, that the Father alone is the source and origin of the divine will, while nevertheless the Son himself personally wills the same. The Arians' proof for the Son's subordination, his obedient work, itself becomes now the mystery of oneness of will between the Divine Persons, based on their oneness of essence. The Arians say "obedience" and mean "compulsion", while for us, it is specifically the Son's obedience that represents the image of the Father, because the Son in his entire filial existence absorbs the entire will of the Father, to such a degree as to *become* or rather to *be* this will himself. For this reason, the unity of will does not exclude the distinction of Persons but rather reveals it in all its fullness; as it is precisely the Son in his *own* will, in his individuality and personhood, who is the image of the Father's will.

2. *The Divine Persons and Their "Mode of Existence"*

Gregory of Nyssa has already been accused, during his lifetime, of overemphasizing the distinction of the Divine Persons to the point of incurring the danger of "Tri-theism". He defends himself against such accusations in his short treatise, "There Are Not Three Gods". In it, he discusses the question that we deal with here: he takes as starting point the oneness of God that comprises also the oneness of will and of work, and then demonstrates that this oneness does not exclude the individuality of the Persons. For the power of God is indeed one, but "it flows, as out of a well, from the Father; it is exercised through the Son, and it actualizes grace in the strength of the Spirit. Yet none of its effects can be attributed to only one or the other of the Persons."[54]

This applies to every work of God, especially to his will: "There is [in God] but one, and only one, movement of the will, in beautiful harmony; it moves from the Father, through the Son, to the Holy Spirit."[55] Gregory states the same in view of God's inner life: "There is but one and the same life, generated by the Father, expressed by the Son, and dependent on the will of the Spirit."[56] In summary, this means: "There is but one Redeemer of all, the God of all, and his salvation comes about through the Son in the grace of the Holy Spirit."[57]

Is this not, once again, the danger of the Son and Spirit, in the Arian sense, appearing to be of inferior essence? Gregory demonstrates that the opposite is true, and thus shows that the Trinity is *the archetype of all person-based community,* or else, as some Russian philosophers of religion are wont to say, *the archetype of every social program.* For here, in the archetype of the divine Trinity, it is made visible that equality and order go together and need each other. Gregory then sets out to show that the Father is indeed the sole originating cause of everything, even of the Son and the Spirit; and yet, *this order does not imply subordination.* The Church Fathers do not hesitate to underline this order among the Divine Persons; for, as Gregory says, "the Gospel itself reveals a certain order [*taxis*], according to which the Faith, originating from the Father and mediated through the Son, arrives at the Holy Spirit".[58] The error of the Arians consisted in considering this order among the Persons as an ontological and hierarchical order. It is true, the Son originates from the Father, and thus is second in the "order" of the Persons. And yet he is inferior to the Father in nothing.

Gregory made further efforts to penetrate rationally this paradox of order and equality. And so he shows that the relation between a cause and what is caused does not determine anything

[54] PG 45, 128C.
[55] PG 45, 128A.
[56] PG 45, 125D.
[57] PG 45, 129B.
[58] Ep. 24 PG 46, 1092A.

regarding the nature of either, but merely indicates their origin. Whether a tree grew by itself or was planted does not say anything about the nature of the tree but only about the ways and means of *how* it became a tree.[59] The order of the Divine Persons, which the Arians made into a *subordination,* therefore does not say anything about their nature, their essence, but only indicates their relationship as to their origins. The Son is of the same essence as the Father, and also of the same will, but he possesses this essence and this will in a *manner* different from the Father; he possesses them *as Son,* in his own manner. This proper mode of existence [*tropos tês hyparxeôs*] of each person is at the same time the specific mode of origin and the specific mode of manifestation.[60] Thus the Son is the image of the Father because he is "begotten of the Father" and works in everything *as Son.* Now we see even more clearly in what way the Son is the perfect image of the Father: *in his own mode of existence as Son.* Basil, in his treatise on the Holy Spirit, interprets the word, "He who has seen me, has seen the Father", in this same sense:

> This does not refer to the form or shape of the Father, since the divine nature is in no way a composite. Rather, in the Father and in the Son we behold the good of the *will,* which coincides with the essence, and which is similar and equal, or more correctly: identical. . . . That the Father works through the Son does not imply that the work of the Father is less than perfect, nor does it reveal the effectiveness of the Son to be weak; it rather shows the *oneness of their will.*[61]

We have seen that Athanasius interpreted this passage in John as an indication of identity of essence between Father and Son. Basil extends its meaning to include the will as well, "because this will is identical with the essence". He shows that Christ not only acted as obedient servant but could also speak "as absolute and sovereign

[59] PG 45, 133C.

[60] Extensive details on this in F. Heinzer, *Gottes Sohn als Mensch. Die Struktur des Menschseins Christi bei Maximus Confessor* (Fribourg, 1980), 32–58.

[61] De Spiritu Sancto PG 32, 105AB; trans. M. Blum, *Basilius von Cäesarea, Über den Heiligen Geist* (Freiburg, 1967), 83f.

Lord" without creating a contradiction between the one and the other: for whenever he spoke with power and authority he did so "for us to recognize our Lord and Creator"; and whenever he acted as obedient servant he did so to reveal to us "the Father of our Lord and Creator".[62]

3. *Obedience and Freedom*

The Son's mode of existence, his way of being God and of possessing divinity, is also the foundation and manner of his being image. The mark of his mode of existence consists in not willing anything different from the Father's will, or as Gregory puts it: to *be* this will.

One final danger must be avoided here. For one could raise this objection: if the Son's mode of existence consists in doing the Father's will, then the Son would *by necessity* be obedient to the Father. Eunomius did not let this objection slip by without using it to affirm the subordination of the Son. In his "Profession of Faith", he states: "The Son has become obedient in word and work *because* he is the only-begotten Son and he is God."[63] Gregory of Nyssa succeeds in showing that here a questionable notion of obedience (as though it were a natural necessity) is presupposed. The *obedience* of the Son extends only to the salvation history of his Incarnation, especially his "obedience unto death on the cross" (Phil 2:18). In *this* we find the obedience of the Son, because prior there was the disobedience of man. In contrast, regarding the work of creation we can no longer say that the Son accomplished it "in obedience", as Eunomius holds; otherwise the apostle could not have said that the Son "upholds the universe by his word of power" (Heb 1:3). Even less can we speak of the Son's "obedience" when considering the inner life of the divinity:[64] within the perfect unity of essence and will of the Trinity there does not exist command and obedience, only the common will.

[62] De Spiritu Sancto PG 32, 105AB; *Basilius,* 83f.

[63] Refut. Conf. Eun. 133 PG 45, 528C.

[64] Gregory of Nazianzus: "The Logos as Logos is neither obedient nor disobedient" (Or. Theol. IV, 6; PG 36, 109B).

But how are we to understand the line, "through him all things were made"? How are we to interpret this instrumentality of the Son? For Eunomius, this is simple: according to him, "the Son is generated in such a wise that his nature is destined to nothing else but obedience."[65] If this were so, Gregory replies, then the Son would be inferior even to man, he would be a mere tool (*organon*), able to work only passively and within the narrow confines of his instrumental purpose.[66] Man at least has "a free soul, which according to its independence and proper ability determines its own choices. He who is by nature subject to necessity, on the other hand, follows—or rather: suffers—the requirements of obedience, and even should he try to escape obedience, his nature would not permit it."[67] To reduce the Son to a mere instrumental power would amount to denying him the freedom that distinguishes even man. It is not possible to speak of obedience without including freedom. Eunomius' argument cannot hide its inner contradictions.

And yet, how are we to interpret "*through* the Son" in positive terms? The Father working *through* him can only mean: the inseparable unity of both in one identical will; in a will that proceeds from the Father and is perfectly appropriated by the Son. The words "*through* him" ultimately refer to the Son's *mode of existence*. For the identifying mark of the Son's personhood consists in being entirely "from the Father", in *being* as well as in *work*. *In this manner* is the Son the image of the Father: the Father works *through* the Son, and for this reason the Father is known *through* the Son.

The difficulties we inevitably encounter when we attempt to discuss the mystery of the Trinity spring above all from our own limited conceptual framework. The mystery of God's Trinity goes beyond these limits; we can approach it only gropingly, in darkness enlightened by our Faith. How are we to combine the thought of God as Father with that of the complete equality of essence? Should we think of a perfect union with an order but no

[65] Refut. Conf. Eun. 138 PG 45, 532A.
[66] The same reproach is found in Basilius PG 29, 617B.
[67] Cf. C. Eun. III, IX, 47–50 PG 45, 876AD.

domination? A union in which total self-surrender is identical to total self-possession? A union in which each exists totally from the other and for the other, and yet remains absolutely free? Such a triune God is too incomprehensible as to be conceived according to the ideal desires of human projection, but at the same time, he is the epitome of everything human yearning longs for in terms of community, oneness, and love, so much so that it seems only reasonable to look on man as created after the image and likeness of precisely *this* God (cf. Gen 1:26).

An exceptionally dense and beautiful text of St. Basil's shall close this chapter on the trinitarian foundations of icon theology. This text sums up once more what we, guided by the great theologians of the fourth century, have tried to set forth:

> For it is impossible to behold the image of the invisible God [Christ] except in the light of the Spirit. Contemplating the image, we cannot separate the light from the image. The cause that makes us see is beheld, by necessity, together with what we see. And so we behold in proper and logical fashion the "reflection of God's splendor" [Christ] through the inspiration of the Spirit; through the "imprint" [= Christ; cf. Heb 1:3], then, we are lifted up to the glory of the Father, to whom belong both the imprint [= the Son] and the printing block [= the Holy Spirit].[68]

---

[68] De Spiritu Sancto 26 PG 32, 185BC; *Basilius,* 97, with a correction in the last three lines.

Chapter Two

The Christological Foundations
of the Icon

Jesus Christ, "in whom are hidden all the treasures of wisdom and knowledge" (Col 2:3), is the "image of the invisible God" (Col 1:15) in whom the life-giving knowledge of the Father is revealed to us. The term "image" proclaims something essential about Christ: his intimate relationship to the Father. Throughout the painful and often obscure passage through the Arian crisis, the Church held fast to this truth by professing the Father and the Son to be of one essence.

For any theology of the icon, the concept, paradoxical as it might be, of a "consubstantial and perfect image" remains fundamental. Up to now, however, we have not yet discussed where and how the Son manifests himself as the image of the Father: in his Incarnation. We spoke only about trinitarian theology in our reflection on the way in which the eternal Son is image of the eternal Father. What about the Incarnation? Is Jesus Christ, true God and true man, still the "image of the invisible God" even in his "form of a slave" (Phil 2:7)? And if so, is he such still in the same, perfect measure as he is in his being the consubstantial, eternal Son? Paul has indeed spoken of "him who became man" when he referred to the "image of the invisible God". But what does "image" mean here? Is the Son, even in his humble state, in his Incarnation, still the *perfect* image of the Father? And does he in his Incarnation reveal the Father perfectly? Or does his "form of a slave" not intrude, like a separating wall between God and us? Does not this limited state, in its natural imperfection, also limit the revelation of the Father? One further question is tied to this: Can the Eternal Word still completely be known even in his temporal human form, in the weakness of his Incarnation, or is the "form of God" concealed by the "form of a slave" (Phil 2:6)? Does the Incarnation reveal or conceal the Son?

Such questions may well be too probing or too inappropriate, demanding to know too much about things that can only be accepted as mysteries and through faith. Yet these questions have been posed *in fact,* not out of an addiction to speculation, but because, in the great christological debates of the fifth, sixth, and seventh centuries, they had become decisive questions whose purpose, over and again, was to reformulate the original proclamation about Christ ever anew, and to safeguard it from the distortions of the time. For the development of an icon theology, these christological controversies are of utmost importance. Let us remember what has been said in the introduction to this book: the theology of the image in the Eastern Church will remain incomprehensible without a reflection on the christological underpinnings of the icon. How else could we understand why the Byzantine discussion of icon veneration was conducted mainly as a christological discussion, while comments on aesthetics, artistic theory, or style are all but absent? We shall investigate this phenomenon more closely in Part Two. First, in this chapter, we are about to retrace, with broad steps, the more important stages of this christological debate. Our aim in this is not to paint a historically complete picture, but rather to highlight those aspects of the development that would become important for the theology of the icon. We shall concentrate on four authors whose contributions to Christology are especially consequential: Origen, Eusebius of Caesarea, Cyril of Alexandria, and Maximus Confessor.

I. Origen — An Iconoclastic Christology?

The great Russian theologian and historian, Georges Florovsky, in a stimulating yet controversial essay,[1] maintained that the Byzantine icon controversy had one of its strongest roots in the theology of Origen (c. 185–254 A.D.). In the Christology of this great Alexandrian above all, Florovsky is convinced that one finds the example of a theology containing the premises of iconoclasm. In what follows, we shall try to pursue Florovsky's suggestions by providing a brief sketch of Origen's Christology.[2] Yet we are well aware of the difficulties inherent in such an endeavor: Origen has always been a highly controversial figure. Even early on, his teachings were either passionately attacked or defended, either accused of heresy or absolved from such suspicion, until they were finally condemned by an ecumenical council (553 A.D.). All the same, his work, more than any other, retained its influence in all areas of theology, despite its preservation only in fragments. Origen's work shows an incredible depth and scope. He was an incomparable exegete, a genuine mystic, a great homilist, a profound theologian. His disciples, as happens so often in the history of human thought, usually could not emulate the wide horizon of their master and so pressed his teachings into a system. "Origenism" as a system, or else as a theological mentality, causing heated debates in subsequent centuries, indeed represents a narrow version of Origen's theology, and yet does not without justification rely on certain teachings of the master.

First of all, this applies to how he understood the Incarnation of the Divine Logos, so consequential for the icon theology. Origen sees the "flesh" of Christ, his body, as belonging to the

---

[1] "Origen, Eusebius and the iconoclastic controversy", *Church History* 19 (1950): 77–96; in agreement is A. Grillmeier, *Der Logos am Kreuz* (Munich, 1956), 49–55; raising objections is Stephan Gero in *Byzantine Iconoclasm during the Reign of Leo III* (Louvain, 1973), 105; idem, *Byzantine Iconoclasm during the Reign of Constantine V* (Louvain, 1977), 103–5.

[2] Two studies should be mentioned here: H. Crouzel, *Théologie de l'image chez Origène* (Paris, 1956), and M. Harl, *Origène et la fonction révélatrice du Verbe incarné* (Paris, 1958).

world of sensory perceptions, and therefore assigns it to the realm of "shadows" and images, as opposed to the truth. Accordingly he states in his commentary on John:

> The Lord is called "without deceit" (Dt 32:4) in contrast to the shadow, the likeness, the image; for thus exists the Word in the eternity of heaven. But on earth he is not the way he is in heaven; for since the Word became flesh, he manifests himself by means of shadows, likenesses, and images. The multitude of those who think themselves believers are instructed through the shadow of the Word and not by the true Word of God, which is in the immensity of heaven.[3]

"Origen sees the Incarnation as God's pedagogical adaptation to the level of our human capacities."[4] If, then, we have to understand the Incarnation in a pedagogical sense, we ought to look beyond and grasp its purpose: to make palpable the Word himself, which human weakness, through its own devices, cannot comprehend. Thus Origen holds that Jesus, while here on earth, and according to this pedagogy, manifested himself under varied appearances adapted to the different capacities of different people.[5] As true and profound as this thought of a divine pedagogy connected with the Incarnation may be, it becomes somewhat disturbing if it implies that the events in Jesus' life would mean nothing more than representation of the first and most elementary step of initiation, of induction. This conception becomes even more disturbing if it considers the suffering and Cross of Christ as merely the lowest level of this initiation process, whose highest level would be Christ's Transfiguration and Resurrection. Origen puts Isaiah's words in 53:2-3 ("There was in him no pleasant form, nor beauty; nor comely appearance that would make us draw to him. He was despised and avoided by men . . . ") on the lips of those who remained caught in their earthly mentality and were unable to climb the mountain of the Transfiguration.[6] Indeed, the mes-

---

[3] In Joa II, 6, 49–50 SC 120, 239; cf. Harl, *Origène,* 191.
[4] Harl, *Origène,* 114.
[5] CC II, 64 SC 132, 435–37; cf. Grillmeier, *Der Logos,* 52–55.
[6] CC IV, 16 SC 136, 221–23.

sage of the Cross—for Paul, the quintessence of the Gospel—is in Origen's eyes only for those yet "in the flesh", not for the initiated:

> We ought to be Christians in the spirit and in the body. Wherever it is appropriate to proclaim the gospel according to the body, and wherever it is advisable to say, in company of people still "in the flesh", that we know Jesus Christ only as the crucified (cf. 1 Cor 2:2), there we have to leave it this way. But when these people have been instructed by the Spirit, bring fruit in the Spirit, and yearn for heavenly wisdom, then they must be allowed to partake of the Word, which after the Incarnation has returned to its prior state as it was "in the beginning with God" (Jn 1:2).[7]

This rather esoteric text depicts the Incarnation as a simple transition, after which the Word returns to his "original state".[8] For Origen, the aim of our knowledge of Christ is to behold the Logos "uncovered", without the wrapping of the flesh. In this very sense, Origen interprets John the Baptist's confession that he is not worthy to loosen the sandal straps of Jesus (cf. Jn 1:27): the Word, by becoming flesh, went into hiding, as it were, and "strapped" down; therefore, the task is to loosen the sandal straps in order to see the Word "without sandals, stripped of everything inferior, and in his true intrinsic reality—as the Son of God".[9] In this perspective, the body of Jesus is but "the earthly image" of the "higher reality", that is, of the Word, which "appears to us in Jesus".[10]

Origen leaves something of a distance between the man Jesus and the Word: Jesus is not entirely identical with the Word; he is its instrument;[11] the Word uses the man Jesus in order to avoid working in its "naked divinity".[12] Jesus is the manifestation of the Word, he is not himself the substance of revelation.

[7] In Joa I, 7, 43 SC 120, 85; cf. I, 9, 58 SC 120, 91.

[8] Cf. In Joa XXXII, 25 (17) GCS 10, 470, 17, 27.

[9] In Joa VI, 35, 179 SC 157, 263; cf. Harl, *Origène,* 194f. Origen, however, does not teach the absorption of Christ's humanity, but its total divinization (In Matth XV, 24 GCS 14, 419).

[10] In Joa VI, 34 SC 157, 261; cf. the texts in Harl, *Origène,* 203, note 61.

[11] CC II, 9 SC 132, 303.

[12] In Joa, fragm. 18 GCS 10, 498, 13.

It is interesting, in this context, to realize how Origen interprets Christ's word, "Whoever sees me, sees the Father" (Jn 14:9).[13] On occasion, he interprets it in an exclusively trinitarian sense, without any reference to the Incarnation.[14] In other instances he applies it to the theophanies of the Old Covenant.[15] But quoting it in the context of the Incarnation, he resolutely refuses to understand it as a reference to a physical beholding of Christ: "No rational person would ever affirm that Jesus referred to his physical body and the beholding by human eyes when he said, 'Whoever sees me, sees the Father.' Otherwise, even all those who yelled, 'Crucify, crucify him!' would then have seen the Father (Lk 23:21)."[16]

Origen, for this reason, instead of the all-too-physical concept of "seeing", prefers the more spiritual concept of "contemplating" (*theorein*):[17] "He who looks at the body of Jesus with his physical eyes does not yet, in this alone, see the Father, his God. For I think time and practice were needed to see Jesus in such a way as to see the Son and thus contemplate the Father."[18]

Origen even states that "seeing" here would not mean a physical perception but "cognition": "For he who has known the Son, has known the Father."[19] This approach by Origen is admittedly open to a christologically correct interpretation, and it does not lack a deeper mystical sense. The texts quoted, nonetheless, demonstrate in Origen a distinct tendency to see in Jesus of Nazareth more the revelatory form of the Logos, marked by this accidental appearance, than the authentic subject of revelation itself.[20] Not without reason would the Origenism of the subsequent centuries

---

[13] Cf. Harl, *Origène*, 183, 186.

[14] For example, CC VIII, 12 SC 150, 201; In Gen Hom I, 13 GCS 29, 17, 8; In Lev Hom XIII, 4 GCS 29, 473, 15 and 474, 7; In Joa XIII, 25, 151 GCS 10, 250, 2; cf. also note 17 below.

[15] PA II, 4, 3 GCS 22, 130, 2.

[16] CC VII, 43 SC 150, 116f.; cf. In Cant III GCS 33, 215, 16–28, and In Luc Hom I GCS 49, 7, 14–8, 2.

[17] For example, In Joa XIX, 6, 35 GCS 10, 305, 9, and XXXII, 29, 359 (475, 4).

[18] In Joa, fragm. XCIII GCS 10, 556, 17.

[19] PA II, 4, 3 GCS 22, 130, 29.

[20] Cf. Harl, *Origène*, 209.

be criticized for blurring the difference between the presence of the Logos in Jesus and, on the other hand, in the sanctified human soul.

In such a conception of the Incarnation of the Word, it is only natural that the New Testament, the written testimony about Jesus' words and deeds, as well as the body of Christ, will appear merely as "shadows of the spiritual realities". According to Origen, it is not sufficient to go by the "bodily" meaning of the gospel; one has to go beyond in order to arrive at the "spiritual" or "eternal gospel", of which the "bodily" gospel is but a shadowy image. It does not come as a surprise, then, that Origen neglects or downgrades the importance of those New Testament texts that depict Jesus' coming into this world as fulfillment, completion, and perfection of revelation, which the Old Testament had offered only as a promise. Origen prefers to interpret such "fulfillment" passages (for instance, Rom 5:16; Heb 10:1; Jn 1:17, 6:55, 15:1; remarkably, Col 2:17b is *never* quoted!) as predictions of the good things to come in the world.[21] This spiritual exegesis is obviously intimately tied to Origen's Christology: just as his Christology sees the earthly life of Jesus mostly as a shadowy image of the hidden truth of the Eternal Word,[22] so too does his exegesis see in the words of Scripture mostly the shadow cast by the truth of the Eternal Word.

This parallel is once more confirmed by Origen's comments on sacred art. Origen holds that just as the words of Scripture remain dead unless we enter into their spiritual meaning, so also a merely physical picture remains dead and lifeless and subject to the ravages of time. For this reason, Origen contrasts the dead images of the pagans with the true images of God; for him, these are the Christians who have imprinted in their souls the beauty of the divine virtues:[23] the true image of God is within! Behind this polemic against idol worship, the outlines of a certain anthropology and doctrine of creation appear in Origen that may very well provide the background for his Christology and exegesis. This

[21] Ibid., 212–14.
[22] Cf. A. Grillmeier, *Jesus der Christus im Glauben der Kirche,* vol. 1 (Freiburg, 1979), 275.
[23] CC VIII, 18 SC 150, 213–15.

anthropology, moreover, we encounter again in the attitude of certain later iconoclasts who made it the predominant reason for their rejection of images (cf. pp. 159–67).

The most serious shortcoming of this anthropology consists in its inability to assign a clear and positive meaning to man's physical nature within God's plan of creation and salvation. In this thinking, man is primarily the soul, the "interior man". For this reason, all material visual expressions are considered occasions for distracting man from his true destiny, for "they divert the eyes of the soul away from God and toward the world".[24]

Against this way of thinking, an objection had already been raised by the pagan philosopher, Celsus (c. 178 A.D.), clearly spelling out the dilemma inherent in the early Christian iconoclasm: he detects a contradiction when Christians, on the one hand, reject anthropomorphic depictions of the divine, yet on the other hand declare man himself an "image of God". In the image controversy of the eighth and ninth centuries, this argument will reappear— this time in defense of Christian icon devotion. Origen, however, rejects it: man, so he argues, is not the "image of God", but created *"in* the image of God", according to the exact text of Genesis 1:26. He reasons that man could not possibly be *"in* God's image" if based on his body, since the body is corruptible; nor based on his body *and* his soul, otherwise one would have to think of God as also being composed; but only based on "the interior man" (Eph 3:16), that is, the soul. Only the soul is able to become "imitator of God" (Eph 5:1), which means, to assume God's qualities (*charaktêras*) and thus to become his image. Scripture calls the body, on the other hand, the "temple of God" (1 Cor 6:19), not his "image".[25]

Since only thus is the soul "in the image of God"—an image "whose painter is the Son of God"[26]—therefore the only appropriate devotion is the one offered on the altar of the Christian soul; and the only images and statues to be erected are the virtues

---

[24] CC IV, 31 SC 136, 261.

[25] CC VI, 63 SC 147, 335–39; CC VII, 66 SC 150, 169.

[26] In Gen Hom XIII, 4 GCS 29, 119, 24.

that mold the soul in the image of God (an argument the icono-clasts later will love to use!): "We are convinced", says Origen, "that only through such images are we to honor the original of all images, 'the image of the invisible God' (Col 1:15), God the only-begotten Son."[27] This, then, is Origen's reply to Celsus, who criticizes the Christians for refusing to erect altars, statues, and temples.

In Origen, without doubt, we witness a tendency that every now and then will reappear during the following centuries: the tendency to see what is visible *only* as shadows of what is invisible, to emphasize in the image primarily the *shortcomings* in relation to the original, and to deemphasize its function of being *revelation* of the original. This tendency is not without its dangers: "The heavy emphasis on the invisible threatens to lessen the importance of Jesus' salvific Incarnation and his human nature."[28] An entire current of spiritual and theological Christian tradition can be assigned to this tendency, and it is not without reason that this tradition is again and again connected with the name of Origen. The highest aim here is the image-less, purely spiritual contempla-tion. The image, and everything connected with symbols and imagery, is then readily reserved for the "uneducated". This tradition, in its extreme forms, leads to the rejection, or at least the disparaging, of all that is sacramental and symbolic, even of the "embodiment" of the Faith in institutions, dogma, and Church. Iconoclasm thus can become the expression of an inimical attitude toward every-thing that is incarnational. In the second part of our research, we shall show evidence of such tendencies surrounding the viewpoint of the iconoclasts. There we shall also identify the connections to Origenism. This Origenism, of course, with its heavy spiritualism, is but the epigones' impoverished version of the Alexandrian's great work itself.

Origen is much too universal, too biblical, too ecclesiastical, too "Catholic", to allow the reduction of his work to only *one* of

[27] CC VIII, 17, trans. Koetschau, BKV, "Origenes", vol. 3, 318f.
[28] So maintains J. Kirchmeyer, in *Dictionnaire de Spiritualité* (Paris, 1932–), vol. 6, col. 816.

its dimensions. It is a misrepresentation when Origen, time and again, is seen primarily as one of the spiritual Fathers of iconoclasm, or else, of a form of Christianity opposed to rituals and ceremonies, to images and sacramentals, and advocating an exclusively spiritual cultus.[29] As is the case with his famous predecessor, Clement of Alexandria, the spiritualism here is embedded within a sacramental and ecclesiastical realism.[30] Though Origen displays, without doubt, a tendency toward spiritualizing (not even foreign to St. Paul; cf. 2 Cor 4:18), yet must this be seen in conjunction with the opposing tendency toward "embodiment". This latter tendency is evident even and especially in those passages that time and again are quoted to show Origen as an enemy of images. In answer to Celsus' criticism that the Christians refused to erect altars and statues, Origen emphasizes indeed the "interiority" of the Christian ritual, but he also goes beyond this by employing the metaphor of the sculptor in order to explain how God is practically "incarnated" in the human virtues, and how man, completely incarnating within himself the will of God, becomes the perfect "statue of God", the *true* image of God:

> Among sculptors and painters there are some who create marvelous works; for instance, among the first, there are Phidias and Polycleitus, among the latter, Zeuxis and Appelles. Others, however, produce lesser pieces, and still others, works inferior even to the lesser artists. There are altogether great differences among those who create statues of idols and paintings. Just so there are some who are better able [than others] to represent with perfect awareness "images" of the almighty God, so that the Olympic Zeus, created by Phidias, cannot even compare with someone who is made "in the likeness of God, the Creator" (cf. Col 1:10). Yet infinitely more precious and splendid than all those images inherent in created things is the one image that

[29] Cf. the outstanding study by H. J. Vogt, *Das Kirchenverständnis des Origenes* (Vienna, 1974).

[30] Greatly emphasized by Clement of Alexandria with his concept of "baptismal realism"; cf. *Paidagogos* I, 6.

dwells in our Savior who testifies about himself, "The Father is in me" (Jn 14:10).[31]

The most perfect "divine image" is the one in which God himself is a *living* presence. Could any pagan idol ever declare about itself, "The Father is in me"? Origen's argumentation cannot be interpreted as a strict rejection of artistic representation and images.[32] He criticizes the divine images of the pagans rather for being "lifeless and unfeeling", or worse even, for harboring demons (as Origen, with Paul, presumes; cf. 1 Cor 10:20; 2 Cor 6:14–16), while the "divine images" of the Christians are dwellings of the Holy Spirit:

> You are entirely free to . . . compare the "images" in the souls of those who devoutly worship Almighty God with the "images" created by the likes of Phidias and Polycleitus; and you will see, clearly and distinctly, that the latter are without life and bound to disappear in time, while the former remain in the immortal soul for as long as the rational soul desires to harbor them within itself.[33]

Origen in this stands on the common ground of the early Church: Christ's advent, so the conviction goes, is the fulfillment of all the promises. Just as the cultured Christians of the early times were convinced they had found, in Christianity, the *true philosophy* that provides answers to all our groping and searching, and directions to all the tortuous pathways of human thought,[34] so they were also certain of having found here access to the *most sublime art,* the *ars divina* itself, which always remains the unreachable model of all human artistic endeavor: in *this,* so we believe, we

---

[31] CC VIII, 17; trans. Koetschau, BKV. "Origenes", vol. 3, 319. The metaphor of "God as artist" is found frequently in early Christian writings; cf. notes 26 above and 37 below; cf. also the excursus XXI in E. R. Curtius, *Europäische Literatur und lateinisches Mittelalter* (Bern, 1948), 529f. ("Gott als Bildner" — God the Imager).

[32] As we find it, for example, in H. Koch, *Die altchristliche Bilderfrage nach den literarischen Quellen* (Göttingen, 1917), 20–22.

[33] CC VIII, 18; trans. Koetschau, BKV, "Origenes", vol. 3, 320.

[34] Cf. G. Bardy, " 'Philosophie' et 'philosophe' dans le vocabulaire chrétien des premiers siècles", *Rev. d'asc. et myst.* 25 (1949):97–108.

have discovered the "spiritual atmosphere . . . in which the Church's interest in images became acceptable, even necessary". Origen contributed to this atmosphere, as K. Holl rightly points out, no less than Irenaeus before and Athanasius after him.[35] We do not believe, however, that this constituted "a process of secularization and paganization of Christianity",[36] rather a process of *integration* and *transformation* of all areas of human life, including the arts, resulting from the mystery of the God-made-man and his creative work of salvation. In conclusion we listen to St. Methodius of Olympus (3rd century A.D.) who frequently employs metaphors taken from the fine arts. Would not man's transformation according to the image of Christ, discussed in the following text, necessarily bring about a change in the conception of the arts and in the self-awareness of the artist as well?

> Man had indeed been brought forth "after the image" of God (Gen 1:26), but he still had not yet achieved such "likeness" itself. In order to complete this task, the Word was sent into the world. First he assumed our human form, a form marred by the scars of many sins, so that we, for whom he took this form, would be enabled on our part to receive his divine form. For it is possible to achieve a perfect likeness of God only if we, like talented and accomplished painters, depict in ourselves those traits that characterized his human existence, and if we preserve them (in us) uncorrupted, by becoming his disciples, walking the path he has revealed to us. He who was God chose to appear in our human flesh so that we could behold, as we do in a painting, a divine model of life, and thus were made able to imitate the one who painted this picture.[37]

---

[35] Karl Holl, *Gesammelte Aufsätze zur Kirchengeschichte*, vol. 2 (Tübingen, 1928), 389.
[36] Koch, *Die altchristliche Bilderfrage*, 88.
[37] *Das Gastmahl* I, IV, 23f. SC 95, 62–64.

II. An Iconoclastic Theology:
Eusebius of Caesarea (c. 264–340 A.D.)

Origen's vast and multidimensional work provided the impetus for the most diverse developments. One form of Origenism offered itself for a determined iconoclasm, and it is this line of development we will now consider as we take a somewhat closer look at the icon theology of Eusebius of Caesarea,[38] which derives in many respects from Origen without following him in every detail. Then, in Cyril of Alexandria and Maximus Confessor, we shall come to know two great figures whose theology would develop further the pro-image elements of the Christian tradition.

1. *Eusebius' Letter to the Empress Constantia — A Theological Blueprint of Iconoclasm*

In their search for iconoclastic pronouncements of the Church Fathers, the opponents of images in the eighth century discovered a text that seemed custom-made for their intentions. It was a letter by Eusebius to Constantia, the Great Constantine's sister. This letter is known to us only through the debates of the image controversy. Because of its late attestation, and also because of intrinsic reasons, the authenticity of this document has been questioned. But we believe that the letter's style and theology fit into the work of this great Church historian well.[39]

---

[38] Regarding the work and the theology of Eusebius, cf. the article "Eusebius von Caesarea" in TRE X, 537–43 (1982) by D. S. Wallace-Hadrill, and Grillmeier, *Jesus der Christus,* vol. I, 300–326.

[39] The authenticity of this letter was not doubted for a long time. It was questioned more recently by Sr. Charles Murray, "Art and the Early Church", JTS, NS 28 (1977):303–45, especially 326–36. Stephan Gero attempts to defend its authenticity again using arguments referring to its style and the history of art and theology; "The True Image of Christ: Eusebius' Letter to Constantia Reconsidered", JTS NS 32 (1981):460–70. K. Schäferdiek, "Zur Verfasserfrage und Situation der epistula ad Constantiam de imagine Christi", in ZKG 91 (1980):177–86, however, would attribute this text to the Arian court Bishop Eusebius of Nicomedia. A

Constantia had asked Eusebius to send her an image of Christ. The answer was a clear and rather curt "No". Should this "No" on the part of the theologian of Emperor Constantine I not be seen as an ideal foundation for the "No" that the later emperor, Constantine V, would try to enforce regarding the icon cult? Did this letter not confirm anew that in Constantine V the mentality of Constantine the Great had once again come to life? Eusebius' letter offered even more: a theological, or more precisely, a christological argumentation against any depiction of Christ. Could anything be changed in Byzantium without christological argumentation? No wonder, then, that Eusebius' letter[40] became the principal testimony for the accusers of icon devotion, and that Patriarch Nicephorus, in his defense of icon devotion, dedicated an entire book to refute Eusebius? This text is of central importance for us, too, as it shows, for the first time, the connection between the attitude toward images and Christology, which after all is also the topic of this present work. But let us here quote the more decisive passages from the letter in question:

> You wrote to me regarding a certain icon of Christ and your wish for me to send you such an icon: What did you have in mind, and of what kind should this icon of Christ be, as you call it? . . . Which icon of Christ are you looking for? The true, unchangeable image that by nature shows the likeness of Christ, or rather the other image that he has taken on for our sake when he clothed himself with the form of a servant (cf. Phil 2:7)? . . . I cannot imagine you are requesting an icon of his divine likeness. Christ himself has instructed you that nobody knows the Father except the Son, and that nobody is worthy to know the Son except the Father alone who has begotten him (cf. Mt 11:27).[41]

---

meticulous study of the historical aspects of this manuscript might yield new insights. The text undoubtedly originated during the *time* of Eusebius. But we also maintain that the letter's theology can be shown to be entirely in line with the theology of Eusebius of Caesarea; cf. for example note 41 below.

[40] The text of this letter has been preserved only in the opposing treatise of Nicephorus: "Contra Eusebium", ed. J. B. Pitra, *Spicilegium Solesmense*, vol. 1 (Paris, 1852), 383–86 = PG 20, c. 1545–49. An edition with text revisions is found in H. Hennephof, ed., *Textus byzantinos ad Iconomachiam pertinentes* (Leiden, 1969), 42–44.

[41] Almost the identical wording in HE I, 2, 2 (10, 11–16); cf. DE V, I, 25 (214, 26–31).

Thus, I presume, you desire the icon of his form as a servant, the form of the humble flesh with which he clothed himself for our sake. Yet about this we have learned that it is intermingled with the glory of God, that what is mortal has been swallowed up by life (cf. 1 Cor 15:52–54; 2 Cor 5:4).[42]

What makes this text so interesting is the strict line of theological argumentation: an icon of Christ? Which form is it supposed to show? The divine likeness is ineffable and inscrutable, the human likeness has been "swallowed up", as it were, by the glory of its divine counterpart.

To forestall any possible misunderstanding here, we do not believe that this text can be read as a *general* rejection of all Christian art. Symbolic and allegorical renderings of Christ, of which we have numerous examples already from the time of Eusebius, are not rejected (See illustration no. 4). The discussion centers rather on the idea of an icon that is supposed to depict Christ *accurately,* in his true likeness:[43] *such* an expectation is rejected by Eusebius; for precisely this accurate likeness cannot be "captured" artistically. Yet it is this very question that will later stand at the center of the image controversy; this very question already occupied Origen: Is it at all possible to capture the *true* likeness of Christ through "dead and lifeless colors and designs"?[44] Is Christ not now glorified, is his earthly form after the Resurrection not now "transfigured, rendered immortal, incorruptible"? From that moment on the "servant's form has been transformed, entirely and thoroughly, into ineffable and intangible light, the same light that equals God the Word. . . . How could anybody presume to paint an icon of this marvelous and unfathomable form, provided such divine and spiritual essence can at all be called a 'form'?"[45]

Should the one making the request invoke the notion of expecting an image of Jesus' earthly form, *before* the transfigura-

[42] PG 20, c. 1545AB.

[43] Here we agree with C. Murray, if the rejection in question is limited to "a true portrait claiming to represent the actual features of Christ" ("Art and the Early Church", JTS NS 28 no. 39, [1977]:329.

[44] PG 20, c. 1545C.

[45] PG 20, c. 1445C–1548A.

tion of the Resurrection, an image, therefore, of "Jesus the man", she will have to be reminded that, on the one hand, God's law (Ex 20:4; Dt 5:8) prohibits fashioning a *likeness* of anything in heaven above or on earth below, and that St. Paul, on the other hand, has taught us that now we do no longer know Christ according to the flesh, even though we knew him so at one time (2 Cor 5:16). In his sharp rebuke of the empress, Eusebius' declared intention is to avoid public scandal; no use of such images should ever give the impression that the Christians, in the manner of idol worshippers, would carry their God around in an image.[46]

Such concern might not have been without foundation. It reflects a situation where the reproach, as voiced by Celsus as late as in the second century, that the Christians would spurn statues and altars, no longer applied; but the opposite reproach, that the Christians would not be different from the pagans in the way they worshipped the image of *their* God, was the danger.

Eusebius knew all too well that such "pagan customs" were not unknown in the Church even in early times.[47] But what really aroused the interest of the iconoclasts of the eighth century was his theory of images, in which the opponents of images found their convictions vindicated. We shall attempt to sketch this theory of the image in broad strokes, following four steps: (a) the trinitarian application of the icon concept; (b) the *Logos* in his manifestations; (c) man as the image of God; and (d) the sacramental concept of the image.

2. *"The Image of God"—Indicating the Subordination of the Logos*

How does Eusebius interpret the Pauline description of Christ as the "image of the invisible God" (Col 1:15)? In contrast to Athanasius, whose writings are of a later period, Eusebius takes the term "image" as a clear indication that the Logos is subordinated to the Father. Thus, for example, we read in his *Demonstratio evangelica:*

[46] PG 20, c. 1548BD.

[47] Cf. the report on the statue of Christ in Paneas, and the images of Peter, Paul, and Christ among converted pagans, in HE VIII, 18, 4 (673).

Illustration 4

Illustration number 4: Christ heals the hemorrhaging woman. Wall-painting, Catacombs of SS. Peter and Marcellinus, Rome, late 3rd century.

Photo: A. Held (Lausanne).

Eusebius reports on an ancient depiction of this scene. His text is an important testimony on the beginnings of Christian art: "Since I have mentioned this town [Paneas = Caesarea Philippi], I do not deem it advisable to skip a tale that should be known to those coming after us. For the hemorrhaging woman, about whom we know from the holy gospels (Mk 5:25–34) that she was healed of her sickness by our Savior, is said to have come from Caesarea Philippi. Even her house is shown there, and other precious reminders of this miracle worked in her by the Savior are kept there as well. On a tall stone in front of the door to the house where the woman had dwelled, there stands a bronze statue of a woman who, genuflecting on one knee, extends her hands forward as if in prayer. Opposite her is placed the figure of a man, of the same metal, appealingly wrapped in a cloak, and reaching out toward the woman. At the feet of the man, on the column, a mysterious plant is growing, even up to the hem of his bronze cloak, said to be a remedy against all kinds of maladies. This statue is said to be the image of Jesus. It is still there nowadays; we have beheld it with our own eyes when we visited this town. It is no surprise that the pagans, to whom our Savior in times past has extended his benevolence, would erect such monuments in his honor. For we have also seen the images of his apostles, Peter and Paul, and even the image of Christ himself, painted in colors. It had to be expected, of course, that these early people would consider them their saviors and, following their pagan customs, would honor them in such a way" (*History of the Church,* VII, 18, 4; from BKV).

Some historians think that this may have been a statue of Asclepius, the god of healing, only "reinterpreted" by that time as a statue of Christ. Does our fresco here from the Roman catacombs also depict Christ as if he were a youthful god?

(See pages 59 and 78.)

Though we openly profess two Lords (that is, the Father and the Son), we nevertheless do not apply the same theological predicates to both. As the true faith teaches us, we employ an order: first, there is the heavenly Father, the Lord and God, who is also Lord and God of the second one, that is, of the Logos of God, of the second Lord, who is Master of everything under him, but not over the one who is greater than he (cf. Jn 14:28); for God the Logos is not the Lord of the Father, nor the God of the Father, but *his image* and Word, his Wisdom and Power.[48]

Here, the subordination of the Son is shown through the proper names given the Son, and the characterization as "image", listed first, is thought to indicate this subordination with special clarity: the Logos is not consubstantial with the Father, he is *only* his image. In this, we are far from the paradoxical concept of the "consubstantial image", developed by Athanasius much later. Here, the philosophical (Neoplatonic) concept of image has not yet been purified in the fire of trinitarian theology. Admittedly, though, Eusebius too conceives the icon character of the Logos in decidedly "spiritualized" terms:

Everyone will join in the profession that the Father exists and dwells *before* the Son. For this very reason is the Son the *image* of God, an image that for us is ineffable and incomprehensible, a living image of the living God, an image existing unto itself, immaterial and incorporeal.... It is unlike earthly images, in which the substance and the image expressed are two different things; rather his form and his substance are one and the same, for the Logos is the complete likeness of the Father.[49]

Eusebius here rejects the purely material notion of the image. Nonetheless, the aspect of what is *missing* is decisive in this conception. The Son is image because he is *second* to the Father.

[48] DE V, 8 (230, 19–30)
[49] DE V, 1, 20–21 (213, 29–35).

Eusebius considers the Son as an image *made* by God and thus as essentially *inferior* to the Father. This is manifested, for instance, when Eusebius employs the comparison with the image of the emperor, a comparison we have already encountered when we discussed Athanasius and Gregory of Nyssa. But Eusebius draws a conclusion contrary to theirs: the latter two used this comparison to show Father and Son as *consubstantial.* For Eusebius, it only demonstrates that the Son can be called "God" because the Father "made him God",[50] and that we may worship as God, "after the Father", the Son as well ("because God is indwelling in him")[51] without their becoming two Gods; this in fact is illustrated through the comparison with the image of the emperor:

> And so, the image of the emperor is venerated because it possesses the features and likeness of the emperor: if you venerate the image, and if you venerate the emperor, you venerate not two but *one* and the same. The true and first emperor and the one depicted on the image are, of course, not two different emperors; they rather are recognized as one and the same, and moreover are so named and venerated. In the same way, the only-begotten Son, who alone is "the image of the invisible God" (cf. Col. 1:15), is rightly so named because of him whose likeness he possesses; for he is made into God by the Father.[52]

It is revealing here how Eusebius uses the image of the emperor as a point of comparison: image and original, in relation to each other, are at the same time close and distant. One can indeed consider and venerate the image as "the emperor", since the emperor is truly depicted in it; yet nobody would ever claim that the image is the emperor himself, because it remains *only* his image. The comparison with the image of the emperor eminently shows that, for Eusebius, Christ was "made God by the Father", in the same sense as the emperor's image was made into the "emperor" himself. This conception remains by and large within the confines of the philosophical definition of the image at that time: no matter

[50] DE V, 4, 10 (225, 24).
[51] DE V, 4, 9 (225).
[52] DE V, 4, 11 (225).

how close the likeness, the image always remains *in essence* inferior to the original. Athanasius, as we have seen, was to be the one who would eventually break open these narrow confines and develop a concept of the image that avers a paradoxical consubstantiality between original and likeness in God the Father and God the Son.

3. *The Universal Activity of the Logos*

Eusebius developed his conception of the image above all within the context of describing the work of Christ as the work of the universal Logos. This approach shall now be considered in more detail. Thus we shall understand more readily why Eusebius opposed Christ's depiction in the icon.

Like most Arians, Eusebius too could not conceive of creation as an act directly accomplished by God. The distance between the divine and the created realms is so vast that it requires the Logos as intermediary, almost in the sense of "dampening" the power of almighty God. No created being is able to be in direct contact with this almighty God, except the Logos, which "the Father himself, through his providence, has called into being before all other creatures".[53] Because the distance between the weakness of the creature and the power of God is unbridgeable,[54] the Logos, like an everlasting, inexhaustible wellspring, gushes forth from the Father.[55]

Eusebius, time and again, describes the universal mission of the Logos, sometimes in rather tiring detail, yet most often in a fascinating cosmic perspective: the Logos is the heart of the universe, he unites everything like an unbreakable bond, he is the all-governing providence;[56] he permeates everything, and on all matter, he imprints form, life, and beauty; he moves the elements, orders everything in harmony, and confers perfection: "Through

[53] DE IV, 6, 6 (159, 22).
[54] DE IV, 6, 6 (159, 24–26).
[55] Ths I, 23 (45).
[56] Ths I, 24 (47).

his divine power of reason he scans everything, penetrates everything, accomplishes everything, without ever being injured by
anything, and without ever being polluted in his own nature."[57]
In short: what the soul is for the inanimate body, the Logos is for
the entire cosmos.[58] A fascinating perspective of the cosmos,
indeed; yet the question arises whether this Logos could be identified with the Word of God in John's prologue, or rather with the
Logos of the Stoics. The Arian flavor of this conception of the
Logos, moreover, will become quite obvious in what follows.

Eusebius likens the world of the senses to a multistringed lyre,
which—plucked by the Logos—emits a glorious song in honor of
the Father, the King of the universe:[59] "The almighty Logos . . .
grasped the breadth and the length of the universe with both his
hands, as it were, brought and bound the universe together in
unity, secured for himself this abundantly assembled instrument,
and elicits . . . the essence of each bodily unit."[60] The cosmos,
then, is the instrument of the Logos. The Logos, in turn, is the
living, divine, life-giving, and wisdom-endowed instrument of
God the Father.[61] If there is one concept at the core of Eusebius'
thinking, it has to be that of the *organon,* the instrument; he has
developed this concept like no other theologian before him.[62] In
view of this concept, his notion of the image, too, will find clarification, for Eusebius explains the image-character of the Logos in
relation to his role as instrument of the Father: "The Logos contains in himself the image of the ineffable and inscrutable Godhead,
and so he too is God and called God, because of his likeness to the
original. For the *same* reason do we say that he is begotten by the
Father as his faithful servant, so that he may govern everything
through a wise, living, and obedient instrument."[63]

[57] DE IV, 13, 2–3 (171, 3–15).

[58] Ths I, 25 (48, 4).

[59] Ths I, 18–19 (50, 6–17).

[60] Ths I, 15 (43, 26).

[61] DE IV, 4, 2 (155, 2).

[62] Cf. W. Metzger, *Der Organongedanke bei den griechischen Kirchenvätern* (Münster-
schwarzach, 1969).

[63] DE IV, 2, 2 (152, 8–14).

The characterization as image already indicated the Logos' essential subordination; now the concept of *organon* emphasizes this further. Eusebius interprets the entire history of salvation through his understanding of the Logos as the instrument of the Father. The infinite power of God is indeed unbearable for all things created; yet the instrument of the Father, the Logos, makes it possible to adapt this immensity to the weakness of the creature. The Father employs this instrument not only while creating and sustaining his creation, but also while revealing himself to the just of the Old Testament. Thus Abraham, at the oak of Mamre, experienced the visit of the Lord who was accompanied by two angels.[64] Who, then, was the person addressed by Abraham as "Lord"? It certainly was not an angel such as the two companions. Was it God himself? "One must not suppose that the all-transcending God should so manifest himself. For it is not proper to say that the divine undergoes change and assumes a human form and countenance. We have to admit, therefore: it was the Logos of God."[65] Since God is himself inscrutable, he uses an instrument in his dealings with man; thus Eusebius explains the frequent theophanies in the Old Testament: "The visions seen by the prophets in their bodily existence were all of human forms, yet it was God who, as through an instrument, spoke by means of these visible forms."[66]

Among the many theophanies worked by God through his Logos, there excels one because of its unique character: the Incarnation. Unique as it may have been, though, Eusebius understands it first of all as a special instance of the Logos' all-pervading presence in the cosmos; witness how Eusebius, in the text quoted

---

[64] Eusebius does not yet understand this as a foreshadowing of the Trinity, the way it would soon be interpreted in later exegesis and art; cf. L. Thunberg, "Early Christian Interpretations of the Three Angels in Gen. 18", in *Studia Patristica,* vol. 7 (Berlin, 1966), 560–70.

[65] DE V, 9, 7 (232, 1–4).

[66] DE V, 13, 3 (236, 18). Eusebius applies Jn 14:9 ("Whoever has seen me has seen the Father") to the previous theophanies of the Old Testament; cf. DE V, 13, 6 (237, 11); VI, 4, 2 (255, 16ff.). Later on, Eusebius will even quote Jn 14:9 without any reference to the Incarnation; cf. ET III, 21 (181, 13); III, 19 (180, 15); II, 7 (106, 16).

above (see note 57), makes the transition to the topic of the Incarnation:

> Through his divine power of reason, the Logos scans everything, penetrates everything, accomplishes everything, without ever being injured by anything, and without ever being polluted in his own nature. *In the same manner,* he dwelled among men; at one time, he appeared only to the few, to prophets and the just, about whom Scripture testifies, and this in manifold ways. In these last times, however, he offered himself as the Savior to all, to those who are evil and godless, the Jews and the Greeks, thanks to the overflowing kindness of the Father.[67]

Thus the Incarnation is part of the sequence of manifestations on the part of the Logos, which is the living instrument of the Father.[68] As the entire cosmos is seen here as the obedient instrument in the hand of the Logos, we should not be surprised that Eusebius now interprets the body too, a part of the cosmos and assumed by the Logos, as an instrument of the Logos. Farther along in the text quoted above, Eusebius returns to the image of the musician, this time applying it to the humanity of the Logos: "The Logos generously calls and heals all men by means of the human instrument he carries, like a musician who proclaims his wisdom by means of the lyre."[69]

The everlasting and inscrutable Father has brought forth the Logos to be the mediating power in the creation and governance of the world. On his part, the Logos reveals himself not primarily "in his divine, incomprehensible, immaterial, and invisible essence", he rather makes himself visible and knowable by using a "bodily instrument" to make possible his dealings with the human race:[70]

> Indeed, how else could our corporeal eyes behold what is incorporeal in God? How else should our mortal nature discover something that is hidden and invisible, which was not discovered even in the myriads of created things? For this

[67] DE IV, 13, 3 (171, 15–21).
[68] Ths III, 39 (140, 23–141, 11).
[69] DE IV, 13, 4 (171, 25–27).
[70] LC 14,1 (241, 18).

reason, the Logos needed a mortal instrument and an appropriate medium to deal with men; for this was to their liking. It is correctly said that *all* love what is similar to themselves. And so, just as the great king utterly needs an interpreter who proclaims the king's words to the multitudes of different tongues and to the cities, so also did the Divine Logos need a medium, an interpreter as it were, and a bodily vehicle, as he made ready to heal the souls in the bodies of men, and to appear on earth. This was to be a human instrument through which he revealed to mankind the nature of the mysterious depths of God.[71]

In the two passages quoted, the Incarnation appears above all as a concession to human weakness. His purpose consists in leading man to a higher level of knowledge where the instrument is no longer needed, where he will have reached reality itself. The Incarnation, therefore, is shown here as a concession above all to those who can comprehend the Logos only according to their bodily, earthly ways:

Furthermore, the Logos concerned himself with the bodies no less than with the souls, and made sure that the bodily eyes of man would behold what he was doing in the body: astonishing miracles and divine signs and powers. To the bodily ears, then, he proclaimed the message, in the flesh, by means of the tongue. Truly, all this he accomplished through the body he had assumed, as if through an interpreter, *for those who in this way, and in this way only, are able to perceive his divinity.*[72]

The ultimate goal is always to arrive, beyond the instrument, at the knowledge of the Logos himself. Eusebius follows here the trail opened by Origen: those who have reached perfection relate directly to the Logos; what is seen in the flesh is for the weak, for those who are incapable of beholding the Logos directly. In all this, however, the relationship between the "bodily instrument" and the Logos is entirely a "one-way road": "Whatever was of the Logos, this he gave also to the man he appeared in (that is, to the instrument, the body), but whatever derived from what was

---

[71] Ths III, 39 (141, 19 – 142, 2) and parallel texts.
[72] Ths III (143, 21–28) and parallel texts.

mortal (that is, from the body), nothing of this he assumed for himself."[73] Since the Logos is not touched nor polluted while filling the entire cosmos with his presence, neither is he affected by the things his body, his instrument, is made to suffer. Eusebius once more returns to the image of the musician plucking the lyre when speaking about the suffering of Christ:

> The One without a body was not polluted through the birth of the body, the One who could not suffer was in his essence not affected by suffering when the mortal part [the body] was again separated from him. It is the same as it would be for a musician who would himself not experience pain should his lyre break or its strings tear.[74]

Eusebius is thus able to describe the entire Passion of Christ as the sole affair of the "human instrument" employed by the Logos: after having rendered the required service to the Logos, the instrument was allowed to die.[75] Yet in order to prevent this death from being considered a weakness of the Logos, the instrument was not to remain in death:

> Someone who wants to show a vessel to be fireproof and its nature to be superior to fire, will demonstrate this marvel in no other way than by committing whatever he holds to the fire and then retrieving it, intact and undamaged, from the fire. Just so did the life-giving Logos of God determine to show the mortal instrument used for the salvation of man to be superior to death, and to be participating in his own life and immortality. Thus he arranged the events, appropriately and eminently and as a benefit for us, in this way: the Logos departed from the body for a short time and surrendered what was mortal to death in order to show *proof* of its mortal nature; yet shortly afterward, he raised this mortal thing out of death to show proof of the divine power through which he manifests the eternal life he proclaimed to be superior to any death.[76]

[73] DE IV, 13, 7 (172, 20).

[74] DE IV, 13, 7 (172, 22–26). This does not imply that Eusebius considered the Incarnation an illusion. The body of the Logos is a true body; cf. DE IV, 10 (168, 15–169, 5; HE I, 2, 23; 24, 20–22; but it remains extrinsic to the Logos!

[75] Thgr fragm. 3 (6, 23–7, 1 = Ths III, 55).

[76] Thgr fragm. 3 (8, 18–9,8 = Ths III, 57).

Christ's suffering is presented here like the triumphant parade of a king who went into battle already a victor, but allowing some time in order to make his sovereignty all the more obvious.[77] In all this, we only hear about the Logos and his flesh, never about the soul of Christ. In death, the Logos leaves the flesh, which— without the Logos—is conquered by death. We gain the impression that the Logos, for Eusebius, simply stands for the soul of Christ. Other passages reinforce this impression.[78] The flesh without the Logos would remain "without reason and motion".[79] Yet the Logos does not abandon it to its dead state, he restores it again to life in the Logos. Now "the corruptible has put on incorruptibility, the mortal has put on immortality" (1 Cor 15:53). Eusebius comments on this passage in Paul: "This means that the whole man was 'swallowed up' by the divinity (1 Cor 15:55), and that therefore the Divine Logos returned to being God, the way he was before he had become man, and that the Logos subsumed his human nature into his divine nature as the "first fruits" (1 Cor 15:20) of our hope."[80]

This passage coincides in all respects with the main argument of the letter to Empress Constantia: the flesh, after the Resurrection, is no longer bound by its own weakness but is "swallowed up" entirely by the divine life. Eusebius, in his letter to Constantia, speaks of a "total transformation". This is not a chance, isolated statement. Elsewhere, too, he speaks

---

[77] Eusebius sensed the inadequacy of this interpretation of the Passion. He therefore adds the biblical notion of the expiatory sacrifice. Occasionally, he also quotes the Servant songs and other Passion-related texts, even saying that the Logos "has made our suffering his own" (cf. Is 53:4); DE X, 1, 22 (450, 12–16). "But this line of biblical exegesis remains a foreign element within the context of this theology" (H. Berkhof, *Die Theologie des Eusebius von Caesarea* [Amsterdam, 1939], 135).

[78] Cf. ET 87, 26: "The Logos animated the flesh in place of the soul." More details on this in H. de Riedmatten, *Les actes du Procès de Paul de Samosate* (Fribourg, 1952), 68–81. Here Eusebius lags considerably behind his teacher, Origen!

[79] CM II, 4 (57, 3–4). Eusebius arrives at obviously "monoenergistic" conclusions (assuming only one—the divine—activity): "The incorporeal One donned an image consisting of a human nature, and the God in him activated his image (that is, the body)" (Ths III, 40 [146, 2–7]).

[80] DE IV, 14 (173, 12–15).

of the "ineffable transformation of our Savior into divinity, after the Resurrection".[81]

How shall we sum up the Christology of Eusebius? Perhaps what is most to the point is the observation that his Christology moves entirely within the context of his cosmology. His doctrine of salvation is part of his cosmology. The purpose of the Incarnation consists in leading mankind back to knowing the truth.

The Logos, through the instrument of his flesh, has manifested himself above all in order to instruct, to move man's free will toward conversion. The aspects of redemption, of ransom, of the gift of grace, are substantially deemphasized. What remains is mainly an ethical and intellectual interpretation of the Christian life. The abyss between God and creation is never bridged. True, God appears in the world of man through the manifold theophanies of his Logos; yet never does God *truly* become man. That the supreme God, in Christ, should himself have appeared on earth is for Eusebius a philosophical impossibility. How could this supreme God, who himself is the denial of all limitations, ever be confined within the limited form of a man? This is not only impossible, it is also unnecessary. For mankind is not so much in need of liberation from death—on the contrary, death renders the soul the invaluable service of freeing it from the oppressive clay of the body[82] —rather, it is in need of being led to a genuine knowledge of the divine truth and of the ethical ideal. In order to mediate such knowledge, a being inferior to the supreme God is quite sufficient. The Logos provides this knowledge without really and ultimately becoming man, rather by using the flesh as instrument. On our way toward the true knowledge, an icon of this mortal flesh would be but a hindrance.

---

[81] DE III, 2, 26 (100, 21); cf. VII, 1, 25 (302, 20); ET III, 15, 11 (173, 20–23); ET III, 10, 1–2 (166, 1–14).

[82] Death is "the Liberator of the soul from the body" (Ths I, 75; 77, 15–31).

4. *The Icon of Christ and Anthropology*

Eusebius, as we have seen, opposes the painting of icons depicting Christ, not only of his invisible divine form but even icons of his human form. The essential reason for this is Christ's Resurrection: through it, his flesh has lost its own subsistence, it has been, as it were, "swallowed up" by his divinity. If, then, Christ's humanity can thus lose its own subsistence, the question might be appropriate whether it ever possessed such subsistence at all. Underlying Eusebius' Christology there appears the outline of a certain anthropology that provides the framework for his conception of Christ's human nature. In what sense does Eusebius understand the creation of man "in God's image and likeness" (Gen 1:26)? The answer to this question will help us comprehend better the deeper reasons for Eusebius' opposition to icons.

God created man through the mediation of his Logos, his image. If man is therefore called the "image of God", then this can only mean that he carries within himself the image of the Logos. The notion of Logos and the notion of creation explain each other. Interpreting John 1:9 ("He was the light enlightening every man who comes into the world"), Eusebius emphasizes that the light here is not the light our eyes perceive but is the Logos himself. "Yet this light was the spiritual illumination only for men. For this reason did the Logos create the spiritual and rational souls by means of his spiritual and rational power according to his own image and likeness."[83] This brief passage, explicitly referring to Genesis 1:26, contains three important affirmations: while the text from Genesis speaks of the creation of *man,* Eusebius only mentions the creation of the *soul;* we shall find out why. As Eusebius speaks of the light of men and then immediately speaks of the soul, he seems to identify man with his soul. The body does not appear to be part of his definition of man; for this, too, we shall shortly find the reason. The third affirmation determines what constitutes the image of God in man: by comparing the properties of the soul with those of the Logos, Eusebius shows

[83] ET I, 20, 7–8 (81, 7).

that the soul is the image of the Logos, because the soul, like the Logos, is spiritual and rational.[84]

Before we draw more specific conclusions regarding the conception of man as God's image, we shall consider three more texts that are essential for Eusebius' anthropology. The first text offers a more detailed exegesis of the creation account:

> Of immortal nature, and comparable to the citizens of heaven, there exists among all the beings on the earth only man, because of this spiritual and rational substance in man. He is the beloved offspring of the Logos, of the common redeemer of all, who perfects him as to his nature according to the image and likeness of his own Father. If this rational being, therefore . . . would have lived in conformity with his nature . . . he might perchance have been free from all earthly and corruptible life. . . . But thus the transitory and corruptible man, through the mercy of the Father, was necessarily clothed with a body, so that he would not be for ever tainted by evil and chained without end to what is transitory, but rather that all that is transitory be soon dissolved and he be received into the community of those who live for ever.[85]

Eusebius then compares man's life on earth to the life of a fetus, saying that the body would be like the "corruptible skin" enveloping the fetus within the womb, the skin that is discarded when he sees the light of day. This conception of man clearly shows the influence of Origen. The creation of the soul is the only true creation, when the soul, through the mediation of the Logos, is made into the image of God the Father.[86] The body is merely added, as it became necessary in consequence of something like an "occupational accident": because of the irrational behavior of man, that is, of the soul. In a different passage, Eusebius formulates this viewpoint in philosophical terms:

> Man is not a unified reality; he does not consist of one nature only, but is *composed of two opposite realities:* body and soul. The

---

[84] This comparison is found even more specifically in ET II, 14, 22 (118, 10ff.).

[85] Ths I, 68–69 (70, 18–71, 14); cf. Ths I, 64 (69, 9): the body is corruptible, but "what is inside" (that is, the soul) is incorruptible.

[86] Cf. also Ths I, 47 (61, 12–28).

body is joined to the soul in an accidental manner and like an instrument, while the spiritual essence [of the soul] is autonomous and substantial. The body lacks reason, the soul is gifted with reason; the body is transitory, the soul is everlasting; the body is mortal, the soul is immortal.[87]

While the previous quote argued its point from the background of the creation account, this text employs more philosophical terms. The body was not created together with the soul; it was added to the soul as an instrument and always remains extrinsic to it, as it were, even though body and soul now form a unity. In this unity, however, only the soul is the image of God.[88]

The third text denies explicitly that the body could ever be an image of God. Eusebius, in refuting a passage from Porphyry's treatise, "On the Veneration of Divine Images", writes:

What similarity could a human body have with the Spirit of God? I hold that the body does not even possess a likeness to the human spirit. For the latter is incorporeal, uncomposed, without parts, while the handiwork of ignorant men imitates the nature of the mortal body and *depicts the barren and mute likeness of the living body in inanimate and dead matter.* In contrast, I deem it appropriate to state that the immortal and rational soul and the dispassionate spirit represent in human nature the image and likeness of God, insofar as the essence of the soul is immaterial and incorporeal, spiritual and rational, and capable of virtue and wisdom. *Should anybody be able to depict in an icon the image and form of the soul, then, and only then, could he also depict the higher beings.*[89]

The conclusion is obvious: if not even the soul has either form or shape, then it is all the more preposterous to set out to depict

[87] PE VI, 6, 26 (303, 24); cf. Ths I, 75 (76, 10–20); cf. also de Riedmatten, *Les actes,* 8off.

[88] This opinion is not specifically Eusebian; it is quite common among the Church Fathers. A case in point is for instance the 10th homily on the Hexaemeron by St. Basil (chaps. 7–8; SC 160, 181–87). Specifically Eusebian, though, is the viewpoint that the creation of the body is a consequence of sin. In this he follows his teacher Origen.

[89] PE II, 10, 15–17 (133, 8–20).

God's likeness. The path through anthropology thus has led us back to our initial question: Is it possible to paint the icon of Christ? The soul cannot be represented in a painting, only the body. Yet even an image of the body would be questionable, since it would represent but a mute and barren imitation of the mortal body. The body appears mostly as the outward cover, as the dwelling place of the soul, which constitutes the true nature of man. Only in this outward sense can the body also be called the image or the likeness of the soul; and this image is different from pagan statues insofar as in them no life at all is found, while the body at least harbors the immortal image of the Logos, the soul. Since the body can be called a "statue" of the soul only in this weaker sense, and cannot be called the soul's image in a true sense, how much more does this apply when in this body dwells not a mere human soul but the Divine Logos himself?

Admittedly, the body of Christ is endowed with incomparable dignity because it shelters the Logos, who bestows on it immortality.[90] Yet this dignity remains on the outside; this Eusebius shows by comparing pagan idols and the body of Christ:

> Those who delight in the things perceived by the senses, and who search for gods in images and carvings of inanimated idols, and who fantasize that God dwells in material and bodily things, and who because of their weakness and insanity of mind declared mortal humans to be of divine nature, those were given, in just such a way, to behold even the kindly and benevolent Logos of God. For this purpose he fashioned for himself a bodily instrument as a most sacred temple, a visible dwelling place for his rational power, an untainted and eminent image, more precious than any inanimated idol.[91]

[90] Cf. DE IV, 13 (172, 20).

[91] LC 14, 2–3 (241, 24–31) = Ths III, 39 (142, 3–12); cf. LC 15, 2 (244, 17–20) = Ths III, 55 (149): "He employed a mortal instrument like an image worthy of God; by this means he entered the life of men as a great king enters through the good services of his herald"; Ths III, 39 (142, 16–23); cf. LC 14, 3 (242, 3–6); cf. also Ths fragm. 3 (4, 12). It is significant that Eusebius calls Christ's body, not *eikôn,* but *agalma* of the Logos: this term emphasizes more the extrinsic nature of the relationship between body and Logos.

Christ's body surpasses the images and idols of the pagans only because it is the dwelling place of the Logos, while those idols are "the homesteads of demons".[92] This dignity is at the same time a limitation. The letter to Empress Constantia shows it clearly. Eusebius, after having explained that, following Christ's Resurrection, his body, being his human form, was "swallowed up" by his divinity, immediately proceeds to refute one other possible argument:

> Should you, however, declare that you do not desire from me an image of his human form as it was transformed into God himself, but rather the icon of his mortal flesh as it consisted before its transfiguration, then my reply is this: Do you not know the passage where God commands not to fashion any image neither of things in heaven nor of things on earth (Ex 20:4)?[93]

Christ's body is indeed a statue (*agalma*) in which the Logos himself dwells. Yet whoever would concentrate on this image and make it an object of devotion would turn into an idolater, and the statue would become an idol. Eusebius sees idolatry as a consequence of man's turning toward all that affects his senses and is earthly.[94] To worship the image of Christ as it is perceived through the senses would be pure idolatry. Eusebius, in the same letter to Constantia, adds that he rejects the custom, the way he has observed it in many places, of displaying icons,

> so that we might not pass for servants of idols, as if we would carry around our God in pictures. I hear St. Paul's teaching about not being absorbed by the things of the flesh. For he says that "even though we once knew Christ according to the flesh, yet now we know him so no longer" (2 Cor 5:16). . . . Since we profess our Lord and Savior to be God, we hasten to know him also *as God* by purifying our hearts with great zeal so that we, thus cleansed, may behold him. Does it not say, "Blessed are the pure of heart, for they shall see God" (Mt 5:8)?[95]

[92] LC 14 (242, 3) = Ths III, 21 (142, 15).
[93] PG 20, 158BC.
[94] Cf. Ths II, 1–82 (81–119) and LC 14 (214, 16–242, 3).
[95] PG 20, 158D–159A.

Eusebius does not deny that the imaging arts are possible. He even sees them as signs of the great power of the human spirit.[96] He himself reports on images of the apostles and of Christ and seems to assume that they go back to the earliest times and are true likenesses of the apostles and of Christ (see illustration no. 4; see above, page 61).[97] But this is precisely not the issue here! We are to seek the Lord *as God,* and this requires purity of heart, a pure soul, which as God's image is alone able to behold the invisible image of the invisible God. Since the Logos is this invisible image, only the spiritual soul, which is the image of the Logos, can know the full and true reality of the Logos.[98] Flesh can know only flesh. The icon, insofar as it is a sense-related representation of the flesh assumed by the Logos, keeps us imprisoned within the very bonds from which the Logos wants to liberate us: the bondage of the flesh.

5. *Eusebius' Sacramental Conception of the Image*

Eusebius' anthropology inevitably leads to an iconoclastic attitude. Is this confirmed also in the area where the interconnection between things of the senses and things of the spirit is especially relevant: in sacramental theology? If Eusebius was indeed the main patristic witness for the opponents of images, if on the other hand the iconoclasts declared that the Eucharist is the only true icon of Christ, then it should be of some interest to take a look, at least briefly, at Eusebius' eucharistic teaching. In fact, Eusebius, too, calls the eucharistic species an image (*eikôn*), and he is moreover one of the few Church Fathers doing this. He sees the Eucharist above all as memorial; the eucharistic symbols make present the memorial of the unique sacrifice of Christ:

[96] By his artistic activity, man demonstrates "that his own capacity is superior to the god fashioned by him" (Ths I, 53 [69, 3]).

[97] Cf. note 47 above.

[98] Cf. ET III, 21, 1 (181, 13f.), where Mt 5:8 is interpreted entirely in the sense found in the letter to Constantia.

It has been passed on to us to perform on the altar the memorial of this sacrifice employing the symbols of his body and his salvific blood, according to the laws of the New Covenant.[99]

Christ himself has entrusted to his disciples the symbols of the divine economy of salvation, and given the command to transform them into *the image* of his own body. For he no longer takes delight in the bloody sacrifices nor in the holocausts prescribed by Moses; rather, he commanded the use of bread as a symbol of his own body.[100]

In an even more general sense, the eucharistic bread and wine are called "the symbols of the ineffable words of the New Covenant".[101] Thus Eusebius interprets Jesus' discourse on the Bread of Life (Jn 6) in the sense of a spiritual partaking of God's Word and not of consuming the "flesh" of the body that the Logos has donned, nor of drinking the "visible, bodily" blood.[102] This spiritual, memorialized interpretation of the Eucharist differs markedly from the sacramental realism of most Church Fathers of that epoch. While these usually emphasize the reality of the actual physical sacrament, Eusebius understands the sacrament first of all as one of the elements constituting the entirely mental and spiritual life of Christians and of their liturgy, which has superseded the physical and bodily sacrifices of the Old Covenant.

The influence of Eusebius on the eucharistic doctrine of the eighth-century iconoclasts has been demonstrated.[103] The connection between his rejection of the Christ icon, his general attitude toward images, and his predominantly spiritualistic conception of the sacraments illustrate in a typical fashion that the ancient Church's struggle about icons has always and foremost been a theological struggle. Eusebius was able to show us precisely this: the attitude

---

[99] DE I, 10, 28 (47, 32–35).

[100] DE VIII, 1, 79–80 (366, 21–26).

[101] DE VIII, 2, 119 (389, 23–25).

[102] ET III, 12 (168, 27–169, 5).

[103] S. Gero, "The Eucharistic Doctrine of the Byzantine Iconoclasts and its Sources", *Byzantinische Zeitschrift* 68 (1975):4–22.

regarding Christ's icon is determined by the concept one has of
Christ himself as "image".

III. "God, Visible in the Flesh": Cyril of Alexandria (d. 444 A.D.)

The guiding question of this chapter is this: Is the Logos even in
his Incarnation still "the image of the invisible God" (Col 1:15)? Is
the Incarnation indeed the manifestation of God's Son himself?
The exposition on Origen and Eusebius has shown that the answer
to this question also determines the attitude toward the arts as a
means of religious expression. For Eusebius, the reality of the
image is necessarily a lesser reality; the artistic image is therefore,
as it were, the lowest and least valuable level of representation: a
portrait, especially an image of Christ, is to be seen as merely "a
deaf and mute picture set in inert and dead material" representing
an earthly body, which itself is corruptible and mortal and hardly
indicative of the invisible reality of the soul, which in turn is the
image of the divine original, the Logos, which again in turn is the
"image of the invisible God", who is utterly beyond the realm of
images, in the transcendence of the Almighty. Within this cascad-
ing system—which descends from one level of image to an even
lower level, down to the ultimate border where being image
represents no more than a distant, feeble echo of the archetype of
all images—in such a system the icon of Christ can be seen only as
a fixation on what is least important.

What kind of iconology would result, in contrast, if the
Christology applied would hold fast to the basic thought of
Athanasius: the concept of an image *in its essence identical* to
the original, an image containing the "undiminished" original?
Would this not imply that a specific human nature, the humanity
of Jesus of Nazareth, is then the "human expression" of this
"co-essential" image? That "God is seen in the flesh"? This very
same conclusion was drawn by Cyril of Alexandria, the great

master of Christology in the fifth century. We now shall consider his Christology insofar as it has a bearing on the conception of the Christ icon.

Cyril, the faithful disciple of the great Athanasius, like him considers the eternal Logos to be the perfect and consubstantial image of the Father, "for the very character of the Father's substance is by its nature transmitted to the Son, so that the Son reveals in himself the Father".[104] As a result of this substantial identity, the Father is entirely in the Son, and the Son is perfect in everything, "because in himself he contains the Father, who is perfect, and because he is the imprint [*charaktêr*] of the Father".[105] We now face the task of investigating how Cyril interprets the Incarnation of this Logos that is in every respect consubstantial with God. It is already obvious that the Logos, for Cyril, cannot be an intermediate entity, the way he was for Arius (and, somewhat less pronounced, for Eusebius). The Logos is God undiminished, the perfect offspring of the perfect substance of the Father. The greatest paradox of the Christian revelation lies in the fact that God himself became man, and that this Incarnation does not represent merely one, albeit the highest, among many manifestations of the Divine Logos, one among many "irruptions" of the absolute into this finite world; rather, that this Incarnation means the true identity between the Logos and a historical, individual man. Cyril incessantly dwelt on this great mystery and proclaimed it in impressively realistic terms.

1. *"The Glory of God Shining on the Face of Christ" (2 Cor 4:6)*

Once the Incarnation is accepted as reality, it follows that "the flesh assumed by the Word does not remain foreign and accidental to this Word but becomes one with it".[106] The flesh is not "an extrinsic cover" but belongs to the very identity of the Logos. For

[104] PG 73, 180C.

[105] PG 73, 53C.

[106] PG 69, 561B. Cyril employs the term "flesh" in the same sense as the gospel of John; cf. note 117 below.

this reason is "the Lord Jesus Christ one undivided identity",[107] for the Word "did not dwell in a man—it *became* man".[108] " 'The image of the invisible God' (Col 1:15), the reflection of the Father's substance and his imprint (Heb 1:3), has assumed the form of a slave (Phil 2:7), not by adding a man unto himself, as the Nestorians teach, but by making himself into such a form and yet at the same time preserving his likeness unto the Father."[109]

To take the Incarnation seriously means: not to take the humanity of the Logos merely as an instrument, a garment, an extrinsic dwelling place, but rather as "the flesh of the everlasting God".[110] Therefore, if the flesh is intrinsic to the Word, and if the Word remains consubstantial with the Father, then the Word, even *in his Incarnation,* "preserves his likeness to God the Father".

At this point, it is already evident that here we are dealing with a conception of the Incarnation essentially different from the one Eusebius held. Eusebius was concerned with transcending the human instrument of the Logos in order to reach the Logos himself, which was hidden in this instrument. Cyril sees the mystery of the Incarnation in the very fact that on the human face of Jesus there irradiates the glory of God:

> "For God who said, 'Out of darkness light shall shine' (Gen 1:3), has shone in our hearts in order to irradiate the knowledge of God's glory that shines on the face of Christ" (2 Cor 4:6). Note that "on the face of Christ" there radiates the light of the divine and ineffable glory of God the Father. For the only-begotten Son reveals in himself the glory of the Father, *even after having become man.* Only in this and in no other manner is he recognized and named the Christ. If not, then let our adversaries tell us how an ordinary man could ever reveal to us or make known to us the light of God's glory. For, surely, we do not behold God in just any man, except he be the Word incarnate, having

---

[107] PG 69, 576BC.
[108] PG 76, 261C.; M. de Durand (SC 97, 522–24) considers this text as inauthentic.
[109] PG 75, 1329AB.
[110] PG 75, 1265A.

become one like us, which even in his Incarnation still preserved the true nature of the Son.[111]

If the Word identifies with the flesh and entirely appropriates
it, then this flesh must, in a certain sense, participate in the
innermost essence of the Son, in his hypostasis. This also changes
the conception of the image. Cyril at one time comments on "the
Day of your countenance" (Ps 21:9) in these words: "Rightly can
we understand the 'time of the Father's countenance' as the time of
the Incarnation, for the Son, after all, is the face [prosôpon] and the
image of the Father."[112]

The notion of "image", unlike in Origen and Eusebius, is here
no longer reserved for the invisible Logos but applies equally to
the incarnate Word. We therefore behold in the incarnate Word
the glory of God. To believe in Jesus Christ does not merely mean
to believe in a man, Cyril explains, but to believe in the Father
himself through Jesus Christ (cf. Jn 12:44f.). So Jesus does not
reject the faith that is directed at him in his Incarnation; rather, he
"accepts it without making a separation or distinction [between
his divinity and his humanity], as faith in his person, regardless of
his being in the flesh".[113] Believing in Jesus of Nazareth is the same
as believing in the person of God's Son. *Those who see Jesus in faith,
see God's Son himself.* Cyril of Alexandria has emphasized this
with unsurpassed clarity. And in this lies his fundamental importance for the development of a theology of the image. This, for
example, is shown in Cyril's interpretation of Jesus' encounter
with the man born blind after he had healed him:

> "Do you believe in the Son of God?" When he exclaimed,
> "Who is he, Lord, that I may believe in him?", Christ answered:
> "You have seen him; the one who speaks with you is he." The
> other then said, "I do believe, Lord!" and he worshipped him
> (Jn 9:35–38). It is evident to everybody that the divine nature is
> invisible—"Nobody has ever beheld God" (Jn 1:18). If the Logos

[111] PG 75, 1329BC.
[112] PG 69, 132AB.
[113] PG 75, 1236B.

of God the Father would have separated his humanity from himself like a phantom form, and if he would have wanted to be believed uncovered and unveiled, why then did he not ask the one who was healed to explore the nature of God, whatever it be, by way of analogy and reflection, instead of pointing to his bodily reality, implying that the very eyes can see it? Does he not say, "You have seen him; the one who speaks with you is he"? Should we therefore not say that the Logos has shown his flesh? —Of course we do! —But then, *how could the Logos himself be in the flesh,* except if we assume that *through this union he became the very same thing he had made his own.*[114]

Christ's flesh, therefore, does not merely represent an opportunity, a suitable circumstance in the area of created things, through this analogy, to ascend to the creative Logos as he is "in himself". Faith has no need to strip Christ of his humanity in order to discover his divinity,[115] faith rather concentrates on the one and inseparable reality of the God-made-man. Christ's humanity thus is not a veil concealing his divinity; instead, it is "the flesh of God", it is in a certain sense the Logos himself—to such an extent does the Word identify himself with the flesh.[116] Cyril explains this strong emphasis on the unity of Word and flesh in view of the purpose of salvation: the Word became flesh not in order to liberate souls from the shackles of their bodies, but to save the body, which through the disobedience of sin is condemned to death. Cyril sees, in a very realistic sense, that our bodies since the fall have lost the breath of life, while our souls have preserved their immortality:[117]

The flesh alone was addressed with the words, "Dust thou art, and to dust thou shalt return" (Gen 3:19). What was most

[114] PG 75, 1236CD.

[115] PG 75, 1233C.

[116] Cyril frequently speaks of "assuming-as-one's-own" (*idiopoieisthai*): PG 72, 906A; 76, 193B, 205D, and elsewhere.

[117] This does not exclude salvation relating also to the soul, since Cyril applies the concept of "flesh" in a biblical sense and *pars pro toto* to the whole human person; PG 73, 160A. Man is in need of salvation primarily insofar he is "flesh," and as such weak and sinful.

endangered in us, therefore, had to be salvaged and had to be called back to immortality by means of a union with him who in essence is Life itself. . . . This was accomplished by uniting the corruptible body with the life-giving Logos in a manner inexpressible in words. For the flesh, having become the property of the Logos, thus was to participate in his immortality.[118]

The work of our salvation is voided if the Word did not become flesh; if there was no death then there was no Resurrection either.[119] Cyril views the subsumption of the mortal flesh by the eternal Word in a very realistic sense. United with the flesh, "the Word pours out on the flesh the splendor of his own glory".[120] In this miraculous exchange, the flesh obtains the life, the glory, the incorruptibility of the divine nature; it is being "filled with the life-giving power of the Logos".[121] The reason for this exchange is our salvation: "The Logos must obtain what belongs to us, in order to give to us what belongs to him."[122] Christ, by assuming our flesh, has in a certain sense entered into a union with all of mankind. All of us, by means of his flesh, have been made his kin (*syngeneian*),[123] and because of this kinship we have been given anew access to "the glory of the sons of God" (Rom 8:21), to which glory we had been called from the beginning:

> "In him the whole fullness of the divine nature dwells in bodily form", says Paul (Col 2:9). And the theologian [John] reveals to us this sublime mystery when he states that the Word has dwelt among us (Jn 1:14). For all of us are in Christ, and this "collective person" [*koinon prosôpon*] of mankind has been revived anew in him. . . . The Word has dwelt in all through the one, so that the dignity of divine sonship might pass from the one true Son of God to all of mankind, through the Spirit of sanctification, and

118 PG 73, 160BC.
119 PG 75, 1265BC.
120 PG 75, 1288C.
121 PG 75, 1360D.
122 PG 75, 1268C; cf. PG 72, 444D–445A.
123 PG 73, 161D; PG 73, 869D.

that through the One among us these words should come true:
"I said, 'You are gods and sons of the Most High'" (Ps 82:6).[124]

To extend the divine sonship to us, it was necessary for the
flesh of the Word himself to share first in the Word's divine
sonship. Cyril, therefore, again and again rejects the idea that
there could be two sonships in Christ, the eternal sonship of the
Word, and the temporal "of the assumed humanity".[125] Rather,
the human flesh of Christ is the flesh of the Son of God: there is
only one sonship; and the mystery of the Word's freely willed
self-abasement consists in the eternal sonship's becoming a property of the Word's humanity: "In Christ, being the only-begotten
Son became a property of his humanity, because of this humanity's
union with the Word . . . , and conversely, being the firstborn of
many brothers (cf. Rom 8:29) became a property of the Word,
because of the Word's union with the flesh."[126] The original fall
from grace has subjected us to corruptibility and death. We carry
in us the image of the earthly Adam (1 Cor 15:49). This corruptibility, once again, affects above all our flesh and makes it
"earthly", dust returning to dust. Having become corruptible, the
image of God in man is also distorted.[127] For the image of God in
man was originally "an imprint, the seal of God in us, a sanctifica-
tion, which makes us partakers of the divine nature and therefore
of its incorruptibility".[128] Our nature, in order to regain the
original fullness of the image and likeness of God, must be imprinted
anew with the seal of the Holy Spirit, so that the Spirit may again
dwell in it. Indeed, since the advent of sin, "the Spirit could no
longer find a dwelling place in man." It was only after the Son of

[124] PG 73, 161C; further patristic texts on the topic of "the unity of mankind" are
found in H. de Lubac, *Glauben aus der Liebe,* 2nd ed. (Einsiedeln, 1970), chap. 1,
note 46; idem, *Die Kirche. Eine Betrachtung* (Einsiedeln, 1968), chap. V; G. Larentzakis,
Einheit der Menschheit, Einheit der Kirche bei Athanasius (Graz, 1978).

[125] Cf. PG 73, 10009D.

[126] PG 75, 1229B; cf. ibid., 1275A: "In him [Christ], human nature has for the
first time received this privilege [that is, sonship]."

[127] Cf. W. Burghardt, *The Image of God in Man according to Cyril of Alexandria*
(Woodstock, 1957).

[128] de Durand, in SC 97, 88.

God had become man that "the Spirit once again dwelt in human nature, first in Him as the new firstfruits of humanity, and then dwelling also in us."[129] Thus we are to be remolded after the incarnate Word, which is "the image of the heavenly Adam" (1 Cor 15:49). Only through his flesh does mankind obtain "the remedy of immortality":[130]

> A body that had become the body of him who did not know sin was well able to discard the tyranny of sin. This body, united to the Word in an ineffable manner, was ennobled by the Word's very own nature: it became holy, life-giving, filled with divine power. We, too, are being transformed in Christ, the firstfruits, so that we can overcome all frailty and sin.[131]

The greatness of salvation history, the salvific effectiveness of the Incarnation, consists in the mystery that Jesus was not a "mere man" but God's Son. "How could 'the blood of Jesus cleanse us from all sin', if it were the blood of an ordinary man, who is subject to sin"?[132] In him, and in him alone, was human nature, as a natural consequence, transformed into the humanity of God's Son. We, on the other hand, can *through grace* become sons of God, thanks to his human nature now taken up into "sonship". This grandiose view on the part of Cyril of Alexandria demands further investigation into its full existential implications.

2. *"Whoever Sees Me, Sees the Father" (Jn 14:9)*

In the mystery of the Son's self-abasement in his Incarnation, his sonship became a property of his humanity. For this reason is it in truth possible for us to behold the Son of God when beholding Jesus of Nazareth. This is the meaning of Jesus' remark to Philip,

---

[129] PG 70, 313CD.

[130] This is especially accomplished by the Eucharist; cf. A. Stuckmann, *Die Eucharistielehre des heiligen Cyrill von Alexandrien* (Paderborn, 1910).

[131] PG 75, 1269DC; the eucharistic body possesses the same power to transform. PG 73, 585D.

[132] PG 75, 1269B.

"Whoever sees me, sees the Father" (Jn 14:9), so frequently quoted and discussed by Cyril:

> Nobody can see the divine essence in itself, for it is entirely invisible and beyond all comprehension and power of reasoning: it is known in itself only by itself. This very truth is expressed by Christ: "Nobody knows the Son except the Father; nobody knows the Father except the Son, and to whom the Son wishes to reveal him" (Mt 11:27). The only-begotten Son shows us the exceeding beauty of God the Father whose radiant image he himself represents. For this reason he says, "Whoever sees me, sees the Father" (Jn 14:9). True, we behold the Son above all with the eyes of our hearts, but also with our bodily eyes; for he has humbled himself and has descended among us, while at the same time dwelling in the form of God and equal to God the Father, because according to his nature he is born of the Father.[133]

These words by our Lord, without doubt, refer to the Incarnation, and Cyril employs them in this sense almost without exception. And yet, is it really possible to say that the Son is the perfect image of God, even with regard to his humanity? After all, God is invisible! Could his image then be visible? Cyril, in the text just quoted, states that we behold the Son even with our bodily eyes. Which, of course, does not mean that we would be able to recognize him as the Son of God immediately through our bodily sight alone. Without faith, we are not able to see that Jesus is the Son of God.[134] For Christ's humanity remains a common humanity with regard to its properties, it is not "remade" into God[135] by becoming the flesh of the Word: the Son is the perfect image of the Father because he is perfectly like the Father, "not based on the characteristics of the flesh, nor on the form of his body", but in view of his divine power and glory. Still, his humanity should

---

[133] PG 69, 465D–468A; cf. PG 75, 1205BC: "The Son presents himself to us as the image that shows us in all clarity the Father: 'Whoever sees me, sees the Father' (Jn 14:9)."

[134] "We who have accepted the faith have seen the Father in the Son . . . " (PG 69, 468B).

[135] Cf. PG 75, 1289D.

never be considered without reference to his being God's Son.[136] The flesh of Christ is not made into "the image of the invisible God", for no *nature,* be it human or divine, can ever be an image, but only a *person.* The *Son* is the image of the *Father.* If Christ is to be image of the Father *as man as well,* then this is possible only because, through the self-abasement of the Incarnation, the properties of his humanity reveal the qualities of the eternal Son as well.

> Let us direct our attention to the specific and true image of the Father, which is the Son. For in him we behold the image of the Father whenever we lift up the eyes of our souls to his qualities: God the Father is by nature good; so is the Son. How could he not be good, he who has willingly accepted such a humiliation, who has come into this world to save sinners, who has given his life for them? Mighty is the Father, and so is the Son. . . . The Father is life itself, and so is the Son, he who gives life to those who perish, he who destroys the power of death and raises the dead. With good reason, therefore, he tells Philip, "Whoever sees me, sees the Father" (Jn 14:9). For in me, so he says, and through me you can see the Father.[137]

It is especially in his becoming man, in his work of salvation, in his sacrifice, that Christ is recognized as the image of the Father. Whoever sees his love for all people, sees the Father. His deeds reveal the love of the Father. Thus the very immensity of his self-abasement reveals the immensity also of the Father. It is true, the flesh as such is somewhat "opaque": the Incarnation veils and hides the glory of the Word.[138] The incomparable beauty of Christ's divinity makes his humanity appear as all but an "outward ugliness".[139] Yet this outward humbleness is the very revelation of the greatness of love from which it flows. The self-abandonment even to the point of the ugliness of death makes visible the love of

[136] PG 73, 484AB.

[137] PG 74, 209D–212A; cf. PG 73, 420B; PG 74, 193BC.

[138] PG 75, 1333B.

[139] PG 69, 396B; cf. PG 70, 1169C–1172B. On the topic of the ugliness of Christ, cf. A. Grillmeier, *Der Logos am Kreuz* (Munich, 1956), 42–47, and idem, *Mit Ihm und in Ihm. Christologische Forschungen und Perspektiven* (Freiburg, 1975), chap. 1.

the Father, a love willing to give the Son in sacrifice.[140] Thus the Son reveals the Father through the very lowliness of taking "the form of a slave": the one on the Cross is "the image of the invisible God" (Col 1:15).

Cyril has repeatedly been considered one of those theologians who propound a theory of "physical salvation", according to which the Incarnation itself would immediately constitute the fullness of salvation; for the union of divinity and humanity in Christ would, in a way, extend the fruits of salvation "physically" to all of mankind.[141] There is no doubt, really, that Cyril emphasizes the Incarnation in no small measure, especially after the onset of the Nestorian crisis (428 A.D.). And yet, it would be entirely mistaken to interpret him as setting the Incarnation and the Passion, the becoming man and the paschal mystery, over against each other. Rather, Cyril shows with great skill that the Incarnation is itself a salvific act, and that, on the other hand, the Cross and the Resurrection receive their significance only in light of the Incarnation. He interprets the Incarnation as the first step in the Son's self-abasement, which would culminate in obedience unto the Cross. In this sense, the Incarnation already contains what the Cross will later reveal in its fullness: the child born of Mary is the beloved Son who has become man out of obedience and love. The Cross, therefore, completes the Incarnation: "With the shedding of the blood, the mystery of the Incarnation found its completion, if it is to be true that Christ was obedient to the Father unto death, even death on the Cross, and that he has redeemed the world through his blood."[142]

Whoever sees the incarnate Word sees the obedience and the love of the Son, and in this sense, the words of Christ "Whoever sees me, sees the Father" (Jn 14:9) also apply to the humanity of the Logos: his humanity, indeed his flesh, is the *visible* manifestation

[140] Cf. PG 69, 645D–648A.

[141] On the history of this line of questioning, cf. R. Hübner, *Die Einheit des Leibes Christi bei Gregor von Nyssa. Untersuchungen zum Ursprung der physischen Erlösungslehre* (Leiden, 1974). Regarding Cyril, de Durand, in SC 97, 93–95, and 137ff.

[142] PG 69, 628D.

of his union with the Father; it is the "radiant image of the Father's beauty".[143] A wonderful conception of Christ's humanity is outlined here: it is the Father's love in visible form, *the human translation of the eternal sonship into human terms;* the "incarnate" image of God. Later we shall discuss in more detail the significant implications regarding the concept of "image" and the theology of the image.

The Incarnation, in Cyril's view, is not the ultimate goal. It points beyond itself: its objective is that "marvelous exchange", in which the willingly accepted poverty of the Son is providing us with the richness of our adoption as sons.[144] Still, the objective, once accomplished, does not devalue the way and the means: the Incarnation is no mere transitory stage, superseded as soon as the objective is reached. For the risen Son is now "the firstborn of many brothers" (Rom 8:29). "Since he has assumed our human nature, and since he has clothed us, through the work of salvation, with his own properties, he is not ashamed to call us brothers: for through him we are destined to become sons."[145] He *remains* our brother, as he is the "firstborn from the dead" (Col 1:18); for "risen from the dead, he ascended *in the flesh* to the Father".[146] This emphasis on the *lasting* significance of Christ's humanity would necessarily have important consequences for the question of Christ's depiction in an image.

Let us now try to summarize the previous insights gleaned from Cyril's Christology as they relate to our topic:

I. Cyril, with incomparable clarity, focused his theological investigation on the unity, the inseparable identity, that exists between Word and flesh based on their intimate union. The flesh has been wholly appropriated by the Word, so that whoever sees Christ, truly sees the Son of God. The terminology employed, however, was often not yet as precise as it would become in the course of later developments (not always constituting a theological improvement!). But it was Cyril who, with his emphasis on

[143] Cf. note 133 above.
[144] Cf. PG 69, 325D; 368D.
[145] PG 69, 436B; cf. 437A.
[146] PG 69, 476C.

the *hypostatic union,* showed the way: the hypostasis, the Divine Person of the Son, became man; the flesh, appropriated by the Word, became the flesh of the second Divine Person.

The concept of "hypostatic union" in Cyril's writing is not yet as specifically defined as in later theology. This term, for him, means above all the "real and true union".[147] And yet, on the other hand, Cyril understands "real union" in a very specific sense: he rejects unambiguously all talk of two hypostases in Christ and emphasizes untiringly that it is one and the same Son to whom all christological attributes apply: "There is only *one* Son, the Word, that became man for us; it is to him everything is ascribed: words and deeds, things divine and human."[148] This conviction, that all of Christ's attributes refer ultimately to one subject only, the Person of the eternal, incarnate Son, was to become *the foundation for the theology of the icon,* according to which the icon allows us to encounter the Person of the Son.

2. Cyril differs from Origen and Eusebius mainly in his *anthropology.* In a nutshell, one might observe that Origen sees man as incarnate soul, Cyril as "animated flesh". The only item in Origen's teaching explicitly rejected by Cyril is his doctrine of the dual creation: for Cyril, the body was not added to the soul because of sin; rather, body and soul form one unity because they were created together.[149] After all, Cyril employs the term "flesh", as we have seen, in the biblical sense of "actual living being" that is subject to mortality. The grandeur of creation lies specifically in the fact that some "flesh" is destined for the immortality of divine life. Before the fall, indeed, man possessed immortality through grace, in spite of his being mortal by nature.[150] The flesh, in order to regain immortality, had to be revived again by means of the union with the Word. Rarely does Cyril fail to mention that the object of interest is not the flesh "without soul" but "the flesh animated by the spiritual

[147] PG 76, 400D–401A.

[148] PG 75, 1325.

[149] Cf. PG 73, 132C–145B; also PG 73, 956C; 74, 796B; 77, 373B: here Origen is explicitly mentioned.

[150] PG 73, 145A.

soul", as he is wont to say. Still, the focus remains on the concrete reality of the flesh.

This realism may perhaps best be recognized in Cyril's eucharistic doctrine: precisely through the Eucharist, through "eating the flesh of Christ", man is made into a "living flesh". The union between Christ and the partaker, effected by the Eucharist, is of such reality that Cyril compares it to the fusion of two globs of sealing wax.[151] Small wonder, then, that on the whole, Cyril attributes to Christ's flesh a far more essential role in salvation history than do Origen and Eusebius.

3. Consequently, it is not without reason that certain ancient traditions attribute to Cyril the introduction of *icon devotion.*[152] No matter how things may have developed historically, Cyril without doubt is one of the fathers of icon devotion: his insistence that there is identity in one person between the humanity of Jesus and the Son of God opens the possibility for an *image* of Christ, the possibility actually to depict the real and individual humanity of Jesus and yet to present this very humanity as the human likeness of the eternal Son of God (see illustration no. 5).

3. *The Flesh of the Word*

One question though, a rather consequential question, is somewhat neglected by Cyril: Of what kind is the participation of the flesh in the Word? What relationship consists between the two? This question, no matter how much it smacks of importune curiosity on the part of prying theologians, is nevertheless important for our topic. For if the flesh retains its own proper nature, how can it then become the place of revelation and activity for the Son of God without itself becoming God? How can God's activity be revealed in Jesus' human activity without the latter losing its human character? In other words, how can the Word's humanity,

---

[151] PG 74, 341D.

[152] This is the legend among the Coptic and Syro-Malabar Christians; cf. E. von Dobschütz, *Christusbilder,* 2nd ed. (Leipzig, 1909), 33; also, Gero, "Cyril of Alexandria. Image Worship, and the vita of Rabban Hormizd", *Oriens Christianus* 62 (1978):77–97.

as humanity, make the Son visible and be his image? Cyril has encountered this question. He interprets Christ's saying, "The words I spoke to you are spirit and life" (Jn 6:63) as follows:

> He fills his entire body with the life-giving energy of spirit. For henceforth he calls his flesh spirit, without denying that it is flesh. . . . Since the flesh cannot give life of and by itself, what does it gain by being in the One who verily is God? . . . It is united to the Word, which by its own nature is life itself. If, then, Christ declares his flesh to be life-giving, he does not with this declare that it possesses the same life-giving power as he himself possesses, or the Holy Spirit. Through Christ himself, therefore, is his body life-giving; for he has "transposed" it onto the level of his own power. *How* this happened remains inaccessible to our mind and inexpressible for our tongue; it must be honored by silence and by faith that transcends all knowledge.[153]

The mystery of the union between Word and flesh demands silence. And yet, the heresies falsifying it nevertheless require discussion. The ensuing debates will always return to Cyril. He will be invoked as the main witness in favor of Monophysitism, which holds that the flesh all but loses its own identity as it is totally permeated and determined by Christ's divinity, like iron by red-hot heat. Cyril would later be invoked as a witness also for Monoenergism, which concedes in Christ only one power and one mode of action—the divine. Did Cyril himself proclaim the flesh of Christ to be totally passive, without any initiative flowing from Christ's humanity? If so, Cyril's contribution to a theology of the image would be less important than we assumed so far; for a purely passive humanity would not be a "living image" of the Son.

True, Cyril at times sounds like a Monoenergist. The flesh of Christ seems frequently so totally "permeated" by divine energy that its own reality is all but lost. Sometimes Cyril even speaks of "the one and only energy" of Christ, as when he comments on the resuscitation of the synagogue official's daughter: "He, as God, restores life anew through his almighty command, and he also restores life anew through the contact with his holy flesh: in both

---

[153] PG 73, 604BD.

Illustration 5

Illustration number 5: Christ the Pantocrator. Detail of a ceiling painting in the Catacombs of Sts. Peter and Marcellinus, Rome, late 4th century.

Photo: L. Hilber (Fribourg), after J. Wilpert, with permission of Herder-Verlag, Freiburg.

During the fourth century, the uniform type of the depiction of Christ begins to emerge, familiar to us from the icons (cf. illustrations numbers 1, 6, 7, 8, 10, and 11). It gradually replaces the symbolic image of Christ, typical for the earliest Christian art (cf. illustration number 2, perhaps also number 3). The artists strive to capture the individual and unmistakable features of Christ's human face. The conviction spreads that these were Christ's outward looks: long parted hair; a full beard; delicate, elongated facial features; large, serious eyes, gazing at the onlooker.

Our fresco from the turn of the fourth to the fifth century, constitutes one of the most impressive testimonies to this development, which determines for centuries the way Christ would be depicted. Some art historians (i.e., A. Grabar, *Christian Iconography: A Study of Its Origins* [London, 1969]), still count this depiction among the symbolic types. In an attempt to emphasize Christ's divinity, they say, he is shown in the iconographic manner of the full-bearded Zeus or Jove. We think the first opinion is more probable.

(See pages 14 and 93.)

ways he thus manifests the one and same effectiveness."[154] Cyril, it should be noted, uses this text to show that the Eucharist, the Body of Christ, possesses this life-giving power. He further underlines that this *one* effect springs from divinity and humanity, both.

Reviewing the healing of the leper, Cyril says: "Admire together with me how Christ is acting here at the same time divinely and bodily: divinely as regards his will, so that everything he wills does happen; and bodily in his human gesture of extending the hand—yet Christ is one and the same in both."[155] Cyril thus recognizes clearly that the properties of both natures are active, yet he wants to underline ever again the *unity* of the subject accomplishing all these actions, be they divine or human.

Still, the question remains whether Cyril attributes to the flesh of Christ as its own activity only its own passiveness. Cyril in truth discusses occasionally, just as Origen and Eusebius, the role of the flesh as consisting in being the instrument of the Logos.[156] It might above all have been the Nestorian crisis that convinced Cyril to drop the concept of "instrument" in his Christology. In his "Letter to the Monks", he cautions against possible misunderstandings based on this term:

> Anybody who should assign to Christ the role of instrument only, would he not, even without such an intention, deprive Christ of his true sonship? Suppose someone has a son who knows how to play the lyre and who sings beautifully. Would he ever treat the lyre with the same respect as he treats the son? Wouldn't such a thing be absurd? The lyre is used to display one's artistry. But the son remains son even without his instrument. If, then, certain people declare that the man born of the woman was assumed (by the Logos) as instrument, in order to work miracles through this instrument and to proclaim the gospel, should they not consider every one of the holy prophets equally as an instrument of God . . . ? In this case, Christ would of course be in no respect superior to them; in no way would he have surpassed his predecessors, if Christ would have been used

[154] PG 73, 577C.
[155] PG 72, 556B.
[156] For example, PG 75, 1212D.

as instrument in the same sense as the prophets.[157] . . . For this reason, we avoid saying that the temple [meaning, the flesh] taken from the Virgin Mary was used as an instrument. We rather follow the Faith proclaimed by the Sacred Scriptures and the Fathers and declare that the Word has become flesh.[158]

Cyril's chief argument here points out that Christ's humanity, understood only in an instrumental sense, would not be the flesh of the Word: it would remain extraneous to the Word, as extraneous as a lyre to the musician. This is the very same argument used by Eusebius, but in reverse. Eusebius used the example of the lyre in order to show that the Logos remained untouched by the suffering of his instrument, the flesh, the same way the musician is not hurt when the strings of his lyre snap. The same point Eusebius is making with this comparison prevents Cyril from applying this comparison to Christ. What would happen to the Easter mystery if the Word himself did not suffer in his flesh? This proves, once again, that Eusebius, in rejecting the icon of Christ, was entirely consistent: the Logos himself is already the instrument of the Father; the flesh of the Logos, insofar as it is his instrument, remains extraneous to him, a mere tool. Cyril, in contrast, sees the intimate union between Word and flesh in the fact that the flesh does not remain extraneous but is totally appropriated by the Son. The flesh, as it is intimately united to the Son who is consubstantial with God the Father, thus becomes "the flesh of God". It is this absolute union that makes it necessary not to degrade Christ's humanity by seeing it only as a purely passive instrument, nor simply to transpose it into God himself. Cyril sees this paradox symbolized in the image of the burning bush: the divinity of the Word, like an all-consuming and unendurable fire, has "moderated" himself to such an extent as to become endurable for the human flesh, yet at the same time he rendered the flesh more powerful than death.[159]

Did Cyril attempt to describe this relationship, this mutual

[157] PG 77, 32D–33B.
[158] PG 77, 36B.
[159] PG 69, 413CD.

permeation of Word and flesh, also in positive terms? He emphasizes that the flesh is not transformed into God and yet is totally appropriated by God. He does not say more, as he did not feel it necessary to say more. The Church Fathers were not so curious as to push theological questions any farther than required by their catechesis. His implications, however, point in the direction in which a later theology would be able to develop this question further.

We owe it to his doctrine of *man as image of God* that we can see how in Cyril's conception the cooperation between the divine and the human nature in Christ finds its interpretation. For the reason why it is possible for the Logos to adapt and unite his divinity to the flesh lies in the fact that human nature has already been created in God's image: "Man, through the Holy Spirit, has received the seal that makes him into the image of God. This is shown by Moses when he says, 'And he breathed into his nostrils the breath of life' (Gen 2:7). For it was the Spirit that conferred life on the creature and imprinted into him the features of the divine likeness."[160] "Participation in the Holy Spirit confers on man the grace to be formed into a perfect likeness of the divine essence. . . . As we receive the Spirit from the Son, we are being molded toward the image of God."[161] Without the gift of the Holy Spirit, "the features of the divine image cannot be restored in man."[162] By means of the Holy Spirit, we carry inside us the image of the Son, for the Spirit is the image of the Son,[163] just as the Son is the image of the Father.[164] Thus human nature is destined to be the image of God through the sonship conferred by the Holy Spirit, for this Spirit forms man according to the image of the Son. The original fall into sin has robbed man of the Holy Spirit's presence; therefore, it is only in Christ that the Holy Spirit is able to dwell

[160] PG 73, 204D.

[161] PG 75, 228B; cf. 225C–228A.

[162] PG 73, c. 205B.

[163] PG 75, 572A.

[164] "Whoever receives the image of the Son, that is, the Holy Spirit, also possesses through him in total measure the Son and the Father who is in him" (PG 75, 572A).

in man in fullness:[165] in this way, Christ has restored his image in man.

Thus there exists a profound relationship between the Son and human nature; the latter is fashioned entirely in view of the Son; and in orientation toward the Son, it finds its essential fulfillment in him. Created in his image, human nature can fully actualize itself only if it fully fashions his image within itself. Still, the gift of the Holy Spirit effecting this image in no way implies the changing of human nature into something extraneous to it: "If we say, we are united with God, this does not mean that our nature is changed into the divine essence; rather, we are united with God through grace and virtues."[166] Our *likeness to God* is real, but this does not change our proper nature. For the image of God in us does not produce an essential similarity with God; the difference between the natures of God and man is infinite: "There is, therefore, in the created beings no natural similarity with God; this similarity rather shines forth in the activity and the quality of our comportment."[167] "For it is the quality of our comportment that makes us similar to God, and it is the exercise of the virtues that imprints on us the features of the divine image."[168] There is indeed such a thing as "participation in the divine nature" (2 Pt 1:4), but it is actuated in the human nature precisely through actualization of those things essentially proper to man:

> Man is the only living being on earth endowed with reason and capable of exercising mercy and all other virtues, also entrusted with dominion over everything on earth, as he is the image and likeness of God. Man is said to be created in the image of God because he is endowed with reason and insofar as he loves virtue and has dominion over everything on earth.[169]

That which defines human nature and constitutes its essence also makes it into the image of God. Yet it can actualize this very

---

[165] Cf. note 129 above.
[166] PG 75, 205C.
[167] PG 75, 673D–676A.
[168] PG 75, 673BC.
[169] PG 76, 1068C–1072A.

reality only if the gift of the Holy Spirit imprints onto it the seal of likeness unto the Son. Cyril, for this reason, would say that it is grace *and* the virtues that unite us with God. In our divine transformation, therefore, there is at work a *synergism,* a cooperative action: grace confers the divine seal, and practicing the virtues imprints on us the features of God's image.

Considering the unique function of Christ's flesh in the work of salvation, we may conclude that Cyril of Alexandria could never attribute to the flesh of Christ a lower function than the one proper to it in the process of man's own divine elevation. To understand Christ's humanity merely as a passive instrument would be degrading to human nature, as it is fashioned to cooperate in the work of salvation. Christ has assumed the total reality of the human condition and has made it his own. True, Christ's humanity, through its union with the Logos, possesses by nature a dignity obtainable to us only through grace and virtues: but neither in him nor in us is the human nature in its divine status "dehumanized". Christ's humanity, after having become "the flesh of God", not only remains human, it fully actualizes the ultimate ideal of being human: the perfect image of God.

Cyril's teaching on the divine elevation of man thus proves to be an important corollary to his Christology. Man is the image of God insofar as the quality of his behavior makes visible this image, which is imprinted in him by the Holy Spirit. Man is capable of receiving this imprint, the features of the divine image, because the Son, through the union with his human nature, has first impressed on it his sonship, and in the works of his love, even unto the Cross, has *in his humanity* made visible the Father: "Whoever sees me, sees the Father."

IV. Love as the Icon of God:
Maximus Confessor (580–662 A.D.)

The importance of Cyril of Alexandria for Christology is comparable to the prominent place St. Athanasius occupies in the area of trinitarian theology. Gregory of Nyssa and Maximus Confessor can be compared to each other in similar fashion: in the discussions following the Council of Nicea (325 A.D.), it fell to Gregory of Nyssa to interpret the Creed of the Council in such a way as to render it fully acceptable to the Church. It is possible to compare the role Maximus played for Christology with the role Gregory played for trinitarian theology. In large measure, it is due to Maximus, the outstanding and perhaps greatest theologian of the late patristic era, that the Council of Chalcedon (451 A.D.), the most important Council of the ancient Church, met with such widespread and thorough acceptance on the part of the Church. We have to thank Maximus for *the most wonderful christological synthesis of the ancient Church.* His theological acuteness guides him to the highest peaks of speculative theology, and our modest attempts to retrace his thoughts cannot entirely avoid the strenuousness of this mental effort. Yet Maximus is not only the speculative theologian, he is equally one of the great mystics and spiritual guides of the Christian Orient. His theology never loses itself on the conceptual and speculative level. It invariably finds its way to the simplest and clearest insights of practical Christian life. This path we intend to retrace in what follows, at least in general outline. Our starting point in this will be rather difficult, at first sight even thoroughly abstract, problems of Christology. The farther we advance, however, so we hope, the more transparent these perplexing questions will become, until we arrive at Maximus' central spiritual vision, which finds its ultimate and most significant subject in the concrete manifestation of love.[170] Those readers

[170] Of the rich literature on Maximus, we single out only the "classic" text, H. U. von Balthasar, *Kosmische Liturgie. Das Weltbild Maximus des Bekenners,* 2nd ed. (Einsiedeln, 1961), and the new collection, *Maximus Confessor. Actes du Symposium*

who deem this approach too arduous may wish to skip ahead to the third section of this chapter (p. 113).

1. *Nature and Person—A Detailed Analysis of Their Correlation*

In his "38th Letter", Gregory of Nyssa formulated, in terms that would remain the standard for the Christian orient, the relation between nature and person in view of the theology of the Trinity. Maximus Confessor, better than any of his predecessors, succeeded then in applying Gregory's insights to Christology as well. Maximus formulated his thoughts on the matter in several letters, which, resembling Gregory's "38th Letter", should be considered theological treatises rather than mere letters. In what follows here, we focus especially on the 15th letter, which expands, explicitly in line with the Cappadocians, the question of nature and person from trinitarian theology into Christology. We enter here the somewhat rarefied field of exact conceptual investigations; yet we shall soon find that we are dealing with clarifications of extreme importance for our topic.

Maximus begins his analysis of the relation between nature and person, like Gregory of Nyssa, with a clarification of the concepts, but within the horizon of a theological view of the mystery. He writes to Cosmas, the deacon:

> You are asking me, what is general and in common, and what is particular and specific, so as *to gain a clear insight about the entire question regarding this union* [between both natures in Christ]. I shall say nothing thought up by myself, but only what I have learned from the Fathers.
>
> Well, then, according to the Fathers, what is common and general is the essence and the nature; for, as they say, these two are identical. What is particular and specific is the

---

sur Maxime le Confesseur, Fribourg, 2–5 Septembre 1980, eds. F. Heinzer and C. Schönborn (Fribourg, 1982).

hypostasis and the person, and again these two on their part are identical.[171]

Maximus then quotes a selection of texts, especially by Basil, but also by Gregory of Nazianzus, in order to show that the Fathers all agree on their teaching on this. Maximus continues with a detailed analysis of the implications of this teaching, a teaching summed up in one of Basil's statements quoted by him: "Nothing can be co-essential with itself, but only one being with another",[172] for which Maximus gives the reason: "If, on the one hand, essence and nature are identical; and if, on the other hand, person and hypostasis are identical, then it becomes obvious that those that are of the same essence and the same nature, are distinct according to the hypostasis."[173]

This rather formalistic principle finds a practical explanation as follows: "For an angel is distinct from another angel, a man from another man, an ox from another ox, a dog from another dog, by reason of their hypostasis, not their nature and essence."[174]

Though this list may not be very flattering for those named first, Maximus is first and foremost interested in clarifying the conceptual relation between nature and hypostasis. *Hypostasis* is used here in a wider sense than "person", since every individual being can be called a hypostasis. Still clarifying the concepts, Maximus applies the distinction also to the discourse about God:

> And if I may be so bold as to mention what is supreme, I would say that even in the highest, uncreated yet all-creating, first cause we see that nature and hypostasis are not identical; for we recognize the one and only essence and nature in the divinity, unfolding in three hypostases distinct from one another by their properties . . . in particular by being unbegotten (the Father), by being begotten (the Son), and by emanating (the Holy Spirit): these properties do not divide the one nature and power of the ineffable divinity into three essences, or dissimilar—

[171] PG 91, 544D–545A.
[172] PG 91, 545B.
[173] PG 91, 549B.
[174] PG 91, 549C.

or even similar—natures, but they denote the Persons in whom the one divinity resides, and who are themselves this one divinity.[175]

Maximus here sums up what we already know from Gregory of Nyssa. The new element consists in his applying the concept of *hypostasis* (in the sense of what is specific because of its distinctive properties) to Christology, where the question evidently is formulated in terms different from those found in the theology of the Trinity: How is it possible for two totally and essentially different natures, divinity and humanity, to form one hypostasis and person? Maximus, before addressing this specifically christological question, tries by a lengthy logical chain of reasoning to determine the principle of different essences being united in one person, in contrast to different persons being united in one essence. We shall merely attempt to repeat the main results of these rather dry reflections.[176]

A distinction has to be made between two kinds of unity:

1. The unity of beings having the same nature, such as men or animals: this is the unity of the species; for example, within the one human nature. For several beings to be united in one nature, it is necessary for them at least to be distinct from one another numerically, through their hypostases. The respective hypostases differentiate between several beings of the same nature, whereby the hypostasis consists in those properties that differentiate the individual being.

2. The other kind of union refers to beings of different natures. Maximus undertakes this entire analysis in view of this kind of union, since the Incarnation of the Logos, in logical terms, constitutes just such a union. In this, Maximus has contributed decisively to the theological clarification. Due to his Aristotelian mentality, but also in reference to his theology of creation, Maximus maintains that every nature is constituted by its own essential principle (*logos*), which retains its identity unchangeably, and which sets its own nature apart from every other nature. This explains why

[175] PG 91, 549D–552A.
[176] Cf. PG 91, 552B–553A.

Maximus clings so emphatically to an axiom that flows from this conviction, an axiom that has played such an important role in Christology: "No nature, as far as nature (that is, on the level of being this nature), can ever have union with another nature. It is, without any participation, in its essence absolutely distinct from every other nature."[177]

A union of the essences of two essentially distinct natures (this is the question regarding the Incarnation) would only be possible if one of the two were totally transformed into the other. Yet this, of course, would not at all be a union but a transformation. Hence, this so very consequential axiom: two essentially distinct natures can be united only if they preserve their *logos*, their essential identity, in this union. Such a union, then, is possible only on the level of the hypostasis. It is decisive for our topic here to note that the hypostatic union of two essentially distinct natures, according to Maximus, is accomplished through the very same elements that are proper to each of these two natures; more specifically, through the very same properties that distinguish these natures from all other individuals of the same nature.

What is said here in rather formal and abstract terms may also be expressed in a more concrete way using an example offered by Maximus himself and employed ever again as a standard model in Christology: the union of body and soul.[178] The hypostasis, say, of the person of Paul, obtains in Maximus' view its identity from the sum total of all those properties that distinguish *his* body and *his* soul from the body and the soul of any other man. On the other hand, the fact that Paul has a *body* and a *soul* unites him with the human nature, constituted by body and soul, common to all other men. The things that distinguish Paul from all other men constitute his personal identity; the things that unite him with all other men distinguish in his very self the two natures present in him.

After these analyses, which still remain all too abstract, Maximus

[177] PG 91, 108CD; cf. 568A.
[178] On the history of this comparison before and in Maximus, cf. K. H. Uthemann, "Das anthropologische Modell der hypostatischen Union bei Maximus Confessor", in Heinzer and Schönborn, *Maximus Confessor. Actes,* 223–33.

enters the area of Christology, the true purpose of all the efforts so far. Similar to Gregory of Nyssa, the philosophical and conceptual clarification is followed by the theological application proper, trinitarian in Gregory, christological in Maximus:

> God's Word himself teaches us that he is perfect in his nature and essence, according to which he is identical and consubstantial with the Father and the Holy Spirit; yet also, that he preserves the distinct difference in personhood, according to which he is in person and hypostasis separate from the Father and the Holy Spirit.
> Through the Holy Spirit, he has taken on flesh out of Mary, the Virgin and Mother of God, and has become completely man; which means, he has become a complete man through the assumption of flesh animated by a spiritual soul, and this flesh receives in him his nature and his hypostasis, that is, being and substance. From the instant of conception on, Word and flesh are one; for the Word himself is in a sense the seed of his own Incarnation. Thus *in his* hypostasis *he has become a compound,* even though in his own [divine] nature he is one and uncompounded.[179]

The initial application to Christology still comes across as rather formalistic: the union of divinity and humanity in Christ can only be of the second kind of union, a unification of realities essentially different; and such a union can only be hypostatic. Maximus now draws from all this certain conclusions that directly apply to the specific mystery of the Incarnation: Christ, in his divinity, is of the same essence as the Father and the Holy Spirit; in his humanity, he is of the same essence as his Mother and we all. In contrast, the properties that distinguish him from the Father and also from us constitute the very realities conveying to his hypostasis and person the distinctive identity. If we now pursue this second aspect more closely, we shall see more clearly its connection with the problem of the icon. For the task here is to determine more specifically the distinctive properties that in their totality constitute, or rather denote, the one and unmistakable hypostasis of Christ.

[179] PG 91, 553C–556A.

Maximus now shows that the very properties that distinguish the Son from the Father and the Holy Spirit link him to his humanity, and that the very properties that distinguish the humanity of Jesus from all other human beings constitute his unification with the person of the Son.[180] This statement, though once again rather abstract, is nevertheless quite consequential in view of the icon problem. The Incarnation then means this: all that defines Jesus' concrete humanity is united with all that defines the Divine Person of the Son, thus creating one common hypostasis and person. The specific properties of Jesus' humanity and the specifics of the Divine Person of the Son form "one unified property that characterizes the hypostasis they together bring about".[181] In other words: the incarnate Person of the Son does not wear his humanity like some outward, extraneous garment under which he would hide; but rather, all that makes it possible to identify Christ as this very specific and unmistakable human being, is a "constitutive element" of the incarnate Person of the Son.

This is extremely important for the theology of the image: it explains why St. Theodore the Studite—whose doctrine on the veneration of images we shall explore further below—could declare that the icon depicts the Person and hypostasis of the Son. In Maximus' terminology, the reasoning for this would be: the specific properties of Christ's humanity, which distinguish him from all other men, denote the hypostasis of the Logos himself. Conversely, this also means that these same properties, which the visual arts try to represent, constitute the *human* properties of the Divine Person.

These considerations are still largely abstract. Their import will become more evident inasmuch as we succeed in filling them with content. Yet before undertaking this task, we have to discuss one other element of Maximus' explorations: the description of the formal difference between the unique hypostatic union of the two natures in Christ, and other unions of

---

[180] PG 91, 556AC.
[181] PG 91, 556C.

different essences in one hypostasis. Here, too, we are forced to penetrate into a thicket of apparently abstract considerations, until we finally reach the bright clearing of beholding the living Person of Christ.

2. The "Composite Hypostasis"

As we have seen, Maximus quotes the "instance" of a united body and soul as the paradigm for the union of different essences in one common hypostasis. The attempt of comparing this paradigm with the union of the divine nature and the human nature in Christ soon reveals the limitations of this comparison. The awareness of such a limitation was further increased by the fact that the Monophysitic movement, spreading vigorously throughout the Near East, paid too little attention to these very limits. Maximus criticizes the Monophysites because, he says, they mistake the composite hypostasis for the composite nature and, because of this mistake, end up holding opinions about Christ that ultimately are blasphemous. We shall now consider Maximus' reasoning in some detail.

Three conditions define a composite nature: (1) the elements of the composition form an involuntary, physically necessary synthesis; (2) one element does not exist without the other, rather, their existence is absolutely simultaneous; (3) this composite nature is part of the natural "components" of the world, which constitute the intrinsic physical order of the world with its species and types.[182]

If these three conditions are present, then it is immediately evident that Christ cannot be called a "composite nature" in this sense, while the hypostatic union of body and soul quite clearly fulfills the criteria for a composite nature. The error of the Monophysites lies in their assuming that *every* composite hypostasis is also a composite nature. Maximus shows that every compos-

---

[182] PG 91, 516D–517A; cf. also 528C; 488D.

ite nature also forms a composite hypostasis, but that the reverse is not necessarily true.[183] This applies at least to the "unique case" of the composite hypostasis of the God-man, as Maximus explains in the following.

The uniqueness of this union of two essentially different natures consists in the fact that these unified natures, divinity and humanity, are *infinitely* different one from the other: "At no time does the divinity become the same in essence as the humanity, so that nothing that is created should, through union with the divinity, turn into that same essence and same nature."[184] The essential identity (*logos*) of everything that exists makes it impossible for any one thing simply to coincide with another thing and become identical with it.[185] This applies eminently to the relation between the infinity of God and the finiteness of all things created: any natural synthesis here is excluded. And precisely in this is the union of the divine and the human natures in Christ radically different from the union of body and soul in man. For body and soul, no matter how different they are in their essence and how impossible it would be for them to coincide and form one identity, nevertheless are directed one toward the other and destined for their union. Body and soul, Maximus explains, correlate according to their natural potencies and are oriented toward one another, so that they do not come into existence except together. This anthropology is substantially different from the one proposed by Origen and Eusebius: body and soul here are no longer seen as opposites, they are not profoundly alien to each other, but on the contrary are essentially directed toward one another.[186]

It is radically different with the union of divinity and humanity in Christ. In no wise at all, neither in its essence nor in its activity, does the human nature possess a natural disposition toward union with the divine nature; and conversely, it has to be stated equally that "there is *no created being* capable of containing the

[183] PG 91, 525D–528A; cf. 489D.
[184] PG 91, 565D.
[185] PG 91, 521A.
[186] Cf. the subtle analysis of "analogies" between body and soul, in Amb Jo 21, PG 91, 1248AB.

Logos".[187] In other words, human nature lacks the natural capability for the hypostatic union, unlike the body's essential disposition for the union with the soul. The hypostatic union in Christ, therefore, is not at all a natural "component" of our world, not even constituting its natural perfection. If it were so, then this union, and consequently the Incarnation of the Son, would be demanded by this order of things; it would be necessary as its inner perfection. Against such tendencies, Maximus emphasizes forcefully that the mystery of the union accomplished in Christ is marked precisely by its character of being absolutely undeserved and freely given:

> God the Logos, existing before all time and being in truth its creator, has effected his kenosis for us men by his own sovereign will. He has become man in order to restore and renew the world, not to contribute to its [natural] immanent perfection. For the Word dwelt in the flesh among men, not because of the laws of nature, but according to the [freely determined] economy of salvation. Thus Christ is not a composite nature . . . , for he exists in a manner not subject to the laws of composite natures. On the contrary, he is a composite hypostasis, which does not correspond to any composite nature relative to its essence. This is the paradox here: to behold a composite hypostasis, which in its essence does not also imply a composite nature.[188]

The paradox of the Incarnation consists in the unexpected, unique, and incomparable way it takes place. Body and soul form a composite hypostasis based on the natural disposition of each part; their union occurs by natural necessity. In contrast, no natural necessity at all determines the union of the Logos with his humanity. And conversely, in this union, Christ's humanity does not find itself under the yoke of a natural domination of what is stronger over what is weaker, the way it is found in the domination of the soul over the body:

> The soul dominates the body without willing it, and in turn is dominated by the body. The soul confers life to the body,

[187] PG 91, 532B.
[188] PG 91, 517BC.

without ever having made such a decision, simply because it is present in the body. On the other hand, the soul participates naturally in the passions and pains of the body, because the soul intrinsically possesses the potentiality for this.[189]

The theology of the Fathers, again and again, had to struggle with the temptation to interpret the Incarnation as some kind of natural "prevailing" of God's omnipotence over the weakness of humanity. Eusebius' Christology clearly is determined by this notion. Cyril of Alexandria is no stranger to it as well, yet he achieves a balance that is no longer present in the later Monophysitism. Maximus opposed this idea vigorously, because he saw it as diminishing the transcendence of God: any dominance, by nature, of the divinity over the humanity basically limits God's omnipotence; for in every natural synthesis, the stronger element indeed dominates the weaker one, but the weaker also dominates the stronger insofar as it co-determines the latter. Such a conception of the Incarnation, consequently, calls into question not merely God's transcendence but the substantial reality of Christ's humanity as well. The result would be not so much a *union* as an intermingling.[190] The unification of body and soul does not result in an intermingling because both elements are by nature oriented toward a union. It is different with the union in Christ; this union cannot be natural, it is hypostatic, effected on the level of the person. Only such a hypostatic union can preserve in its unity the infinite difference between the divine and the human nature: "We must not presume that this difference is relinquished by the stronger element [the divine nature]."[191]

---

[189] PG 91, 488D.

[190] Whenever the two parts are mixed and dissolved, it would be improper to speak of a "union"; cf. PG 90, 713A.

[191] The second letter to Thomas, ed. P. Canart, *Byzantion* 34 (1964): 434.

3. A New Mode of Existence

Our analyses so far may seem perhaps like a pointless ballgame with concepts. As we now try to fill these abstract expositions with content, we shall finally understand better their importance in view of the theology of the Incarnation and the theology of the icon. Let us recall how Maximus described the hypostatic union: that which *distinguishes* the Person of the Son from the Father and the Holy Spirit, *unites* him with the flesh, with his humanity.[192] What else, then, distinguishes the Son from the Father but the fact of being Son? The Son, the Word, is united to the flesh precisely through this distinguishing mark: through being Son. And what else can this mean but that the flesh becomes the flesh of the Word according to the very mode of existence proper to the eternal Word?

The Word is God, within the ineffable communion of the three Divine Persons, in such a way that he receives his divine nature wholly from the Father and receives the entire divine nature without diminution or shortfall. For each of the Divine Persons is God according to the character of his respective originating relationship, or mode of existence:[193] the Father by being unbegotten (he is unoriginated origin); the Son by being begotten; the Holy Spirit by procession.[194] The defining quality of each Person, therefore, consists in his respective relation to the other two Persons: what is specific to each is the character of his *originating relationship.* The specific character, the individuality of the Person of the Son lies in his being God in such a mode as to receive himself entirely from the Father and to give himself entirely to him.

This mode of existence proper to the Son in turn becomes, through the hypostatic union, the mode of existence for his

---

[192] Cf. note 180 above.

[193] Cf. Myst. 23, PG 91, 701A. The significance of *tropos tês hyparxeôs* as originating relation and mode of existence, is discussed in very clear and structured terms in F. Heinzer, *Gottes Sohn als Mensch. Die Struktur des Menschseins Christi bei Maximus Confessor* (Freiburg, 1980), 29–58.

[194] PG 91, 549D.

humanity as well. *The mode of his being God becomes the mode of his being man.* In the following, we shall try to gain a better understanding of this extraordinary, unprecedented mode of being man.

As the *first* and fundamental realization in this context, we have to state this: The Divine Persons, in their existential mode of total mutual giving and surrendering, are nevertheless—and precisely because of this—free, in a way far beyond our comprehension. Their embeddedness in the one divine nature is not a coercion but the sovereign divine freedom of mutual self-giving. Our own bonds to our nature, in spite of all freedom proper to being human, are still marked by those inescapable constraints that within the confines of finite being are always experienced as limitations, often also as burden, sometimes even as oppression. The Incarnation, which is the assumption of the human nature on the part of the Son, implies that the sovereign divine freedom, in which the Son owns his divinity in mutual giving and receiving, now becomes also the mode of his owning his humanity. The relationship in Christ of person and nature is incomparably free; he does not own his humanity under conditions of necessity, the way our own existence as humans is determined—since our existence is defined, as it were, without our "consent", according to necessary and predetermined realities. The Son, in contrast, became man "by his own will",[195] to such an extent that his mode of being man is marked by the same freedom with which he eternally receives and gives himself. In this lies the ultimate reason why the *human* self-giving of Jesus can be for us the perfect human "translation" of his eternal self-giving to the Father: only the Incarnation of the divine freedom in the human condition can result in such total self-giving.

A *second* characteristic of Christ's mode of existence flows from the premises: adopting human nature cannot merely represent some extrinsic condition, as suggested by Eusebius' comparison of a musician playing his instrument. Rather, the analysis of the different forms of union has shown the unity of Word and flesh in

[195] PG 91, 529AB.

Christ to be of such a kind that the properties of the Divine Person and the specific qualities of Christ's humanity form a common hypostasis, a "composite hypostasis", in which the human, "person-specific qualities" become the very qualities of the Divine Person.[196] This means nothing less than this: the unmistakable characteristic of Christ's humanity consists in being not merely the instrument of the Son but being, as it were, *the Son himself:* just as he is himself in his divinity, so is he also now himself in his humanity. Maximus expresses this in a formulation that returns over and again and aptly expresses the basic insight of St. Cyril's Christology: "Christ is not different from his two natures; he is *from* them, he is *in* them, he *is* these natures."[197] Christ *is* God, and he *is* man, and remains such forever.[198] The Incarnation means not simply that the Son also *has* a human nature, but that he *is* man, that he is *this* man.

Now, a *third* observation regarding the Son's mode of existence; indeed, an extremely complicated question whose answer has prompted heated debates among the theologians: in what way is Christ's human nature *individuated* with respect to all other men? It is a rather subtle question, and Maximus did not discuss it explicitly. Yet it is not inconsequential for the consideration of the icon; after all, the visual arts are concerned with the individuality of a person thus depicted: these facial features, this tint of the hair, etc.

The icon, no doubt, depicts such an individualized human countenance. But in what consists this individuality? Maximus, according to the few applicable passages, seems to assume that the principle of individuation in Christ's humanity is his human existence, which nevertheless at no time subsists by itself, that is, without being "en-hypostatized" in the Divine Person, as the theologians of his time put it. Maximus stresses that to each nature

[196] PG 91, 556D.

[197] Cf. PG 91, 121A and D; PG 91, 573A; 572C; PG 90, 121B and elsewhere. The use Maximus makes of this formula is thoroughly researched in P. Piret, *Le Christ et la Trinité selon Maxime le Confesseur,* vol. 69 of *Théologie historique* (Paris, 1983) 203–39.

[198] Cf. PG 90, 1136BC; PG 91, 1309D.

there corresponds its proper existence, which in turn is the condition for its specific activity: "To profess about Christ that his natures are not without their proper existence nor without their proper activities does not mean creating several hypostases or acting subjects; rather, it means, in line with the orthodox faith, affirming their existences and their essential and proper activities."[199]

The paradox of the Incarnation consists in this: that a human existence has been equipped to express, in and through itself, the individual properties of the Divine Person of the Son; that a human existence has become the localized manifestation of a Divine Person, the place, not of any provisional, only didactical and transitory manifestation, but of a permanent and final manifestation: God has become man, and he never ceases to be such. True, the icon presents but a human face. Yet this face, this human reality, has its *existential origin,* not in another human existence, but in the Person of the Son of God: it *is his* human mode of existence.[200]

The created existence of Christ's human nature, from the moment of its conception, is the existence of the Word that has "emptied himself"; it obtains its hypostasis, its ultimate "selfhood", in the Word. In this union, the human existence of Christ is not absorbed by his divine existence; its "essential selfness" (*logos*) remains intact. But it is, according to its origin, transposed as it were into the "key" of the mode of existence proper to the hypostasis of the Son; this is the *new mode of existence* characterizing Christ's humanity: a human existence totally resonating in tune with the eternal sonship of the Logos. "Through the provisions of the Incarnation, the entire personal individuality of the eternal Son has become the individuality of the existence and the heart and the soul of Jesus the man."[201]

[199] PG 91, 205BC; cf. the article by J. M. Garrigues, "La personne composée du Christ d'après S. Maxime le Confesseur", *Revue Thomiste* 84 (1974):181–204.

[200] PG 91, 553C; 560C; 1037A; 821C.

[201] J. M. Garrigues, *Maxime le Confesseur. La charité avenir divin de l'homme* (Paris, 1976), 171.

4. *The Two Activities and Wills in Christ*

At the center of St. Maximus' theological reflection, there lies the theme of the *paradoxical and unexpected way and manner* in which the mystery of the Incarnation unfolded. The *fact* that God became man is a mystery, the *way* in which God became man is perhaps more of a mystery. It was in particular the heresies of Monoenergism and Monothelitism that prompted Maximus to reflect specifically on the *way* the Incarnation happened. Both heresies diminish the true human nature by admitting in Christ only one "energy" (mode of action) and one will, the divine will. In contrast to these heresies, Maximus insists that in Christ the human and created mode of acting and willing is not absorbed into his divinity but operates in union with the latter, in the way of interpenetration and without the one eliminating the other.

In view of a theology of the icon, this dogmatic discussion is of the utmost importance: Monothelitism is the last major christological heresy prior to the iconoclastic movement; both heresies share certain traits. The one denies Christ's human mode of acting and willing, the other denies the possibility to "sketch" or depict Jesus' humanity. Both heresies in their core reject the possibility that Christ's humanity, as created reality, could be the formal expression of the Divine Person of the Son. It is here, in the very question regarding the two modes of acting and willing in Christ, that we see much more clearly how the Person of the Eternal Son can mold the human existence of Christ even to its roots without destroying or altering it. The fight against Monothelitism constitutes a certain return to the realism of Christ's humanity, to this humanity's lowliest and humblest manifestations; it also brings a new and sharpened awareness that the reality of the Eternal Word transpires foremost in his ultimate self-abasement. The image of Christ thus becomes less hierarchical; it loses the traces of Docetism that still were clinging to it. In the dramatic events of Gethsemane and Golgotha, the faith-filled meditation discovers anew the heart of our salvation; in the despised countenance of the Lord, it finds the true icon of God's love. The theological reflection on the two wills in Christ opens our eyes for the theology of the Christ-icon.

Maximus extended his careful analyses of the relation between the two natures in Christ to the relation between the two modes of action and will as well. Here again his often conceptual and formal analysis appears at first rather barren and abstract. Yet Maximus never intends to subordinate the mystery to logic. His interest is always focused on the reality in question, a reality transcending all human concepts, and he would never simply deny this reality.[202]

Every living nature, in order to be truly an individual nature, has to be its own moving self, has to possess its own individual motion, which is constitutive of it.[203] The motion produced by every living nature according to that nature is its specific "energy", its mode of acting, which characterizes the essence of that nature: "Since the mode of acting follows nature, it is therefore the constitutive and defining element of every nature."[204] From this, it follows that nature and action are inseparably connected: "Everybody agrees and is unanimous in teaching that everything of the same nature also acts the same, and vice versa."[205]

When two different natures are united in one person, then the mode of action specific to each nature is not to be changed by this union; otherwise the two natures themselves would be changed. The union of the two modes of action, however, is only possible as a hypostatic union, on the level of the person, not of the natures involved. This the adherents of Monoenergism did not, or would not, see.

According to Maximus, then, the mode of acting is inherent in a respective nature; for every nature acts as its own self. The person does not possess such a mode of action, but rather determines the way and manner (*tropos*) of its specific, proper, and essential mode of action.[206] This applies particularly to the Trinity:

---

[202] Cf. PG 91, 596BC; cf. V. Croce, *Tradizione e ricerca. Il metodo teologico di san Massimo il Confessore* (Milan, 1974).

[203] PG 91, 1052A.

[204] PG 91, 348A; cf. PG 91, 1049C; cf. also the analysis of *energeia* in Sophronius' writings, in C. Schönborn, *Sophrone de Jérusalem* (Paris, 1972), 201–24.

[205] PG 91, 348C.

[206] PG 91, 1052B.

the Divine Persons do not each possess their own operation and will, but only the one, essential, divine acting and willing. Yet each Person actuates this one and essential acting and willing according to that Person's specific mode and manner of being God. The Son does not own an activity and a will different from the Father, but he acts and wills in identity with the Father's will, only in *a way different* from the Father, namely, in the way and manner of being Son.

The same situation is present in the "composite hypostasis" of the Incarnate Word. Christ, as God, operates in a divine manner, and as man, in a human manner; yet his action is special, unique, and distinct insofar as he, as man, operates in a human manner *different* from us, that is, in a way and manner proper to the Person of the Eternal Word. Now we are able to grasp more completely the specifics of the identification of the Word with the adopted flesh, the way it was discussed time and again by Cyril. Cyril still tended to interpret the relationship of the Logos to his adopted humanity as some kind of superiority of what is stronger over what is weaker, which could easily lead to viewing Christ's humanity as entirely passive, and only his divinity as active.[207] Cyril did not yet counteract this peril sufficiently. Maximus has shown more than clearly that this view destroys not only the true humanity of Christ but also the transcendence of God, setting his transcendence in competition to his own creation.[208] Since the Word, in his Incarnation, makes his human nature his very own, to such an extent as to become true man, it will then be meaningless to say that the Logos exerts his power over his human nature; the Logos does not exert some kind of extrinsic causality upon his human nature, the way Eusebius thought, but he operates *in* both of his natures.

In opposition to the teaching of the two modes of acting and willing in Christ, there is raised, time and again, the objection that this leads to an unimaginable double state in Christ, to two lives

---

[207] This is also the thinking of the Monothelitist patriarch, Pyrrhus of Constantinople; cf. PG 91, 349C.

[208] PG 91, 64AB.

lived in parallel, rending Christ's existential unity asunder. In this, Monoenergism and Monothelitism appear to be more coherent, since they assume in Christ a unified action and will. Maximus, in contrast, tried to show that such plausibility is deceiving. By reason of his formal analyses of the different kinds of unions, he is able to demonstrate how a plausible unity in Christ's acting and willing is safeguarded through the very preservation of the difference between divine and human acting and willing. It is not the nature-specific modes of acting that are united and uniform here, but the *way and manner* in which both act as one.[209]

In the person of Christ, there exist the divine and the human acting and willing in mutual correlation, in reciprocating permeation (*perichôrêsis*), yet not on the level of the natures involved but on the level of the person: the common element consists in the personal "twist" bestowed on the divine and the human activity in Christ. Only in this way is it possible for Jesus' human activity to become the expression of his divine activity; for in Christ, a human activity became the activity of the Divine Person of the Son of God. Let us try to specify this reflection in more precise terms so the abstract theological formulae may better yield their simple yet profound faith content.

> Each one of us operates, not inasmuch as "Who" he is, but as "What" he is, namely, inasmuch as he is man. Inasmuch as he is "Who", such as Peter or Paul, he shapes the way and manner [*tropos*] of his activity by being negligent or diligent, and by giving it either this or that expression, according to his free will. Thus in the different manner [*tropos*] of operating we see the difference of persons in their actuality, while in the nature of the operation we see the natural mode of acting common to all men.[210]

In the *nature* of the act, therefore, we see the nature of him who acts. Thus Jesus' human deeds point to his human nature, in the same way as his supernatural deeds reveal his divine nature. On

---

[209] PG 91, 1052BC; cf. 1044D.
[210] PG 91, 137A.

the other hand, the *manner* of acting shows the individuality of the acting person. Since it is the person who shapes this manner of acting, Christ confers on his human acts the very imprint that marks his divine mode of acting: the imprint of his eternal Sonship. *Here* is the place where Maximus finds the key for his Christology: the Eternal Son's mode of existing and acting becomes the mold that shapes the form of his human acts.

The most important conclusion from this, especially in view of our topic, is the certainty that the human acts of Jesus, his *way and manner* of acting, reveal the life of the Triune God. Maximus explains, in a famous and frequently quoted text, how the Incarnation becomes revelation of the Trinity:

> This mystery was known before all ages by the Father and by the Son and by the Holy Spirit: by the Father, because such was his will and pleasure; by the Son, because he himself carried it out; by the Holy Spirit, because of his cooperation in it. For the knowledge of the Father, of the Son, and of the Holy Spirit is one and the same, as is their essence and their power.[211]

There is in God but one action, as there is but one essence; yet each of the Divine Persons acts out this one activity in each one's individual, person-specific manner. In the action of the Son, then, there is manifest, on the one hand, the common, one activity of God; on the other hand, in the very manner of the Son's acting, there is also manifest the Father's way of acting ("his will and pleasure") and the Holy Spirit's way of acting ("co-worker"). The concrete reality of the Incarnation, therefore, reveals the Trinity as well:

> The incarnate Word of God teaches us the theology of the Trinity; for in himself he shows forth the Father and the Holy Spirit also. The entire Father and the entire Holy Spirit are essentially and perfectly in the entirety of the Son, and no less—indeed, especially—in the Son incarnate: the Father as the

[211] PG 90, 624B; E. V. Ivánka, trans., *Maximos der Bekenner* (Einsiedeln, 1961), 80f.

source of the salvific plan, the Holy Spirit as the co-worker with the Son who himself accomplishes the Incarnation.[212]

It is difficult for our thinking, corrupted as its structure is by sin, to grasp the mystery of this joint action of the Divine Persons. For each Person's specific features do not lead to any division, neither in the one essence nor in the one activity. This is based on the paradoxical, divine constitution of the trinitarian unity: just as the person-specific properties of the Divine Persons are defined, not by their *contrast* to the others, but by the type of their *relationship* to each other, so also is the mode of their activity, specific to each Person, defined by the relationship of the Divine Persons to each other. The Father's mode of acting corresponds to his mode of existing: he *operates* in everything as Father because he *is* the Father, source and wellspring of the Son and the Holy Spirit, but also dispenser of the place they occupy within the unfolding of creation, salvation, and fulfillment. The Son, who receives himself entirely from the Father, becomes the "angel", the herald of the Father's great design, which he, together with the Holy Spirit, brings about as well. Maximus sees in this revelation and fulfillment of the "great design" the ultimate and innermost destiny of all things. We quote a passage of his magnificent text:

This is the great and hidden mystery. This is the blessed destiny for which the cosmos was brought into existence. This is the ultimate design which God had in mind before the beginning of anything created—the end foreknown, by reason of which all things exist, but which in turn does not exist by reason of any other thing. With this final destiny in mind, God created the substances of all things. This is the destination and the ultimate purpose toward which the Divine Providence and everything guided by Divine Providence is aimed and oriented, so that everything created by God would finally be in him recollected into the original unity. This is the great mystery that embraces all the eons, and that reveals the infinitely inex-

[212] PG 90, 876CD; the history of this trinitarian formula is briefly outlined by F. Heinzer, "L'explication trinitaire de l'Economie chez Maxime le Confesseur", in Heinzer and Schönborn, *Maximus Confessor. Actes,* 161–64.

haustible and immense design of God, a design eternally beyond all the eons. The "angel" of this design is the Word of God himself, who in his essence became man and (through this very act), we dare say, revealed the heart of hearts of the Father's loving kindness, so that he might show to us, in his own person, the ultimate destiny toward which has been created everything that arose and came into being.[213]

In this splendid conception of God's salvific economy, Maximus identifies the Incarnation as the heart of the divine design. The universal role of the Logos, so emphatically underlined by Eusebius, finds here its true significance in God's design. The Logos is not merely the cosmic instrument of God; no possibility of finding Neoplatonic emanatism here; God's own freedom is completely safeguarded, even—and especially—as it extends to the ultimate obedience of the Son, who himself comes forth from this freedom, so much so that he becomes the revelation of "the heart of hearts of the Father's loving-kindness".

In this conception, the Incarnation is no longer viewed as a mere pedagogical concession to human weakness, a concession to be surpassed by rising onto a higher level of knowledge, where the Incarnation as such would have become obsolete. Similarly, Christ's humanity no longer appears as a passive instrument employed by the Logos only to render his message palpable for the weak human condition. Rather, the Incarnation is in its core that "end, by reason of which all things exist". The Incarnation reveals the meaning and the destiny of all creation. Maximus most assuredly was not the first to proclaim this teaching; Origen and Eusebius both taught it, each in their own way. But especially in Eusebius, we see that the rejection of images is tied to a very specific view of the relationship between creation and Incarnation: the Incarnation is a concession to man's matter-bound spirit, but most certainly it is *not* the intrinsic purpose of creation. Maximus effected a decisive correction of this view, influenced as it is by the speculative system of Origenism. He launches the theology of the Incarnation in a new direction by conceiving the Incarnation

---

[213] PG 90, 621AC; *Maximos der Bekenner,* 77f.

entirely as flowing from the trinitarian "will" (cf. Eph 1:9) of God, whose "messenger" was Christ. Maximus is thus in a position to recognize in the union of Christ's two natures "the blessed purpose" of the work of creation. Creation, in this paradoxical union, finds its natural and its supernatural fulfillment: natural, because it has been created by God for this very union (already in God's image!); supernatural, because the type and manner of this union transcends not only man's fallen state, but the natural order itself. In this union, then, created nature is perfectly preserved and yet at the same time elevated to a mode of existence transcending this nature:

> Yes, for the sake of Christ—rather, for the sake of the mystery that is Christ—all the eons, and all that the eons contain, have received the origin of their being from Christ and find the destiny of their being also in him. For the final purpose as designed in God's mind, and conceived in anticipation from the beginning, was the unification of all the eons: the union of what is specific with what is unspecific; of what is measured with what is unmeasured; of what is limited with what is unlimited; of the Creator with the created; of what is [unchangeable and] lasting with what is [changing and] in motion. And this union has been revealed at the end of time in Christ, who in himself brought God's foreknowledge to its fulfillment.[214]

In Christ, the final purpose of creation has been revealed: the union of humanity and divinity in a paradoxical conquest, which does not transform or dissolve God into man or man into God, which rather renews human nature and imprints on it the mode of existence of the Eternal Son. This conquest, which leads human nature to its ultimate perfection, is called *love*. Maximus is the prominent theologian of love. In this love we can identify, with him as guide, the heart and center of a theology of the icon.

---

[214] PG 90, 621BC; *Maximus der Bekenner*, 78.

5. Christ, "the Living Icon of Love"

Our exposition so far has shown that Maximus encounters ever again, and through different approaches, the mysterious cooperation between God and man as it became reality in Christ. This *synergy*, this combined action, is man's original vocation; it is made possible thanks to the unique gift that man alone has received from the Creator: the gift of freedom, which makes man a true image of God.[215] Freedom is not simply a gift added to an already existing nature, it is fundamental for human nature and an essential property; to be free defines the spiritual nature: "In beings not endowed with reason, nature is in command; but in man, nature is being commanded, because man directs himself in freedom, according to his own will."[216] If freedom is an essential property of human nature, then this free cooperation with the Creator constitutes the full actualization and realization of this nature too. The gift of freedom allows a true interaction between God and man, even though, as to their nature, the two are infinitely distinct from one another.

According to his nature, man is destined for *synergy* with God; yet he actualizes this only if he freely decides to reach out to God. Through the fall from grace and the ensuing proneness to sin, however, the difference between God and man was changed for the latter into *opposition*. The natural movement toward God is no longer fully appropriated by man's free will. The place of "synergy" is now occupied by "opposition", and consequently, man no longer acts as would correspond to the most profound and essential principle of his nature. Maximus expresses this in his precise manner: "Difference does not always mean opposition! Opposition reigns when the free will clearly moves contrary to reason and contrary to its natural disposition; difference, on the other hand, results from the operation of a nature acting in harmony with its natural disposition. Opposition

---

[215] PG 91, 304C; 324D.
[216] PG 91, 304C; cf. 293D.

is a revolt against a nature, while difference undergirds this nature."[217]

Difference, therefore, is positive, a "bestower of being", "a supporter of permanence".[218] Opposition, destroying the interaction between God and man, is an attack on the nature of man. It deforms the true face of man, the image of God. It draws man away from God and toward his own self, and establishes among men the tyranny of egotism.[219] Nothing else could liberate man from this subjection to opposition than a victory over the dynamism of this opposition. To accomplish this, man had to die to self in order to rise to that other mode of existence to which he is called, and in which alone he is able to flourish according to his nature: the mode of synergy with God. This victory was won by Christ, not "from the outside in", but embedded within a human existence, within human acting and willing.

In Christ, all human acting and willing have been restored to their originally intended communion with God's acting and willing. Opposition no longer prevails, but "synergy", interaction. Maximus illustrated this especially with the extreme situation of the Lord's agony in the garden:

> Our Savior, insofar as he was true man, possessed a natural will; yet this will was not in opposition to the divine will but rather formed by it. For nothing that conforms to nature stands in opposition to God, not even the human free will (in which is manifested the distinction between persons) if it acts according to nature. If it were not so, we should have to accuse the Creator himself of having caused the original fall from grace, and of having created something by nature opposed to him.[220]

The mutual interaction of the two wills in Christ, therefore, is not a passive change of the human will through the divine will. This interaction takes place in freedom, at the source of Christ's human will, yet also in such a way that the transition between the

---

[217] PG 91, 193A.
[218] PG 91, 1400C; 1133CD; 249C; cf. von Balthasar, *Kosmische Liturgie*, 153 and 258.
[219] PG 91, 397A.
[220] PG 91, 48D–49A.

two wills from opposition to union is accomplished through the sacrifice of obedience. In the agony of Gethsemane, this transition occurs. Here the spontaneous, natural tendency of the human will, which abhors death, is overcome by the obedience offered to the Father by Christ the man. Maximus interprets Jesus' words in the garden ("Father, if it is possible, let this cup pass me by; yet not my will be done, but yours" [Lk 22:42]) in such a sense that Christ, beset by mortal anguish, still reveals the total movement of his human will to be in perfect accord with the divine will. This would be so because Christ's human will, in its natural orientation, was entirely formed and molded by the manner and nature of the divine counsel (*tropos*).[221]

In Christ, therefore, human nature conforms always and in everything to the counsel of the divine will, without this divine will remaining merely extrinsic to the human will. For Christ's human will never had any stirring of opposition to the divine counsel. Even the spontaneous movement of the will against suffering and death, especially against undeserved suffering, a movement inherent in human nature and manifest as an indomitable drive for self-preservation, was in Christ replaced by the recasting and remolding of the will that characterized his human existence at its root. As we have already seen above, Maximus identifies the reason for this new mode of existence as the fact that Christ possesses his humanity in freedom, and that he, therefore, is not subject to the constraints of self-affirmation and self-preservation so typical of our own mode of existence. By imparting on his human will the new "orientation" of perfect harmony with the Father's counsel, he imprints on it that voluntary, infinite dedication through which he, as Son, is eternally in union with the Father. This "orientation" at the same time liberates the human will for that for which it was created: to be, as the image of God, free for God.

> Christ has restored human nature.... He kept his free will clean of all rage and rebellion against nature; even against those who crucified him he did not harbor adversity; on the contrary:

[221] PG 91, 48C.

it was for them that he suffered death, offering his own life. This he showed by freely accepting his suffering, a suffering he took upon himself because of his love for all men.[222]

This restoration of human nature in Christ, therefore, was accomplished at the price of his suffering. Christ's Passion represents another "exodus" (cf. Lk 9:31), that of human nature, by which it is liberated from the isolation and the slavery of its self-centeredness (*philautia*), to be led back to the love of God. Christ has imprinted on human nature the same love that unites him, eternally and essentially, to the Father and the Holy Spirit. For this purpose, he had to break down the walls of selfishness that imprison man in a vicious circle of cravings and hatred, of the obsession with lust and the running away from pain; the walls that prevent him from achieving true happiness and incorruptible joy, for which he was created.[223]

Christ, by letting his divine love for man embrace even his human death, thus overcame the *diabolos,* the source of that domineering opposition between man and God as well as neighbor:

> This was our Lord's intention: to be, *as man* and in our stead, obedient to the Father even unto death, upholding the commandment of love. He defeated the devil through his suffering, inflicted on him by the scribes and Pharisees, who were spurred on by the devil. Thus, by freely allowing himself to be vanquished, he vanquished him who had hoped to triumph, and he snatched the world away from his tyranny.[224]

In this way, the self-abasement of Jesus becomes the great return, the new "exodus" of mankind. Christ the man, by obeying the commandment of love, even love for enemies, made his humanity into the perfect image of God's love. Maximus constantly employs expressions such as "to imprint", "to form", and "to re-form" to describe how in Christ the human will is directed by

[222] PG 90, 877D–880A.

[223] Cf. our essay, "Plaisir et douleur dans l'analyse de S. Maxime le Confesseur, d'après les quaestiones ad Thalassium", in F. Heinzer and C. Schönborn, *Maximus Confessor. Actes,* 273–84.

[224] PG 90, 921BC.

the divine will. These terms are frequently borrowed from the art of painting. Maximus is thus impressively able to draw a connection, in this context especially, to the world of the icon.

> O mystery, more mysterious than all the rest: God himself, out of love, became man. . . . Without any change in him, he took on the weakness of our human nature, in order to bring salvation to man, and to give himself to us men as ideal image [*hypotyposis*] of virtue and as a *living icon of love* and goodwill toward God and neighbor, an icon that has the power to elicit in us the dutiful response.[225]

In Christ, human nature has been enabled to imitate the love of God. In Jesus' humanity, as it were, the complete fullness of God's love has "dwelled bodily" (cf. Col 2:9).

Love is the icon of God: this is the heart, the central insight, of all our theological reflections concerning the icon of Christ. In love, God is made visible to our eyes; in love, we can communicate with God's life in order to achieve perfect similarity to God:

> Love is a great treasure, of all treasures the first and noblest: for love unites through its power God and man in everyone who possesses it, and it brings about the Creator of man showing himself as man, and man, made divine, becoming in his goodness like unto God, to the extent that this is possible for man. This likeness, it seems to me, is the reason why man can love God with his whole heart, with his whole soul, with all his strength, and can love his neighbor as he loves himself.[226]

It is in love that the "synergy" between God and man reaches perfection. Love gives man this ability; in this mutual relationship, God and man mirror each other insofar as they become the complete image of each other's mode of existence: the mode of love. Maximus even goes so far as to say that God and man, in this, become models to one another.[227] Christ is the "prototype" of this communion; he was the first to enact it in himself: "Through his

---

[225] PG 91, 644B; cf. 404BC.
[226] PG 91, 401C.
[227] PG 91, 1113B.

suffering for us he first achieved the imprint of love [*protypôsas*] in himself, only to give it then to us as the gift of grace."[228]

Christ, therefore, represents for us the mold, the original form of God's image; and man is his image by creation and call. Since the Son's mode of existence bestowed on the human freedom of Christ a new form, we all can from now on in our freedom participate, in grace, in his freedom. In this life already, we can participate in Christ's mode of existence, in his new humanity, if only our humanity is rooted in Christ's humanity. This is the *divinization of man,* so often discussed by the Fathers. It represents the "counterpart", the corresponding reality, to the *humanization of God:* God and man engage in a "wondrous exchange", which does not destroy the specific structure of human nature but rather, through supernatural means, leads it to its completion.

6. *"Image and Symbol of Himself"*

This interchange between God and man was in a special way made visible at Christ's Transfiguration. The Transfiguration on Mount Tabor lets us sense the ultimate purpose of the Incarnation:

> In his outward appearance he was like us; for in his boundless love he took it upon himself to become creature, yet without changing [his divinity], and thus he became the *image* [*typos*] *and symbol of himself:* he has revealed himself symbolically out of his inner being; through himself who is visible he has drawn the whole of creation to himself who is invisible and totally hidden.[229]

This dense text, formulated with the precision of the Greek language, represents in a sense a summary of all that Maximus taught concerning our topic. Closing this chapter, we can let ourselves be guided by this text, in order to recapitulate the results and to compare them with the previous stages of our journey so far.

[228] PG 91, 404C.
[229] PG 91, 1165D–1168A.

At first sight, this text brings to mind Origen's view of the Incarnation: Christ's humanity is the indispensable medium that God had to employ in order to reveal himself to us men who are bound by the realm of the senses; the intention, however, remained always to reach beyond the instrument of the human form and to arrive at the invisible, hidden divinity of the Logos. On Mount Tabor, in Christ's Transfiguration, does not the divine glory for a brief moment break through the obscure veil of the flesh? Yet what precisely did Maximus say? That Christ "has revealed himself symbolically out of his inner being". The emphasis focuses entirely on "himself". In his humanity, he has shown nothing else but "himself". "He himself who is visible" is no other than "he himself who is invisible and totally hidden". The path from one to the other does not lead anywhere but to him himself; this path never leaves its starting point, for the Lord himself *is* this path. Christ's humanity, "he who is visible", is the image and symbol, not of someone other and different in his invisibility, but of "him himself who is invisible". The two sides, the one visible and the other invisible, can never be separated; for both pertain to the *one* Lord.

The visible side, the human likeness of Jesus, is irrevocably the "image and symbol" of the Son of God. The Word became flesh, and remains so. But where does it direct us? To "himself who is hidden". The Word would guide us "from himself to himself", and this journey, this transition, is indeed the "paschal passage" of the Lord, that "exodus" about which Christ conversed with Moses and Elijah at the Transfiguration (cf. Lk 9:31). In his paschal passage, Christ leads "all of creation" *to the Father;* for he, once lifted up from the earth, draws *all to himself* (Jn 12:32). He himself is the way to the Father; to find *him* means to have already reached the Father. There is no other access to God's glory than the face of Christ (2 Cor 4:6). By letting ourselves be guided by him on the way of his paschal passage, we ourselves will be "changed *into his image,* from glory to ever greater glory" (2 Cor 3:18).

7. Summary and Perspective

Maximus' dense and concise text sums up our entire journey through the great patristic tradition, yet also points to the ineffable and boundless character of the mystery that it entails. What conclusion does our effort yield? Whereto are we led by identifying the building blocks of a theology of the image?

In Maximus, we found a christological synthesis rarely achieved with more balance or more mystical and existential content. Maximus searched for the "royal path" that neither lessens the transcendence of God nor surrenders the specific reality of the creature. In the ineffable union of Christ's two natures in the one person, Maximus found the effusive prototype and the ideal of the "synergy" between the infinite and the finite, between the uncreated and the created, between God and man. The different approaches to this one mystery, though, all converge in one central point in which all mysteries are hidden and yet revealed: *in the face of Jesus Christ.* This is the living seal of the interaction between God and man; it is the Word through which God expresses himself perfectly, the incarnate Word; and yet it also is the silent, concealed, unfathomable Word: we shall never cease to walk in the light of this countenance (cf. Ps 89:16).

The christological controversies dragged on through centuries. During all this time, the Church never stopped to *profess* the mystery of Christ revealed and yet hidden in the holy face of Jesus. In Nicea (325 A.D.), she professed Christ as the consubstantial image of the Father; in Ephesus (431 A.D.) as the unchanged Word become flesh; in Chalcedon (451 A.D.) as true God and true man; in Constantinople (553 A.D.) as "one of the Trinity who suffered for us"; and again in Constantinople (681 A.D.) as the Word of God, whose human acting and willing was in perfect unison with God's counsel, even unto death. After these long centuries of turbulent, consequential struggles for the profession of the true Christ, our gaze comes to rest to contemplate a quiet image: *the icon of Christ.*

After Christ's Transfiguration, when the three apostles, in fear and terror prostrated on the ground, lifted up their eyes again, they "saw only Jesus, him alone" (Mk 9:8). Him whom they had beheld, only a moment ago, in blinding splendor, accompanied by the two witnesses, him now they see alone, Jesus of Nazareth who in a short while would be nailed to a cross. The Church, after having for centuries examined and proclaimed the divine glory of Christ, his consubstantiality with the Father, could do only one more thing: profess that *this human countenance,* the face of Jesus of Nazareth, holds in itself the complete mystery of God. Only this remained for the Church: to profess her faith in the "blessed return" of Jesus, for whose face we yearn, patiently guided by the icon: "*This Jesus,* who has been taken from you up into heaven, will return *in the same way as* you have seen him ascending into heaven" (Acts 1:11).

PART TWO

THE ICON OF CHRIST
AND THE IMAGE CONTROVERSY

The essential elements for the construction of a theology of the image have now been discussed. We could have concluded our journey with the word of the angels to the apostles, "This Jesus, who has been taken from you up into heaven, will return in the same way as you have seen him ascending into heaven" (Acts 1:11). Their gaze followed him who had been taken from their midst. The prediction that he would return "in the same way" as they had seen him ascend implies the task for the disciples left behind, really the Church, to keep alive the remembrance of his face (see illustration no. 6). The icon is an expression of his living remembrance: it commemorates not merely a man from the distant past, but him who *as man* was glorified through suffering and the Cross, who is alive *now* and "intercedes for us with the Father", and whose return to us has been promised. The icon is a connecting link between the Incarnation and the return, between the first and the last coming of the Lord. The icon not only perpetuates the memory of the Incarnation, it is also a constant reminder of the promised return of Christ. This is why the Eastern Church considers the icon of Christ an indispensable element of the profession of the Christian Faith. The Eastern Church sees the icon as a *condensed* version of the Creed.

In Part One of this book, we have tried to show that all the elements of the Church's Creed converge in the face of Jesus as their focal point. All the important statements of the ancient Church's christological profession are summed up in this mystery. The defenders of images were well aware of this. For them, therefore, the defense of images and image devotion was not simply a pragmatic and pedagogical matter; at stake was the very center of the Christian Faith. Studying the era of the iconoclastic controversy (726–843 A.D.), we immediately realize that the conflict was above all conducted in theological terms. The icon controversy, in regard to its content, is the last stage of the ancient Church's christological struggles. In what follows here, we intend to discuss this controversy in terms of this last, concluding stage that summed up all the preceding achievements. Our specific task will be to show how the iconoclastic controversy is tied in with the previous stages of the christological development. We will have to show, first of all, how the transition from contemplating Christ's humanity to justifying Christ's representation in image is accomplished. For even though Christ's countenance be "the image of the invisible God" (Col 1:15), as from his face shines the splendor of God (2 Cor 4:6), still the question remains whether human art can really capture this countenance.

May and should Christ be represented in an image? This was the primary question at the center of the icon controversy, as the debate focused not only on the usefulness but especially, and more basically, on the possibility of showing Christ in an image. This question contains two further questions, to which the following pages intend to give at least some approximate answer: *To what extent is the Incarnation a reality? What is the potential of human art, and where do its limits lie?*

Proceeding in chonological order, we begin with listing the arguments of the iconoclasts, especially their christological position; this is followed by the response of the defenders of images, traced in three stages, according to the historical periods: the first stage of the iconoclastic controversy, then the Council of Nicea (787 A.D.), and finally, the second stage of the controversy. Our exposition does not claim to be exhaustive. We will limit ourselves to the more important arguments that in the respective period of the controversy were added to the existing terms of the debate.

Illustration 6

Illustration number 6: The Ascension of Christ. Encaustic icon, 46 × 29.5 cm, 6th century, Monastery of St. Catherine, Mount Sinai.

Photo: J. Galley-Schwitter A.G. (Basel).

This considerably damaged icon, in its original parts, is still imbued with the spirit found in the paintings of the outgoing ancient era (vivid gestures, flowing folds of the garments, eyes pointed in a variety of directions). The Blessed Mother (originally placed in profile), the three apostles on her left, and the larger part of Christ's figure have all been repainted in this century. The original vivacity of expression can best be seen (in addition to the angels, inspired by the ancient forms of genies) in the figure of the Apostle Paul (at the right of the Blessed Mother).

The Apostle of the Gentiles, Paul, belongs in this biblical account of the Ascension no more than Mary. The icon, of course, intends to tell not only about the historical happening but also about its timeless meaning. The apostles with their upward gaze (or gesture; Mary, too, originally appeared in this pose) represent the Church, looking up to her Lord and yearning for his return. Christ, inside the mandorla, is carried aloft by the angels. According to their testimony (cf. Acts 1:11), he will return *in the same way.* The image of Christ here almost appears like an icon within an icon. Thus indeed is the deeper significance of the icon of Christ. It will not merely recall the past, the historical earthly story of Jesus; it is equally some kind of "anticipation" of the contemplation of Christ that will be granted to all men at his return.

(See page 137.)

Chapter One

The Theological Outline of the Byzantine Iconoclastic Controversy

I. The Dispute as to the Causes of the Byzantine Iconoclastic Controversy

What was it that prompted Emperor Leo III (717–741 A.D.) single-handedly to start the icon controversy in 726 A.D.[1] by having the celebrated image of Christ over the main entrance to the imperial palace in Constantinople removed by force? How was it possible for iconoclasm, in the Byzantine realm that in every other respect loved images, to grow, under his son Constantine V (741–775 A.D.), into a mighty and at times very popular movement, which in 754 A.D. received highest ecclesiastical approval from a great council of 338 bishops? Recent research converges on the thesis that Emperor Leo himself was the initial driving force: iconoclasm is "an imperial heresy . . . born 'of the purple', in the imperial palace".[2]

---

[1] There is very extensive, more recent literature available on the Byzantine image controversy. We should mention especially the outstanding historical works by Stephan Gero, mainly his two monographs, *Byzantine Iconoclasm during the Reign of Leo III* (Louvain, 1973), and *Byzantine Iconoclasm during the Reign of Constantine V,* (Louvain, 1977), CSCO 346 and 384. A valuable synopsis is offered in the collection, the result of a symposium, *Iconoclasm,* A. Bryer and Judith Herrin, eds. (Birmingham, 1977). A comprehensive bibliography is found in the article, "Bilder", by H. G. Thümmel, *Theologische Realenzyklopädie* 6 (1980):538–40.

[2] Stephan Gero, *Leo III,* 131. P. Schreiner, "Legende und Wirklichkeit in der Darstellung des byzantinischen Bilderstreits", *Saeculum* 27 (1976):165–79, maintains similarly that "the personal iconoclastic attitude on the part of Emperor Leo was the single decisive force" (178); so also the "Vita" of St. Nicetas of Medikion, in

This thesis, of course, does not yet say a great deal. The question as to the emperor's *personal motives* remains unanswered. We have to clarify further which forces in the Byzantine Empire the emperor was able to mobilize for his project to make it into a popular movement.

For quite some time attempts have been made to explain the emperor's iconoclastic attitude with his oriental origins. Leo III was of Syrian extraction, coming from Germanicia, a city in northern Syria, which for generations knew only Monophysitic bishops and was strongly influenced by the advancing Islam. The assertion of a Jewish influence on the future emperor, though legendary in character, may well contain a kernel of historical truth. Clearly, to identify the motivation for Leo's iconoclasm, many point to influences coming from outside the Byzantine realm, from the "heretical" regions of Monophysitism, of Islam, and of Judaism. Indeed, not too long ago, an outstanding expert on the problem wrote that the icon controversy "was not, strictly speaking, a Byzantine movement but rather a Middle-Eastern, . . . a semitic movement".[3]

The pattern underlying this thesis is, it has to be admitted, much too vague: "Byzantine" does not necessarily imply "pro-icon", nor does "semitic" mean indifferently "anti-icon". The attitude of Judaism toward the visual arts has been shown more and more to be nonuniform, at times even explicitly undecided.[4] Regarding Islam's attitude, Oleg Grabar concludes it to be, not iconoclastic, but at most "icon-neutral".[5] And the reference to Leo's Syrian and Monophysitic background relies on the mistaken assumption that the non-Byzantine orientals (Monophysites, Nestorians) were iconoclasts: Is not the famous *Codex Rabula,* one of the most ancient examples of Christian book illumination (c. 586

Acta Sanctorum, April 1, XXVIII AB. The following reflections are in part taken from our article, "Der byzantinische Bilderstreit—ein Testfall für das Verhältnis von Kirche und Kunst?" *Intern. Kath. Zeitschrift Communio* 11 (1982):518–26.

[3] C. Mango, in *Iconoclasm,* 6. The "oriental" thesis is also advanced by A. Grabar, *L'iconoclasme byzantin: Dossier archéologique* (Paris, 1957).

[4] Cf. J. Maier, "Bilder", *Theologische Realenzyklopädie* 6 (1980):521–25.

[5] "Islam and Iconoclasm", in *Iconoclasm.*

A.D.), of Monophysitic origin? And then, to quote another example, there is in Edessa, Syria, the image of Christ — created, according to the legends of Abgar, by Christ himself — that received equal veneration from the Monophysites and from the Orthodox.[6]

In the search to find reasons for the icon controversy within the Byzantine realm itself, the dualistic sect of the Paulicians is frequently mentioned. This thesis sees iconoclasm as a link between the Paulicians — manicheistic and despising the material world — and the dualist Bogomils. Convincing proof for this, though, is lacking so far.[7] To label the iconoclasts "Manicheans"[8] is part and parcel of the usual Byzantine polemic. Favored to some extent, especially among Marxist authors, is the "explanation" of the icon controversy in terms of class struggle:[9] monasticism and imperial powers, the military and small farmers are interpreted as the social forces engaged in the struggle to resolve society's inner contradictions. This theory disregards the findings of careful historical research: that the monasteries, for instance, were not uniformly in favor of images, as the military and the imperial powers were not uniformly against them.[10] The most widespread thesis by far, identifying the roots of the iconoclastic controversy within the Byzantine realm itself, speaks of an ongoing tradition in Christianity of hostility toward the arts: a period of general hostility in early Christianity was followed, after the "Constantine transformation", by a gradual liberalization of the Church's attitude toward the arts, in spite of some warning voices (names especially cited are those of Epiphanius of Salamis and Eusebius of Caesarea) who unsuccessfully defended the original purity of "worship in spirit and truth". From the sixth century on, so the thesis goes, the veneration of images held sway in the Church

---

[6] Cf. S. Brock, "Iconoclasm and the Monophysites", in *Iconoclasm*, 53–57.

[7] Summary of the discussion provided by Gero, "Notes on Byzantine Iconoclasm in the Eighth Century", *Byzantion* 44 (1974):23–42, esp. 33–36.

[8] Cf. for instance John Damascene, PG 94, 1245C; 1297C.

[9] H. Bredekamp, *Kunst als Medium sozialer Konflikte. Bilderkämpfe von der Spätantike bis zur Hussitenrevolution* (Frankfurt, 1975). Cf. the same line of thought in M. Warnke, ed., *Bildersturm. Die Zerstörung des Kunstwerks* (Munich, 1973).

[10] Cf. Schreiner, "Legende und Wirklichkeit".

everywhere all but unimpeded. Iconoclasm, according to this conception, would have been a last, and once again futile, rebellion of the ancient Christian spirituality against the Church's slow and inevitable "sliding back into paganism" (K. Holl).

This thesis all but assumed the force of a dogma because it was adopted by researchers whose monographs on "The Problem of Images in early Christianity" ("Die altchristliche Bilderfrage", by H. Koch, 1917) and on "The Early Christians' Attitude toward Images" ("Die Stellung der alten Christen zu den Bildern", W. Ellinger, 1930) are still quoted as the standard texts.

More recent research,[11] however, tends more and more to show that the early Church did not at all profess only a purely spiritual, entirely "art-free" Christianity. Even though the *veneration* of images in the early Church seems to have been at home rather in heretical circles,[12] still the general attitude toward the arts might not have been so entirely negative as the "classics" mentioned above assert in this context.

Where, then, do we find the underlying causes for the icon controversy? Should we not look for them where the controversy actually raged: in the area of religious reform? The icon controversy is primarily a religious phenomenon: it is a dispute about the "true religion", the purity of the Church, the "worship in spirit and truth". This certainly does not exclude the possibility that iconoclasm, "like all doctrinal developments in the early Church, had political and social implications".[13] Emperor Leo III saw himself, as far as the documents disclose, as a religious reformer. He felt called to restore in his realm the true religion, which was degraded and betrayed by the cult of images. Such cult of images is pagan idolatry, to be eradicated: "Hezekiah, the King of the

[11] For instance A. Grabar, *Christian Iconography. A Study of Its Origins* (London, 1969); idem, *Les Voies de la Création en Iconographie chrétienne. Antiquité et moyen-âge* (Paris, 1979). Especially impressive and pioneering: C. Murray, "Art and the Early Church", *JTS* 28 (1977): 302–45.

[12] Cf. E. Junod and J. D. Kaestli, *L'histoire des actes apocryphes des Apôtres du IIIe au IXe siècle. Le cas des Actes de Jean* (Lausanne, 1981), esp. chap. 7.

[13] G. Florovsky, "Origen, Eusebius and the Iconoclastic Controversy", *Church History* 19 (1950): 77–96, 79.

Jews, after eight hundred years removed the Bronze Serpent from the Temple; and I, after eight hundred years, had the idols removed from the Church", the emperor reportedly said.[14] Leo III considered himself a priest-king, called by God to cleanse God's house from all idolatry; a new Moses, established by God as shepherd of God's people, that is, the Roman Empire.[15] To what extent religious motives were decisive is shown by the fact that the emperor interpreted the severe earthquake of 726 A.D. as a sign of the divine wrath against the veneration of images.[16]

Seen in this perspective, the seemingly unstoppable advance of Islam and the disintegration of the empire could equally be interpreted as God's punishment chastising the new people of God as thoroughly as it did the Israelites of old when they abandoned the true worship.[17] The almost miraculous rescue of the imperial city from the Arabian fleet (717 A.D.), Leo's and Constantine's spectacular military successes in their wars against Islam, seemed to confirm all too clearly that the iconoclasts brought God's blessings on the empire. This tangible divine approval of the emperor's political and religious reforms may have also convinced many leaders of the Church that the imperial iconoclasm followed the will of God. Thus the bishops of the iconoclastic council of 754 A.D. compared the emperors with the apostles, who were sent by Christ to destroy idol worship everywhere.[18]

[14] Quote from the (inauthentic) letter of Pope Gregory II to Leo III; Mansi 12, c. 966CD. The passage refers to 2 Kings 18:4 (erroneously, King Hezekiah rather than King Uzziah).

[15] Cf. the analysis of Leo's ideology, in Gero, *Leo III,* 48–58. Regarding the precedent of the Old Testament kingship and the arrogation of priestly prerogatives, cf. A. Michel, *Die Kaisermacht in der Ostkirche* (Darmstadt, 1959).

[16] Theophanes reports on this in his chronography (a. 6218), German translation by L. Breyer, *Bilderstreit und Arabersturm in Byzanz,* 2nd ed. (Graz, 1964), 38f.

[17] Cf. on this the stimulating, though not unopposed essay by P. Brown, "A Dark-Age Crisis: Aspects of the Iconoclastic Controversy", *The English Historical Review* 346 (1973):1–34.

[18] Mansi 13, 225D; cf. PG 110, 940A; PG 100, 577D, 601A: "If [Emperor] Constantine [V] had not freed us from the folly of idolatry [the icon cult], Christ would have been of no avail to us", the bishops at the council of 754 A.D. are said to have exclaimed, as Nicephorus reports.

This conviction of leading the Church and the empire back to their original purity provided iconoclasm with its enthusiasm and its persuasive power. Yet this was also its weakness: to what extent were the iconoclasts able to convince themselves and the people that the veneration of images was simply the equivalent of idolatry? At what point does a work of art turn into an idol? Was it necessary to condemn indiscriminately as deviation *everything* that centuries of Christian development had produced in religious imagery? If not, where would one draw the line? In fact, this line was not drawn uniformly. Moderate iconoclasts attacked only images as such. Radical iconoclasts, such as later on Emperor Constantine V,[19] not only rejected images but also the veneration of relics and of the saints, including—so it seems—the invocation of the Blessed Mother, in which direction even his loyal iconoclast bishops were unwilling to follow him.

As much as the iconoclastic reform appeared coherent in theory, it turned out to be unworkable in practice. Or should it not be seen as a contradiction when venerating an image of Christ is prohibited while the image of the emperor continues to receive the traditional reverence? How would it further be credible to put the images of Christ, of the Blessed Mother, and of the saints on the same level as the idols of the pagans? And above all: when would the alleged "deviation" from the original purity of the Church have taken place?

This last question especially brings out the dilemma of the iconoclastic reform (the dilemma of every "reformation"!). The answers here were again quite varied: Leo III seems to consider the entire history of the Church as a time of betrayal, should one take those "eight hundred years" rather literally. But again, when precisely did this "idolatry" sneak into the Church? The bishops at the iconoclastic council of 754 A.D. appear to consider the cult of the images an evil of rather late origin; for they deem the Church of the first six ecumenical councils (325–681 A.D.) still pure and uncorrupted. Only afterward, they say, did the Tempter, the Evil One, "secretly and under the guise of Christianity introduce

---

[19] Cf. Gero, *Constantine V,* 143–65.

this idolatry".[20] Which would mean that this evil penetrated the Church in the short period between 681 A.D. and 726 A.D. This, however, cannot have been the opinion of the iconoclasts; they were well aware of the struggles—without success—on the part of Eusebius of Caesarea and Epiphanius of Salamis in the fourth century to stem the further expansion of the image cult. When indeed did the error make inroads, when was the true tradition severed, a tradition the iconoclasts claimed to restore? They have no precise answer to this question. Yet they are well prepared to describe rather meticulously the evil they are fighting. The few iconoclastic texts that have survived the victory of the defenders of images[21] offer us a clear picture of the accusations leveled against the cult of images. We shall try to list them by discussing them in the order of their importance.

II. The Church Sliding into Paganism?
Theological Arguments against the Veneration of Images

1. *Abuses in the Cult of Images*

No doubt, as the veneration of images grew, so did the number of abuses. Popular religion was certainly not always free of them.[22] Among the numerous miracles reported and believed in connection with icons, there were certainly some whose authenticity was questioned, with good reason, by the iconoclasts: that miraculous image of Mary, for instance, where occasionally milk would flow out of its breasts, but which milk was poured into the image, as research has determined, from behind through a straw.[23] Was it

[20] Mansi 13, 221CD.

[21] The more important texts are in H. Hennephof, ed., *Textus byzantinos ad iconomachiam pertinentes* (Leiden, 1969).

[22] Details in D. Savramis, "Der abergläubische Missbrauch der Bilder in Byzanz", *Ostkirchliche Studien* 9 (1960):174–92.

[23] PG III, 1136D–1137B.

not a questionable custom to choose an icon as baptismal sponsor?[24]
It is reported to have happened that priests at Communion would
mix into the eucharistic chalice some colored dust from an icon,[25]
a superstitious practice that brings to mind the widespread [ab]use
of drinking the oil from the lamps that had burned in front of
icons or relics.[26] Such and similar reproaches were probably not
mere figments of the imagination.

The most objectionable aspect of the icon cult, of course, was
not the ever-present possibility of abuse but the fact that images
were *venerated* at all. The outward signs of this cult: candles or
lamps, incense, kissing, prostration—all these expressions of the
image cult smacked alarmingly of the pagan practices of idolatry.
Could the simple faithful always be aware of the subtle theological distinction between veneration [*proskynêsis*] and worship [*latreia*],
with which the theologians defended themselves against the accusation that the cult of images constituted the *worship* of graven
images? Did not the defenders of images ever and again have to
explain this distinction to monks and laypersons alike, clarifying
that images must only be venerated, while the Lord himself, so
depicted, should alone be worshipped?[27] All of this confirmed
the opponents in their conviction that the veneration of images
was incompatible with the purity of Christianity.

2. *"Thou Shalt Not Fashion for Thyself an Image" (Ex 20:4)*

The Old Testament's injunction against images was one of the
iconoclasts' mightiest weapons: "Thou shalt not fashion for thyself
an image, no likeness of anything in the sky above nor on the
earth below nor in the waters beneath the earth" (Ex 20:4).

The command is clear. Of what use would be further discussion?
Not one image can claim an exception! Let us not try to get away
from the strict demands of this command! In view of this ban, did

---

[24] Mansi 14, 420AB; cf. PG 99, 961BC.
[25] Mansi 14, 420AB.
[26] Cf. PG 87, 3552D–3557C.
[27] PG 99, 1529D; PG 100, 756D–757A.

not the entire dispute about images assume the character of idle sophistry? Was it not a crying shame that Jews and Muslims had to remind the Christians of the seriousness of this prohibition? Here it becomes understandable that iconoclasm was embedded in an atmosphere of a holy war. And since every holy war needs a rousing slogan, what would have been more appropriate than this one: "War on the images! Smash the idols!"

The reality, however, was not as clear and simple as it might have seemed in the initial euphoria of iconoclasm. The iconoclastic emperors were men of war; their political success and their fame rested on their fortunes in war. Warriors do not gladly engage in discussions. A legend—biased, but telling—asserts that Emperor Leo had the "Academy of Constantinople" burned down and with it the entire college of twelve professors who had refused to support the attack on images.[28] This is hardly historical fact, yet we can easily imagine a Leo III wishing to get rid of those "intellectuals" who through their theological distinctions only succeed in complicating everything.

As simple as the rejection of images might have appeared, the matter was nevertheless far from being so clear. Were *all* images banned? Or only images of living things? The interpretation of Exodus 20:4 in Deuteronomy 4:16–18 understood it in this latter sense. The iconoclasts as well did not agree in their interpretation of the ban on images. Obviously tolerated in the arts at the time of iconoclasm, in addition to ornaments, were also representations of animals.[29] Islam was more consistent in this respect and rejected any depiction of living things.[30]

A total ban on images turns out to be impossible. The iconoclasts, in fact, did not simply destroy every image and all visual representations; they rather had their own imagery more in line with their ideas. They accepted above all a decorative art: abstract ornaments

[28] Regarding this legend, see P. Lemerle, *Le premier humanisme byzantin* (Paris, 1971), 89–94, 105–8.

[29] Cf. PG 100, 465A.

[30] Cf. PG 100, 528CD; A. Grabar, *L'iconoclasme,* 103–12. But here, too, one might have to differentiate; cf. M. S. Ipçiroğlu, *Das Bild im Islam. Ein Verbot und seine Folgen* (Vienna and Munich, 1971).

or plant forms, but also depictions of animals, including hunting scenes. The defenders of images were especially angered by the fact that Emperor Constantine V ordered the celebrated pictures of the ecumenical councils in the so-called *Milion* replaced with scenes from the hippodrome and that he even went so far as to add the explicit likeness of his favorite charioteer.[31] Iconoclastic art differed from the conception held by the champions of images, especially in its rejection of any *veneration* of images and its relegating the image to a strictly secular and decorative purpose. And yet, even in this, there was at least one exception of particular importance: the emperors obviously never thought of abandoning, together with the icon cult, the traditional veneration of the emperor's image as well. On the contrary, they fostered this cult, manifest foremost in their minting of coins. It is very telling that the iconoclastic emperors replaced the cross on the coins with their own likeness, which was then stamped on both sides of the coins.[32]

To invoke the biblical injunction against images evidently is not sufficient to sustain the theological foundation of iconoclasm; otherwise this ban would have had to have been observed more consistently and more rigorously. There must have been other, more specific arguments to justify the accusation of idolatry against the icon cult.

3. *Matter and Spirit*

In the "Letter of Pope Gregory II to the Emperor Leo III" we read: "You have written: 'We must not worship anything fashioned by human hands, nor any figure depicting the likeness of anything, according to God's word, neither in the sky nor on the earth'; you further write: 'Explain this to me: who told us we ought to

[31] PG 100, 1172AB; A. Grabar, *L'iconoclasme*, 55–61.
[32] A. Grabar, *L'iconoclasme*, 119–25, 210; L. W. Barnard, "The Emperor Cult and the Origins of the Iconoclastic Controversy", *Byzantion* 43 (1973):13–29.

venerate and worship things fashioned by human hands, when God's law prohibits it?' "[33]

The ban on images is here more specifically interpreted as the rejection of cultic veneration of anything fashioned by human hands; such statements are already found in the biblical polemic against the manufacturers of idols. But here the argument receives a new emphasis: the veneration of images is viewed as *the worship of lifeless, inanimate matter* and set against the authentic devotion of worship "in spirit and in truth". This contempt for matter is one of the most striking traits of iconoclasm. While other arguments underwent profound changes over the 120 years of the image controversy, this one remained constant. Here we certainly touch on one of the fundamental reasons for iconoclasm.

The controversy began in 726 A.D. when Emperor Leo III had the image of Christ over the Chalke palace gate in Constantinople removed by force. This image, in A. Grabar's words, was "the most representative religious portrayal in the empire" (see illustrations no. 7 and no. 8).[34] Its destruction could be seen only as a programmatic declaration. That Leo III intended it to be such is shown by the fact that in place of Christ's image he had a cross fixed, which he wanted to be understood as a "counter-image" to the icon of Christ by adding the following programmatic inscription: "The Lord God does not allow the fashioning of an image of Christ that is lifeless and without breath, made of earthly matter despised by the [Sacred] Writings. Leo, together with his son, the new Constantine, signs the royal portals with the thrice-blessed sign of the cross, the glory of all believers."[35]

God will not permit man to fashion a lifeless image of his Christ; for how could such a material likeness represent a living being, especially one of such high dignity as is Christ? A symbolic representation, the sign of the cross, for example, avoids this

[33] Mansi 12, 959E.

[34] A. Grabar, *L'iconoclasme*, 134; cf. C. Mango, *The Brazen House. A Study of the Vestibule of the Imperial Palace of Constantinople* (Copenhagen, 1959), 108–48; Gero, *Leo III*, 212–17.

[35] PG 99, 437C.

difficulty. It speaks, without depiction, of things that cannot be molded into inanimated matter. The iconoclastic synod of 754 A.D. puts it in similar words:

> Condemned be everyone who attempts to capture the likeness of the saints with material colors in lifeless and mute icons—for such images are of no use. To fashion them is a nonsensical idea and a devilish invention, taking the place of depicting in ourselves the virtues of the saints as told in the Writings, and thus becoming ourselves living icons and being prompted to a zeal similar to theirs.[36]

Even as late as at the iconoclastic council of 815 A.D. the reproach is voiced that the image-loving Council of Nicea permitted, because of the Incarnation, the depiction of the inscrutable Son of God by means "of unworthy matter" and extended to "the lifeless matter of the icons" a veneration due only to God. The council further refused to represent and venerate the saints "in the lifeless rendition of portraits".[37] When compared to the loftiness and dignity of the subjects in question, the ignoble tools of the visual arts seem to be *kako technia,* an evil procedure,[38] a craft that is "dead, even contemptible, never alive".[39] This is a cry of genuine consternation: "How dare they paint in the vulgar art of the pagans the ever blessed and exalted Mother of God?"[40]

A living image—a lifeless image: this is the distinctive criterion for the iconoclasts in separating the image from the idol. But what, then, would constitute a true image? According to the texts quoted here, a true image is one that reproduces the original completely and without any reduction. Constantine V was the first to formulate this definition in explicit terms. This highly

---

[36] Mansi 13, 345CD. This text alludes to a passage in Theodotus of Ancyra, but with revealing changes: the neutral expression, "on icons with material colors", is given a negative meaning by adding, "lifeless and mute"; cf. Mansi 13, 309E–312A. Such slanted changes of patristic quotations are found not infrequently; cf. SC 160, 56 and 209: the rendering of Basilius' text about the creation of man.

[37] Nos. 273 and 274 in Hennephof, *Textus byzantinos.*

[38] Mansi 13, 324E.

[39] Mansi 13, 276D; cf. 229DE.

[40] Mansi 13, 277CD.

Illustration 7

Illustration number 7: Christ the Pantocrator. Encaustic icon, 84 × 45.5 cm, 1st half of the 6th century, Monastery of St. Catherine, Mount Sinai.

Photo: J. Galley-Schwitter A.G. (Basel).

This icon, before its restoration in 1962, was dated approximately to the 13th century. Only after all later layers of paint had been removed did the icon reveal its full splendor and masterful beauty. Kurt Weitzmann, one of the most knowledgeable experts on the icon collection in the Monastery of St. Catherine, interprets the theological meaning of the subtle play of forms and colors as follows:

"The high artistic quality of this icon derives not only from the delicate and most masterful employment of the encaustic technique, but equally from the hieratic composition and the linear rendition of the details. The artist, by positioning the figure of Christ frontally in the center of the image and showing his eyes wide open so they do not focus on any particular point, succeeds in obtaining an effect of remoteness and timelessness, a visual expression of the divine nature. At the same time he avoids a strict symmetry, and adds vitality to the posture by turning Christ's body slightly toward the right. There are other traits as well worth mentioning: the pupils of the eyes are not on the same level; the left eyebrow is curved higher than the right one—an element especially contributing to the vivid facial expression; ... the hair is parted, not at the precise center but slightly to the side, while the beard is combed into the opposite direction, and following its curved flow, the hair falls over the left shoulder, while on the other side it is gathered toward the rear. By combining in such subtle ways abstract and more naturalistic elements, the artist succeeds in presenting in visual form the dogma of the two natures in Christ, the divine and the human natures" (*The Monastery of Saint Catherine at Mount Sinai. The Icons* [Princeton, 1973], vol. 1, 15).

The model for this icon, which reputedly originated in Constantinople, can probably be traced to the famous image of Christ at the Chalke palace gate, an image destroyed at the start of the two stages of iconoclasm (726 and 814 A.D.).

(See pages 24 and 151.)

Illustration 8

Illustration number 8: Christ the Pantocrator. Encaustic icon (detail), 1st half of the 6th century, Monastery of St. Catherine, Mount Sinai (cf. illustration number 7).

Photo: J. Galley-Schwitter A.G. (Basel).

(See pages 24 and 151.)

intelligent warrior and emperor shows himself also an impressive theologian. The defenders of images needed half a century before they would seriously confront and discuss his arguments.

4. The Consubstantial Image

Emperor Leo III rejected the icon because it is "mute and without life breath". His son, Constantine V, provides the reasons for this rejection: "Every image is the copy of an original. . . . In order to be a true image, it has to be consubstantial with what is depicted . . . so that the whole be safeguarded; otherwise it is not an image."[41] This precisely is lacking in icons painted on wood; they are not consubstantial with the original, so they do not even deserve to be called images. It is essential for every true image to "preserve" and represent perfectly the original in the likeness. This definition of the image, of course, renders icons impossible! How did Emperor Constantine arrive at this conception? It seems far removed from the Greek way of thinking, which strongly emphasizes the short-comings of the image in comparison to the original: images are shadows, faint reflections of the lofty original. Where does Constantine find his idea of a consubstantial image? We have met this idea already in the trinitarian theology of Athanasius, for whom the Son is the eternal, consubstantial image of the Father. Should this reversal of the Greek conception of the image in the meantime have taken hold to such an extent that Constantine now accepts as model for any visual representation only the "image of all images", the Son, the "image of the invisible God"?

A different explanation seems to be more convincing. A Muslim text threatens the manufacturers of images as follows: "On the day of the resurrection they will be punished most severely; they will be commanded, 'Give life to what you have fashioned!' "[42] We also know the reaction of an Arab Christian author, a defender of

---

[41] Constantine's texts are partly contained in the refutation by Patriarch Nicephorus; collected by Hennephof, *Textus byzantinos,* nos. 141–87. Our texts are taken from PG 100, 216C, 225A, 228D.

[42] Quoted in A. Grabar, *L'iconoclasme,* 141.

images, to this argument. Theodore Abû Qurra (c. 750–820 A.D.), in his book on the veneration of images, states that such a conception (of no other than living and consubstantial images) will necessarily lead to the demise of any visual art; for even those who only allow the depictions of plants would have to be able to bring them to life.[43] The extent of this conception of the image within the realm of Islam at that time is shown by Grabar also in several other references. Thus the Islamic art of the time is known to have loved certain "consubstantial" images, in the form of artificial representations of plants and animals, "animated" through clever mechanisms.[44] Emperor Theophilus (829–842 A.D.) reportedly tried to imitate at his court those "gadgets", which speak of a rather peculiar mythical notion of the identity between image and original. As long as this was confined to amusing the royal court, no great harm would result. But when such ideas were transferred into the realm of religion, the danger became obvious: how could such illusionary "living" images fail to foster the ever-present tendency to practice idolatry? The Isaurian dynasty came from northern Mesopotamia, an area heavily influenced in those days by a young and vital Islam. Is it conceivable that Emperor Constantine V formed his concept of the image under this influence?

Only this much is certain: he admitted as true images only those in which the one depicted is present as a living reality. No wonder, then, that he considered the Eucharist to be the only true image of Christ: for in the eucharistic offering, Christ is *substantially* present. "The bread we receive is indeed the icon of his body, depicting his flesh, as it has become the figure [*typos*] of his body."[45] "Not every piece of bread is already Christ's body, nor is every cup of wine already his blood, but only when it has been removed, through the sacred action, from the realm of what is made by human hands, and elevated into the realm of what is not

---

[43] German translation in G. Graf, *Die arabischen Schriften des Theodor Abû Qurra* (Paderborn, 1910), 278–333; here, 298.

[44] A. Grabar, *L'iconoclasme,* 169f. and 140f.; cf. O. Grabar, "Islam and Iconoclasm", in *Iconoclasm,* 46.

[45] PG 100, 337A; cf. the article by Gero, "The Eucharistic Doctrine of the Byzantine Iconoclasts and Its Sources", *Byzantinische Zeitschrift* 68 (1975):4–22.

made by human hands."[46] The bread becomes the eucharistic icon of Christ because it is being removed, by divine power, from the confines of human ingenuity and transformed into a gift created by God. The Eucharist was for Constantine V the one and only true icon of Christ, because Christ himself offered here his "image", which was completely permeated by his living reality. We shall later see that icon devotion, especially in its popular form, held a similar view in its assumption that the *true icons of Christ* are not those painted by artists but those miraculously given by Christ himself: the *acheiropoietoi,* icons "not made by human hands".[47]

The demand that an icon, to be a true icon, must represent a consubstantial likeness of the original certainly was in line with the desire to experience the real *presence* of the one so depicted. It would probably not be without merit to pursue the question whether the efforts, active in the Western Church of the Middle Ages, to *see,* to *contemplate,* and to *adore* the Eucharist, did not actually spring from the very same desire.[48] Emperor Constantine's concept of the image, of course, totally disregards one other and rather essential aspect of the image: the aspect of *likeness.* For is there anything that looks less like the visible face of Christ than the forms of bread and wine? The Greeks desire to "behold" (cf. Jn 12:20f.). To behold the figure of Christ only in its "eucharistic veil" would not satisfy them.

5. An "Origenian" Approach

Iconoclasm did not present a united front. The 338 bishops who at the council of 754 A.D. were expected to give their ecclesiastical and conciliar approval to the imperial iconoclasm, no matter how devoted they were to the illustrious imperial desire, nevertheless showed a certain measure of independence by not simply rubber-stamping Constantine's theological texts. It is possible to detect

[46] PG 100, 337C.
[47] Cf. below, p. 240–43.
[48] Cf. E. Dumoutet, *Le désir de voir l'hostie et les origines de la dévotion au Saint-Sacrement* (Paris, 1926).

between these texts and the council's own promulgated decree a number of significant differences.[49] Most important for our topic is the fact that the bishops did not adopt Constantine's notion of the consubstantial image. True, this did not modify anything in the iconoclastic decisions of the council, but these decisions are justified by reasons different from those given by the theologizing emperor. The bishops probably noticed the deficient argumentation in the texts submitted to the council by the emperor. Their reinterpretation of the emperor's arguments reveals something of the complexity inherent in the iconoclastic movement in the Byzantine realm.

Constantine V held a conception of the image, which—with some reservations—we may label "oriental": image and original are all but magically the same. The theologians of the council of 754 A.D. gave the iconoclastic arguments a much more "Greek" twist by positing as great a distance as possible, really an abyss, between original and image. It is fascinating to see how these two tendencies in the image concept, despite their opposing directions, arrive at the same conclusion: the rejection of images. In both cases, images are not possible: in the first, because too much is asked of them (to be consubstantial with the original); in the second, because their ability is underrated (they are infinitely separated from the original).

This second trend is clearly expressed in the deliberations of the council of 754 A.D. It is worth noticing that the extant iconoclastic texts of Emperor Constantine never advance the reproach that icons are mere matter; it is not this material character of images that disturbed the emperor, but the fact that the original is not *present* in these material images. The bishops at the council, in contrast, take offense at the fact that the images of saints "insult" the saints who live in the splendor of Christ, because these images are but "shabby and lifeless matter".[50] Hence the "anathema" of the council: "Should anyone endeavor to capture the divine countenance [*charaktêra*] of the incarnate Word of God by means of *material colors* instead of contemplating him whole-

---

[49] G. Ostrogorsky, *Studien zur Geschichte des byzantinischen Bilderstreits* (Wroclaw, 1929), 15–45, identifies some of these differences.

[50] Mansi 13, 277DE.

heartedly with the *eyes of the spirit,* him who sits at the right hand of the Father on the throne of glory, surpassing the sun in splendor, such a one be banned."[51]

The contrast between material colors and spiritual contemplation illustrates the abyss separating the icon from its heavenly original. The goal of the Christian life is spiritual contemplation, and this requires the exercise of our spiritual eyes, which alone are able to behold spiritual realities. The distance between these spiritual originals and the material means available to earthly art is simply too great.

In contrast to the view of Emperor Constantine, whose interest focused on the presence of the original in the material likeness, the theology of the experts at the council of 754 A.D. moved within a rather Neoplatonic mental structure. The material world is unable to represent the splendor of the spiritual world. Time and again the Platonism inherent in the Eastern image cult has been pointed out. And yet, as it seems to us, the extent to which at least a good number of the iconoclasts were also influenced by Platonic ideas is often overlooked.[52] The "Platonism" of the iconoclasts shows not only in their strong emphasis on separating the spiritual from the material world. The "Testimonies of the Fathers" as well, collected by the iconoclastic council, every so often quote texts that clearly betray Platonic influences: such as the segment from the apocryphal Acts of John (2nd century), which tells of a newly converted pagan who out of gratitude, in pagan fashion, had a portrait painted of his benefactor, the Apostle John, in order to venerate it. The apostle not only rebukes this misguided zeal, he is moreover not willing to recognize himself in the image. Yet one glance in the mirror convinces him that the image really shows his portrait and is like him. "However," he adds immediately, "it is not a likeness of me but of my appearance in the flesh. . . . What you have done here is childish and defective. You have painted a dead image of a dead body." The body is something dead; it is utterly useless to depict it. He who desires to become an authentic and skilled painter should use those colors that Jesus provides

[51] Mansi 13, 336E.
[52] Florovsky has pointed this out, in "Origen", 94–96.

through the apostle, in order to paint the only image approved by Christ: the godly soul.[53]

This text evokes the famous passage at the beginning of Porphyry's *Life of Plotinus*. Plotinus, it says, was ashamed to be in the body and therefore refused to sit for a portrait by a sculptor. Is it not enough "to put up with the likeness [*eidôlon*] nature has clothed us with?" Why should he then desire "that a likeness of the likeness of me be preserved, a likeness more durable, as if this likeness were worth seeing"?[54] We may by all means admire physical beauty, but should never stop there, as it is only an image of the ideal beauty. The danger consists in being satisfied with some beauty "that is present to us in images and bodies", while forgetting the ideal beauty from which flows our love for earthly beauty:[55] "For when we discover physical beauty, we must not draw close to it but acknowledge that it is but a likeness, an imprint, a shadow, and flee to that beauty of which it is the image."[56] Plotinus describes this flight as a purification of our spiritual eyes. We must close our physical eyes in order to open our spiritual eyes:

> Retreat into yourself, and look around; and should you see that you are not yet beautiful, then imitate the sculptor who aims at making a beautiful sculpture by chiselling away something here, smoothing something there, polishing something here, refining something there, until he has completed the beautiful likeness of a statue. Thus should you chisel away all that is idle, straighten all that is crooked, clean all that is dark and make it into light, never tiring to work on the perfection of this your image.[57]

This image is nothing else than the soul. To cleanse it from all darkness so it may shine brightly really means to cleanse it from all

---

[53] "Acta Johannis", 26–29, Hennecke and Schneemelcher, *Neutestamentliche Apokryphen*, II, 147f.; cf. Junod's commentary on this text in *L'histoire des actes apocryphes*.

[54] Trans. R. Harder (Hamburg, 1958), 3.

[55] Enn. III, 5, 1; *Life of Plotinus*, vol. 5, 175.

[56] Enn. I, 6, 8; vol. I, 21.

[57] Enn. I, 6, 9; vol. I, 23.

contamination by elements of the body.[58] How could anybody, then, still insist on fashioning an image of this bodily shell, from which the yearning soul desires to be liberated?[59]

Here we find once more certain thoughts similar to those formulated by another witness to the iconoclastic council of 754 A.D.—Eusebius of Caesarea. He, too, looked at the icon as something senseless, because it perpetuates a condition that must be overcome: bodily existence. For Eusebius, as well as for the synod of 754 A.D., the resurrection constitutes the same liberation from the earthly, bodily existence that Plotinus desires in his own way. The visual arts, for Eusebius and for Plotinus, dwell on a stage that has to be overcome. The council of 754 A.D. agrees. Was there a direct influence of such "platonizing" tendencies on the early Church? Or is the council's iconoclasm rather the manifestation of a certain basic attitude of the Church, coming to the surface every so often? Both reasons might apply; for the return to certain anti-image sources of the early Church means indeed an attempt to bind one's own conviction into the continuing history. Some historians believe that this basic theological position can be shown to be connected to one other, not easily identified current that every now and then appeared in Eastern Christianity, invariably creating conflicts: we speak of *Origenism*.

G. Florovsky detects in the iconoclastic controversy "a new act in the history of 'Origenistic quarrels' ".[60] A. Grillmeier agrees and thinks that Origenism "could not have any interest in a historical image of Christ".[61] The fact that the spiritual movement carrying this label had not disappeared by the time of the icon controversy is proved by the Patriarch Germanus I (d. 733 A.D.), who was the first writer to confront the iconoclasts, and who also had to deal with Origenist tendencies.[62]

[58] Enn. I, 6, 5; vol. I, 15.

[59] *Life of Plotinus*, 57.

[60] "Origen", 87.

[61] *Mit Ihm und in Ihm. Christologische Forschungen und Perspektiven* (Freiburg, 1975), 34.

[62] Cf. the valuable documentation by W. Lackner, "Ein hagiographisches Zeugnis für den Antapodotikos des Patriarchen Germanos I. von Konstantinopel", *Byzantion* 38 (1968):42–104.

So far, we have tried to present the arguments of the icono-clasts at least in rough outlines. The Old Testament's ban on images certainly was important. But more decisive were the funda-mental conceptions of the image and its relation to the original. The emperor's opinion here differed substantially from that of the council. Constantine demanded that reality and image be as one. With this, the image loses its character of being depiction. The "Origenian" tendency of the council separates the material work of art from what is depicted by such a gulf that here, too, the image loses its essence of being a representation. At most, it is the shadow of a shadow. And so it follows that for both, emperor and council, the veneration of images becomes an idolatrous abuse corrupting the pure, spiritual tradition of the Church and regressing to a pagan, earthly stage.

The veneration of images on the part of the iconophiles is contrasted by the iconoclasts with the veneration of the cross. They assert, not without reason, that the veneration of the cross constitutes the most ancient tradition of the Church. Did not the great Constantine conquer "in this sign"? It is part of Constantine V's imperial ideology that he in turn desired to attribute his own victories for the empire to the veneration of this sign. The venera-tion of the cross avoided those aspects that brought criticism to the image cult. The cross is a pure symbol, not claiming to depict anything, only reminding of something. *Cross and icon* thus appear at first as rivals in the image controversy. The defenders of images are accused of substituting the ancient crosses with icons.[63] On their part, the iconoclasts replaced the icons with the cross, and after the iconophiles prevailed (843 A.D.), they occasionally in turn replaced the crosses with icons, which is still clearly dis-cernible in the apse—destroyed in the meantime—of the Church of the Dormition in Nicea (see illustration no. 9). Yet in the end, the veneration of cross and icon were reconciled: the Council of Nicea (787 A.D.) professes equal veneration of cross and image, and Empress Theodora, in 843 A.D., restored the image of Christ, destroyed by Leo III, over the Chalke palace gate, but did not

[63] So wrote Emperor Theophilus to Emperor Ludwig; Mansi 14, 420B.

Illustration 9

Illustration number 9: Mosaic in the apse of the Church dedicated to the Dormition of Mary (*Koimesis*) in Nicea (destroyed in 1922).

Photo: Ecole Pratique des Hautes Etudes (Paris).

The original picture of Mary (reputedly outgoing 6th century) was removed at the time of iconoclasm and replaced by a cross. After the iconophiles had prevailed (843 A.D.), the cross was again taken down (its outlines are still clearly visible on the mosaic), and replaced by an image of the Blessed Mother, modeled after the first picture. Only the original inscription has survived this conflict between cross and icon, so typical for the icon controversy. "In your mother's womb, before the daystar, I have begotten you" (Ps 110:3; cf. also illustration number 10).

(See page 164.)

remove the cross put there instead by Leo III (see illustration no. 10).[64]

Image of Christ, or symbol of Christ: the conflict between cross and icon points to the fact that at the center of the controversy right from the beginning there stood the question regarding the image of *Christ.* The iconoclastic arguments so far focused generally on the veneration of images as such. The most crucial and most consequential argument, however, not discussed up till now, concentrated on the image of Christ alone. For this reason, it was all the more effective. In his "questions" submitted to the council of 754 A.D., the emperor advances a new argument: the veneration of images is not only idolatry but christological heresy; even worse: it is the sum and peak of all christological heresies. No matter how contrived or rhetorical such accusations may sound, one cannot fail to admire the emperor's ingenuity in attacking the icon cult.

After the chapter on Eusebius of Caesarea, such arguments are no longer unfamiliar to us. New in all this is only the fact that between Eusebius and Emperor Constantine there lie four centuries of christological debates, which clarified many points still undecided at the time of Eusebius. Consequently, the christological arguments against images now had become more precise, but so had the counter-arguments of the icon defenders as well, as we shall see. This debate we shall analyze in what follows. Though the debate may appear alien to our modern mind-set, it is nonetheless fascinating.

[64] On the veneration of the cross, cf. Grillmeier, *Der Logos am Kreuz* (Munich, 1957).

III. The Christology of the Iconoclasts

1. *The Emperor Constantine V*

There is much to support the impression that it was the Emperor Constantine himself who made the debate on sacred images into a christological controversy. Those few texts of his that were preserved, but other documents of his era as well, are proof that the emperor was presenting there his own personal theological ideas. He is not the first Byzantine emperor full of enthusiasm for theological speculation: you only have to recall the great Justinian! Constantine wanted to provide iconoclasm with a solid dogmatic foundation. Nothing could discredit the cult of images more than evidence that it conflicted with the important christological councils. Could there be in the Byzantine realm a more serious accusation than to say that all defenders of images are Nestorians and Monophysites? To expose the icon cult as a *christological* heresy — this was the emperor's design. If this was successful, then the support of the bishops was assured. Was Constantine aware of the import his attitude would have? The accusation of christological heresy was bound to awaken again all the ghosts that for centuries had frightened and confused Byzantine history. In the arena of Christology above all, the emperor had to expect a struggle in which would be employed every weapon that the theology of the previous centuries had forged. The arguments, to modern readers perhaps outlandish, briefly explained in what follows, are essential for any comprehension of the Byzantine controversy on images: those involved were well aware that *this* stood at the center of the controversy.

"Those who fashion icons of Christ . . . have not grasped the depth of the dogma regarding the unmixed union of the two natures in Christ":[65] so the handy, aggressive thesis of Emperor Constantine. We shall look at these arguments in detail: How does

---

[65] PG 100, 329A. We quote Constantine's texts from Hennephof, *Textus byzantinos,* with reference to their location in PG 100; a valuable analysis of these texts is given by Gero, *Constantine V,* 37–52.

Illustration 10

Illustration number 10: Ampulla from the Holy Land, 6th century, Cathedral Treasury in Monza.

Photo: J. Jobé (Lausanne).

These ampullae served the pilgrims to bring oil from the sacred places of Palestine. The collections of such ampullae in Monza and Bobbio are among the most important sources of the iconography of the Holy Land. The ampulla shown here may have contained blessed oil from the "Anastasis", the Church of the Holy Sepulchre in Jerusalem. In the lower part of the picture, we see the sacred tomb (with doors closed!), in front of which the angel who announces to the women coming from the left the message of the Resurrection: "The Lord has risen!", as the small inscription over the tomb indicates. At the center there appears Golgotha, the holy cross, which is venerated by two men (pilgrims?) on their knees. On top of the cross, we see the majestic portrait of Christ, surrounded by the sun (at left) and the moon (at right). This unique rendition probably symbolizes that the risen Lord is exalted above cross and tomb and is now enthroned "at the right hand of the Father". The robber at the right looks up at Jesus, the one at the left turns away. At the far left stands the Blessed Mother, at the far right, the Baptizer, pointing at Christ. Cross and icon—this is the message—do not exclude each other. We may surmise that the image of Christ on the Chalke gate, restored in 843 A.D. by Empress Theodora, also combined cross and icon, thus following the same pattern. The circular inscription around the edge of the ampulla reads: "Oil from the life-giving wood at the holy places of Christ."

(See pages 166–67.)

the emperor understand "unmixed union"? What constitutes for him an icon? and Why would one exclude the other?

a. The union of the two natures in Christ

"This is the firm belief of the holy Catholic Church of God: . . . since the two natures come together in an unmixed union, that is, a union of divinity and humanity, Christ is one, in the one hypostasis; and so it follows that he is twofold in the one person."[66]

This is entirely the language of the Council of Chalcedon. Subsequently, the emperor once again emphasizes: "Our Lord Jesus Christ is one person [*prosôpon*] *out of* two natures, one immaterial, the other material, by an unmixed union."[67] A strict Chalcedonian considering this statement would have taken exception only to the unobtrusive "out of", since the Council of Chalcedon, for specific reasons, would have preferred to say, "*in* two natures". The issue here turns more problematical as Constantine continues: "After this union has taken place, the resulting reality has become inseparable."[68] This, too, is still the language of Chalcedon, but Constantine emphasizes "inseparable" so strongly as to make the distinction between Christ's two natures almost indiscernible. In order to avoid the separation of the two natures, their distinctiveness is all but forgotten. Did Constantine teach that, through their union, the flesh of Christ became consubstantial with the Eternal Word? This has been asserted, not without some reason.[69] All this leads to the conclusion that Constantine's christological position was close to that of the Monophysites.[70] This proximity has been pointed out already in his own time. Just as it applies to the Monophysites, so also to Constantine; both hold that the result of the Incarnation is an inseparable reality arising out of the two natures, a reality in which divinity and humanity have become

[66] PG 100, 216BC.

[67] PG 100, 232A.

[68] PG 100, 248D; cf. 236C.

[69] So the Patriarch Nicephorus, PG 100, 248A. Supporting this is the fact that Constantine considers the Eucharist to be the only icon, as he demands that any icon be consubstantial with its original.

[70] Cf. Ostrogorsky, *Studien zur Geschichte,* 24–29.

practically indiscernible: "Christ, out of a duality, has become one person."[71]

b. The concept of the image

We shall now explore the emperor's concept of the image. As mentioned above, he accepted as a true image only that which would be consubstantial with the original. He specifies in what sense he understands this: "If an image does not present the exact shape of the forms making up the 'personal countenance' [*prosôpon*] of its original, then it can never be an icon."[72] The icon, then, must reproduce the countenance of the person so depicted. Constantine repeatedly emphasizes: "The icon is the image of a person [*prosôpon*]."[73] This may sound like a most obvious statement. One has to ask, however, why this was so rarely said with such simplicity and clarity during the entire image controversy. *Prosôpon* seems to retain for Constantine its original meaning: the visible countenance, the face of a person. It is for this reason that we translate this term in what follows as "personal countenance", which might come closest to its specific sense. This may explain why he prefers this term over the more abstract term "hypostasis".

The icon, then, presents a concrete *prosôpon*. In order to fulfill the claim to be an icon, a true image, it must show this *prosôpon*, this "personal countenance", exactly *as it is*. True, Constantine is not really out of line; for how could something be an image if in it we do not recognize the one so depicted? Still, the question remains: What is really meant with "as it is"? Consulting Constantine's first definition (a true image is consubstantial with the original), we have to conclude that the only true icon is that which is identical to the original in everything, or — in Constantine's words — the one "in which the totality of the original is preserved".[74] Constantine, without doubt, is correct in describing the icon as the image of a *prosôpon*. He goes too far in demanding that the icon must show the *prosôpon* "as it is".

[71] PG 100, 301C.
[72] PG 100, 293A.
[73] PG 100, 297A; 301C.
[74] PG 100, 228D.

c. The icon of Christ

We now have specified how Constantine views the union of the two natures in Christ, and what he expects from an image. These two determinations, in order to sustain Constantine's argument, would have to be incompatible one with the other. He poses his question with great skill: "We now ask the bishops, How could it be possible to paint or depict our Lord Jesus Christ, given the fact that he possesses this one 'personal countenance', out of two natures, the immaterial and the material, through the unmixed union?"[75] And he immediately explains the reason for this question: "The fact that something is immaterial implies the consequence that it cannot be depicted, as it is without shape or form."[76] Constantine, based on these premises, then formulates his stringent conclusions:

1. Christ's "*prosôpon* or hypostasis cannot be separated from his two natures."[77]

2. One of the two natures, his divinity, cannot be depicted; it cannot be "circumscribed".

3. It is, therefore, impossible to paint or "circumscribe" the *prosôpon* of Christ.

In order to grasp the more subtle points of the ensuing debates, we should remember, once again, what was said in the chapter on Gregory of Nyssa regarding the concept of *perigraphê*, "circumscription", or "outlining".[78] In this, we always ought to keep in mind the concrete as well as the abstract meaning of these terms: when we hear that the divine nature cannot be "circumscribed", Constantine intends to say that it is beyond our grasp, that is, incomprehensible; but at the same time, in the concrete sense of the word, that it cannot be outlined neither in writing nor in drawing (in the Greek language both use the word graphê!).

[75] PG 100, 232A.
[76] PG 100, 232C.
[77] PG 100, 236C.
[78] Cf. above, p. 20.

Constantine's conclusion contains inescapable consequences regarding the icon cult: "Since that which is painted here represents the one 'personal countenance' [prosôpon], it follows that he who 'circumscribes' this prosôpon has also 'circumscribed' the divine nature, which indeed cannot be 'circumscribed'."[79] Since the one prosôpon of Christ cannot be separated from his two natures, the defenders of icons are unable to take refuge behind the argument that they only depict Christ's human nature. For the icon always depicts a "human countenance". Yet Christ's personal countenance is such that it cannot be sketched or "circumscribed"; "for nobody can picture him who possesses one personal countenance out of two natures, by depicting the personal countenance of the one nature while leaving the other nature without its personal countenance".[80]

The iconophiles, therefore, only have a choice between two heresies, without the possibility of escaping into a third option: if they wish to safeguard the unity of Christ's person, then "with the flesh, they necessarily also circumscribe the [Eternal] Word".[81] If they wish to escape this consequence and maintain the impossibility of "circumscribing" Christ's divinity, then they must say that Christ's humanity possesses its own personal countenance; which means, "they reduce Christ to the level of created beings, separating him from the [Eternal] Word with which he is nevertheless in essential union."[82] The council of 754 A.D. would later state explicitly: the iconophiles must choose between Monophysitism and Nestorianism. They have no other option!

These conclusions proved devastating for the defenders of images. No refutation was advanced for a long time, and only in the second stage of the image controversy (after 815 A.D.) did the iconophile theologians succeed in disproving them. Constantine had been able to create a succinct formulation for the purpose of making it evident to everyone how untenable the image cult really was. He submitted his "questions" to the bishops he had

[79] PG 100, 236C.
[80] PG 100, 296C.
[81] PG 100, 260C–261A.
[82] PG 100, 284D.

summoned to a great synod in Constantinople. We already presented some of the statements of this synod of 754 A.D. It remains for us to investigate to what extent the authors of the council's decrees accepted the christological argumentation submitted by the emperor. The result will be a surprise!

2. *The Synod of 754* A.D.

The 338 bishops summoned by the emperor to the council, seem to have submitted without exception to the emperor's will. Some of them were still alive when the council of 787 restored the veneration of images and had to defend themselves for their stance thirty years earlier. What importance could be seen in a council that practically served as a rubber stamp for the emperor? A closer study of this council's decrees reveals that it did not at all simply repeat the arguments of the emperor. On the contrary, we already pointed out that the council Fathers amended the imperial texts considerably without arriving at different conclusions. This is also true with regard to the christological argumentation. The authors of the decrees coming from the council of 754 A.D. changed the premises of Constantine's arguments carefully yet decisively toward greater orthodoxy. This, however, created a different problem: How could they, based on different premises, arrive at the same conclusion as their patron, the emperor? All of this is a masterful example of Byzantine subtlety!

a. *The union of the two natures in Christ*

Constantine's argument against the icon of Christ asserted: "That which is depicted in the icon is a 'personal countenance'. But he who 'circumscribes' this 'personal countenance' obviously also 'circumscribes' the divine nature, which cannot be 'circumscribed'."[83] The fundamental error in this argumentation consists in the false assumption regarding the *prosôpon* of Christ, and it is rather

[83] PG 100, 236C.

astonishing that the iconophiles needed such a long time to unmask this error; for not until Nicephorus and Theodore the Studite, sixty years later, did they succeed in this. Nearly all of the defenders of images tackle first the question whether one can "circumscribe" Christ's humanity without at the same time "circumscribing" his divinity. They seem to overlook that this question is but an appendix to the infinitely more decisive question as to the *prosôpon* of Christ. To disprove Constantine, it would have been sufficient to disprove his concept of the "personal countenance" of Christ (as Nicephorus and Theodore would later do). For Constantine was right in saying that every icon depicts the *prosôpon* of him whose image it is, and the same applies to the icon of Christ. But it is simply a fallacy to assert that painting an icon of Christ means also "circumscribing" his divine nature, which cannot be done. The first part of this book has shown that the face of Jesus (the very face depicted in the icon) is the face of the incarnate person of the Eternal Word. This human face does not "circumscribe" the divine nature, not even the human nature, but the *prosôpon,* the person of the Word. In the icon, we see neither a divine nor a human *nature,* but rather the face of the *person* of Jesus who is God and man.

The belated insight in the solution of Emperor Constantine's dilemma may find its explanation partly in the fact that the council Fathers in 754 A.D. carefully covered up all tracks that might have led to this solution. One discovers with considerable surprise that the council did not adopt the one element in Constantine's arguments that was the most accurate of all: the definition of the icon as an image of a "personal countenance". The council did not offer a definition of the image at all. Why this strange omission? It is rather improbable that it was an oversight. Did the bishops gathered at the emperor's bidding realize that their lord's theology was not totally reliable? Their subservience notwithstanding, they were not afraid to make corrections where they deemed necessary. Since they were most certainly in broad agreement with the emperor's iconoclastic views,[84] they felt all

---

[84] Gero, *Constantine V,* 61f.

the more at liberty to carry out such changes in the imperial documents. Did this render the argumentation more coherent?

b. A hidden error

Constantine's thesis rests on the alleged impossibility to depict Christ's *prosôpon*, his hypostasis, because it is common to his humanity and his divinity. The council of 754 A.D. shifts the emphasis to the question whether the *flesh* of Christ can be circumscribed or not. It is true, the council followed Constantine in underlining the radical unity of the two natures: "*Out of* the two there arises one unmixed and undivided reality."[85] Constantine drew from this the direct conclusion: since this one reality is the *prosôpon* of Christ, he cannot be depicted. The council employs a different argument, not found in the emperor's text because he did not need it: the icon of Christ is not possible because his flesh is entirely made divine; "all of his flesh is totally assumed into the divine nature [!] and entirely made divine".[86] "Body and soul, both together are made divine, and neither can be separated from the divinity."[87] Incidentally, the Council here assigns to the soul a role of mediation between divinity and the flesh, which once again might reveal a tendency toward Origenism, whose teaching this is.[88] Those who fashion icons, therefore, "take the flesh that is totally intermingled with the divinity and thus made divine",[89] the flesh "made divine by its union with the Divine Word",[90] and separate it again from this very Word.

The conclusions of the council are in unison with those of the emperor. Though the argumentation follows different lines, both start with the same erroneous premise: an incorrect concept of the

[85] Mansi 13, 340C; cf. PG 100, 248D; here, too, we hear "*out of* two natures", instead of "*in* two natures", as the Council of Chalcedon defined it!

[86] Mansi 13, 256E.

[87] Mansi 13, 257A.

[88] J. Meyendorff, *Le Christ dans la Théologie byzantine* (Paris, 1968), 247, note 23; Gero, *Constantine V,* 99, note 150, contradicts Meyendorff, in our opinion, without reason.

[89] Mansi 13, 257E.

[90] Mansi 13, 341E.

hypostatic union. But in the council's text this error is less obvious than in the emperor's text. Did the theologians at the council thus succeed in concealing the weak point in their argumentation? As we read the extensive refutation of this document on the part of the Seventh Ecumenical Council (787 A.D.), this impression is reinforced: nowhere in this eloquent and word-for-word refutation is addressed the central question: the question as to the one person in two natures. This is all the more amazing since the theologians of the iconoclastic council, by correcting the emperor's questions, did not improve the argumentation; they in essence returned to the position of Eusebius of Caesarea, whose letter to Empress Constantia they quote as important evidence.[91] In this they fall short even of the emperor's level of reasoning. Thanks to him, the image controversy was lifted onto a higher level of discourse than it deserved: at its core, it concerns the Incarnation, more specifically the mystery of a human face, the *mystery of the face of Jesus, true God and true man.*

---

[91] Mansi 13, 313AD.

Chapter Two

The Defenders of Images

The final stage of our journey lies before us: the description of the theology developed by the defenders of images. Such a presentation, of course, can never be complete. Between St. Germanus, the first theologian defending icons, and the "victory of orthodoxy" (843 A.D.), there elapsed twelve decades of intensive literary activity, involving the most competent representatives of the Greek Church. Trying to describe here the entire history of this literature on the image debate would far exceed our scope.[1]

To simplify the presentation and avoid unnecessary repetition, we chose a method that proceeds both historically and thematically. We shall introduce the authors chronologically, but focus only on each author's original and specific contribution to the argumentation, without repeating what his predecessors have already stated. In this way, we hope to offer a historical synopsis of the icon theology, and at the same time a summary of the more important topics. Since the most essential arguments of the iconoclasts were of a christological nature, we shall likewise limit ourselves to this perspective, so central for the entire image controversy.

---

[1] Such a comprehensive study is still not available. Except for single monographs, the most extensive study up to now is the series of articles by L. Koch, "Zur Theologie der Christusikone", *Benediktinische Monatsschrift* 19 (1937):357–87; 20 (1938):32–47, 168–75, 281–88, 437–52.

I. The First Period of the Icon Controversy: The Icon, a Monument to the Incarnation

The iconoclastic council of 754 A.D. anathematized three iconophile theologians: "Anathema on Germanus, of divided loyalty, who worships wood! Anathema on George, of like mind, who corrupts the teachings of the Fathers! Anathema on the Mansurian, the infamous, who thinks like the Saracens!"[2] The Patriarch Germanus I of Constantinople, the monk George of Cyprus, and John Damascene, son of Mansur, are the three writers whom the council of 754 A.D. deemed important enough to deserve a condemnation by name. They are indeed the most prominent defenders of the icon during the first iconoclastic period. Consequently, the Council of Nicea (787 A.D.), closing this period, pronounced their solemn rehabilitation: "Everlasting remembrance for Germanus, the orthodox believer; for John, and for George, the heralds of the truth. The Trinity has glorified all three."[3] We now direct our attention to these—rather disparate—stellar three.

1. The Icon as "Representation of Christ's Flesh": Germanus of Constantinople

We owe the first written reaction to the gathering iconoclastic storm to a saint, Patriarch Germanus (715–730 A.D.). He was patriarch of Constantinople when Emperor Leo III began to speak of "the elimination of the sacred images".[4] Germanus is reported to have implored the emperor, "May this calamity, my Lord, not come to pass under your reign. For he who would bring this about is a precursor of the Antichrist, and an enemy of the salvific

---

[2] Mansi 13, 356D.

[3] Mansi 13, 400C.

[4] Theophanes, ad ann. 6217 (de Boor, 404). A translation (with commentary) of the *Vita* of St. Germanus is found in L. Lamza, *Patriarch Germanos I of Constantinople* (Würzburg, 1975).

Incarnation of God."[5] He who rejects the icon, also rejects the Incarnation: this is the common conviction of all defenders of images. Germanus, in one of his letters, explains this view, which would then be repeated unceasingly by the iconophiles of the following years:

> We allow icons to be fashioned and painted with wax and colors, not in order to pervert the perfection of our liturgy. Of the invisible deity we make neither a likeness nor any other form. For even the supreme choirs of the holy angels do not fully know or fathom God. But then the only-begotten Son, who dwells in the bosom of the Father (cf. Jn 1:18), desiring to free his own creature from the sentence of death, mercifully deigned, according to the Father's and the Holy Spirit's counsel, to become man. He took on our own flesh and blood, one like us yet without sin, as the great Apostle says (Heb 4:15). For this reason we depict his human likeness in an image, the way he looked as man and in the flesh, and not as he is in his ineffable and invisible divinity. For we have that urge to depict what pertains to our Faith, namely, the truth that Christ became man not merely in appearance and impression ... but in reality and truth, and complete in everything except sin, which the enemy has planted in us. In conformity with this firm belief, we depict the likeness [charaktêra] of his holy flesh in our icons, which we esteem and honor through appropriate reverence, for they remind us of his life-giving and ineffable Incarnation.[6]

John of Synada, to whom Germanus wrote this letter, was archbishop of a region where certain iconoclastic tendencies had appeared. A bishop of this ecclesiastical province, Constantine of Nakoleia, had voiced to the patriarch his concerns about the veneration of images. This Constantine was a convinced opponent of icons. Even though it is probably an exaggeration to consider him the originator of iconoclasm, it may well be that he

---

[5] Theophanes, ad ann. 6221 (de Boor, 407); trans. L. Breyer, *Bilderstreit und Arabersturm in Byzanz,* 2nd ed. (Graz, 1964), 43.

[6] Mansi 13, 101AC.

did not play merely a subordinate role.[7] Constantine's main objection to images centered on their explicit ban in the Old Covenant (Ex 20:4). He concludes from this that we must not venerate *anything* fashioned by human hands, by human ingenuity.[8] The iconoclasts understood the biblical injunction in a literal and material sense: any image made by man is prohibited, no matter of whom the original might be. Against this, Germanus objected: "One ought to look not only at *what* is done, but also at the *intention.*"[9] Germanus, therefore, sees *who* is depicted in the image as the decisive point. For him, as also for his theological successors, the icon is ever first and foremost the image of a person. Should the image depict a false god, an idol without reality, then it is itself an idol, a graven image.[10] Should the image depict Christ, the Blessed Mother, or a saint, then such images are worthy of veneration, because persons so depicted are worthy of veneration.[11]

The distance between these two viewpoints was so great that mutual understanding seemed impossible. The defenders of images were shocked that anybody would dare to compare the veneration of the sacred icons to idolatry: "Never compare the temple of God, the Church, to idols!"[12] The opponents of images, in turn, demanded a strict application of the Old Testament's injunction. There were endless debates on the extent of this ban. Is it still valid as at the time of the Old Covenant? Is it part of the commands pertaining to the Mosaic Law, and thus superseded by Christ and the New Covenant? This discussion was to continue until the end of the image controversy.[13] The answer given by the iconophiles would remain the same until the end, the one already stated by

[7] Regarding this question, cf. Gero, *Byzantine Iconoclasm during the Reign of Leo III* (Louvain, 1973), 85–93 and 118, note 18.

[8] Mansi 13, 100C.

[9] Mansi 13, 121B.

[10] Mansi 13, 112DE.

[11] Cf. Germanus' appealing texts on the images of the saints: Mansi 13, 101E; 104AB; 113C.

[12] Mansi 13, 120B.

[13] Patriarch Nicephorus dedicated the major part of his central work (Apologeticus major) to this problem; PG 100, 533–850.

Germanus: Christ has brought us the true knowledge of God. With this, he has freed us from all error of idolatry.[14] After Christ, the entire situation is essentially different from the time under the Law. When God, at Mount Horeb, spoke to his people,[15] they did not behold any form nor figure; but in these latter days, God has revealed himself in the flesh, and thus our faith does not come from hearing alone, but also is implanted, through our visual sense, in the hearts of those who gaze on Christ:[16] the Incarnation has changed everything here. From now on, God has assumed a visible likeness, and this "likeness [*charaktêra*] of his sacred flesh" we are able to behold.

Germanus here chooses the term *charaktêr* deliberately. In the previous chapters on Gregory of Nyssa and Maximus Confessor, we already encountered this term as the key concept of trinitarian theology and Christology. In the context of icon theology, it reclaims its original, literal meaning, without losing the abundant theological connotation it had added in the course of several centuries. The "florilegium" collected by the Second Council of Nicea[17] offers a wealth of patristic texts that are instructive regarding the conceptual development of the word *charaktêr*, for which reason we shall quote some of these texts.

As we have shown in the chapter on Gregory of Nyssa, the word *charaktêr* initially means "something carved, imprinted, engraved". The verb *charassein* then assumes the analogous sense of "carving, engraving" visible marks, be they letters or pictures. This is the reason for the dual meaning of this verb: to write, or to draw. (We met the same dual meaning in the words *graphein* and *graphê*.) A text by Cyril of Alexandria, included in the florilegium, demonstrates this dual meaning. Cyril compares the relationship between the Old and the New Covenant to the different layers of a painting (*graph*): "The painters first draw in form of an outline (*charagmata*) the rough figures on the image. When they add the splendor of colors, the beauty of the painting (*graphês*) shines

14 Mansi 13, 112CD; 120E–121A.
15 Mansi 13, 117C; cf. Dt 4:15.
16 Mansi 13, 116B.
17 Mansi 13, 4–128.

forth."[18] *Charaktêr,* therefore, denotes something that makes certain outlines and brushstrokes into an image. For this reason is the term frequently used interchangeably with *ikôn,* icon. Thus the (forged, yet contemporary) letter from Pope Gregory II to the emperor, Leo III, reflects the usage of the time as it reports on the imperial emissary, who was charged with the demolition of the image of Christ at the Chalke palace gate, saying that he "struck with his pickaxe three times the face [*prosôpon*] of the Savior's image [*charakterôs*]".[19] Leontius of Neapolis, who wrote his apology against the Jews in the first half of the seventh century A.D., in his argumentation in favor of images constantly employs the term *charaktêr* in this very sense. He anticipates many of Germanus' arguments. As he explains, Christians do not venerate

> the *charaktêres,* icons, and depictions of the saints like so many gods. For if they would venerate the wood of an icon like a god, then they might as well venerate all other pieces of wood in the same way. If they would really venerate the wood of the icon like a god, they would certainly not burn it in fire once the depiction [*charaktêr*] of the icon has worn off.[20]

Based on this meaning, *charaktêr* can stand for the likeness, the face of the one depicted in the icon. A letter by St. Nilus (fifth century A.D.) contains the report of a miraculous apparition of the martyr Plato to a young monk. The latter immediately recognizes the martyr, "because he has frequently seen his likeness [*charaktêra*] on icons".[21]

We ought to quote here, in conclusion, a text that played an important role in the iconoclastic controversy: the eighty-second

---

[18] Mansi 12B = PG 77, 217C; cf. Mansi 13, 12E = PG 77, 220B (this regards a visual depiction of Abraham's sacrifice; cf. a similar text in Gregory of Nyssa, PG 46, 572CD = Mansi 13, 9CD.

[19] Mansi 12, 970D; ed. J. Gouillard, in *Travaux et Mémoirs,* vol. 3 (Paris, 1968), 293, 222f.

[20] Mansi 13, 44D; cf. ibid., 45BC: "I venerate the icon of God, but, of course, not the wood or the colors as such; rather, because it contains the inanimate expression [*charaktêra*] of Christ, I believe that through it I possess and venerate Christ himself."

[21] Mansi 13, 33A = PG 79, 581A.

canon of the Quinisext Synod, the Synod of Constantinople in 692 A.D., so consequential for Church law in the East:

> Some of the sacred icons depict a lamb, to which the Precursor [John the Baptizer] is pointing: a lamb, which typologically stands for grace, and which in the Law has prefigured the true Lamb, Christ our God. Even though we honor the ancient types and foreshadowings as authentic symbols and anticipations of the truth, in line with the Church's tradition, we nonetheless prefer the grace itself and the truth itself, which we venerate as the fulfillment of this Law. In order to bring this fulfillment before everyone's eyes, at least in image, we command that from now on in the icons there should be painted, in place of the former lamb, the human likeness [*charaktêra*] of Christ our God, the Lamb who takes upon himself the sins of the world. For thus we will comprehend the depth of humility in the Word of God, and will be prompted to remember his life in the flesh, his suffering, his salvific death, and the resulting salvation of the world.[22]

The term *charaktêr* has here, exactly as thirty-five years later with St. Germanus, the dual meaning of "icon" and "likeness depicted on the icon". The analysis, for the time being, does not go further. But the foundations have been laid: the Incarnation means that the Eternal Word has assumed a visible likeness. Pressured by the iconoclasts' arguments, the theology of the image will forge ahead and will show, building on the theology of the Church Fathers, that this likeness of Jesus' distinctive human countenance is nothing else but the likeness of the *Person* of Christ, true God and true man.

2. The Struggle of the Monks: George Cyprius

The second witness of this early period of the icon controversy is quite different from the first. Germanus spoke with the full author-

---

[22] Mansi 13, 40E–41A = Mansi 11, 977E–980B; trans. N. Thon, *Ikone und Liturgie* (Trier, 1979) (= *Sophia,* vol. 19), p. 48.

ity of the highest-ranking Eastern patriarch. The self-confidence of a man belonging to the higher Byzantine nobility shines through. With George Cyprius,[23] we enter a more popular environment: the world of the monks, who from the beginning were the driving force behind the opposition to the imperial iconoclasm. George was an elderly monk living "on Mount Olivet in the Taurus Mountains in Cilicia".[24] When news of the destruction of images reached him, he addressed the people, who admired him as their spiritual father, with a fiery appeal not to be deceived by the manipulations of those whom he sees as the precursors of the Antichrist. He attacked especially the emperor, and this with a bluntness rarely found in official Byzantine ecclesiastical circles.

From the beginning, he emphasized the battle cry of the iconophiles: "Whosoever [in matters of icons] obeys the emperor, sets himself against Christ, who gives to his faithful his immaculate image, and thus shows to us the model of his salvific Incarnation."[25] The opposition of the iconophiles against the imperial iconoclasm drew its vigor from the sharpness of this contrast between Christ and the emperor. You had to make a choice whom to obey. The emperor was seen as being in opposition to Christ by his own doing when he began to destroy the depiction of Christ.

The abovementioned appeal to the people by George Cyprius has been preserved; it is followed by a very interesting public disputation with Cosmas, a bishop at the imperial court. A second speech follows, given by the old monk at a regional synod that took place after the disputation. We are mainly interested in this public disputation, which was probably carefully recorded, and which paints an exceptionally lively picture of the two unyielding opposing camps represented by George, the monk, on the one side, and Cosmas, the bishop, on the other. The two speeches, evidently heavily edited, we shall mainly disregard. The events

[23] Text edition and critical analysis in B. Melioranskij, *George Cyprius and John of Jerusalem. Two lesser known defenders of orthodoxy in the 8th century* [in Russian] (St. Petersburg, 1901); a thorough review by E. Kurtz, *Byzantinische Zeitschrift* 11 (1902):538–43.

[24] Regarding the location of this monastery, cf. Kurtz, in *Byzantinische Zeitschrift*.

[25] Melioranskij, *George Cyprius*, V.

here are assigned to the year 752 A.D., to the time when Emperor Constantine began preparations for the great iconoclastic council of 754 A.D.[26]

We see Bishop Cosmas, the adversary of the old monk, as he set out, armed with imperial authority, to ferret out all nests of iconophile resistance. He summons George in front of a synod and berates him in the presence of the entire assembly:

> It is you, then, who raised his head and spoke ill of the emperor, the same emperor who, we all agree, is guided by God, and who with his most splendid mind examines our orthodox Faith. For the emperor is the imitator of Christ: indeed, when Christ dwelled in Egypt, he toppled the man-made idols there.[27] In the same way does the emperor now smash the idolatrous images here. Who would dare resist the divinely approved teaching and the exalted command of the emperor? Is it not so that every mouth must fall silent, every ear must heed, when his teaching proceeds from his saintly lips? For whoever resists his commands is not worthy to live even one hour longer. Such a one ought to be thrown into the fire and burnt at the stake.[28]

Amazing to hear such words coming from the mouth of a bishop! And yet, without such a testimony it would be impossible to comprehend how it could be that at the council of 754 A.D. *all* the bishops obeyed the will of the emperor and became iconoclasts, and that thirty years later, after the "divine teaching" of the emperor had changed, once again *all* the bishops unanimously signed the decrees of the iconophile Council of 787 A.D. The "arguments" of Bishop Cosmas are valuable evidence for such a "Caesaropapist" attitude; the main accusation against the old monk is that of opposition to the emperor. In the course of the discussion, Bishop Cosmas time and again returns to "the will of the emperor" as the ultimate reason. So also during the discussion about the validity of the Old Testament's ban on images. When Cosmas

[26] On questions of textual and historical criticism, cf. Kurtz, in *Byzantinische Zeitschrift*.

[27] Allusion to an apocryphal gospel, in which such is reported of Jesus' childhood in Egypt.

[28] Melioranskij, *George Cyprius*, VIII–IX.

finds himself in a corner, he simply attacks *ad hominem:* "Our holy and supreme emperor has greater wisdom than you, and he knows God's will and counsel! He is convinced, as a matter of fact, that the words of the Old Testament have to be valid."[29] He goes so far as to instruct the assembled crowd: "Everybody has to believe what God has said and what our holy emperor has commanded!"[30] Since the words of the emperor have become a matter of faith, there remains but a small step for the courtier bishop to make this accusation: "You have *blasphemed* [!] against the emperor; according to imperial law you deserve death!" To which the intrepid old monk replies: "You have blasphemed the Son of God, and nobody executes you. I did not utter any blasphemy, only words of the Apostle, and I should merit death?"[31]

Against the blind submission to imperial power, the monk sets the authority of the Holy Spirit: "I am more ignorant than anybody else, without doubt; but I have on my side the Holy Spirit of Christ, and the apostles, and the Church Fathers, who testify for my cause and teach me knowledge."[32] Here we are not far from someone like Symeon the New Theologian (949–1042 A.D.), who contrasts an unworthy hierarchy with the charismatic gift of the Holy Spirit!

The language of Bishop Cosmas recalls the era of Constantine the Great, when Eusebius of Caesarea saluted the emperor as another apostle. It was against such a surrender of the Faith to the emperor's authority that the iconophile monastics rebelled. For them, the icon controversy was a struggle for ecclesiastical freedom.[33] Were the monks really wrong in viewing the attack on the images of Christ as an attack on the sovereignty of Christ

[29] Ibid., XIII.

[30] Ibid., XVIII; cf. also XII, XXIV, XXVIII.

[31] Ibid., XXIV.

[32] Ibid., XXVIII.

[33] This is shown by the following: K. Schwarzlose, *Der Bilderstreit, ein Kampf der griechischen Kirche um ihre Eigenart and Freiheit* (Gotha, 1890); and P. Brown, "A Dark-Age Crisis"; Aspects of the Iconoclastic Controversy", *The English Historical Review* 88 (1973):1–34. The evaluation of the monasteries' role by H. G. Becks, however, is in our opinion too negative; in *Handbuch der Kirchengeschichte,* ed. H. Jedin, III, I, 31–81.

Illustration 11

Illustration number 11: Anti-iconoclastic illumination. Chludor Psalter, 9th century, Historical Museum, Moscow, fol. 67r. Illustration on Ps 69:22 ("They gave me gall for my food; in my thirst they gave me vinegar to drink").

Photo: Ecole Pratique des Hautes Etudes (Paris).

The depiction of the crucifixion follows closely the texts of the gospels (Mk 15:36f.; Mt 27:48–50; Jn 19:28f.). Iconoclasm and crucifixion are polemically shown to be one and the same thing. Two iconoclasts (a layman whose hair is wildly ruffled and a bishop) are shown as they together, using a sponge, whitewash a round image of Christ (*imago clipeata*). The accompanying text underlines the intent to equate iconoclasts and Christ's enemies: in the same way as the latter offer Christ "gall and vinegar", so also do "the iconoclasts mix water and lime [to whitewash] the image [*prosôpon*] of Christ".

(See page 191.)

himself (see illustration no. 11)? The heated debate between the bishop and the monk ends without a clear winner or loser. The monk at times is no match for the arguments of the bishop. And besides, most of the time, the two talk at cross-purposes. The inability to find a common language is clearly evident. Thus Bishop Cosmas constantly emphasizes the literal validity of the ban on images; he accuses his opponents of allegorizing those passages of Scripture they don't like,[34] while Christ has never abolished this ban.[35] The common people of the Church, he says, have slipped back into pagan idolatry.[36]

In contrast to this, George focuses on the place of Christ in this discussion about idolatry: an image of Christ can never be an idol.[37] And he takes the offensive: the origin of the icon cult goes back to Christ himself. Even though Scripture is silent on icons, Christ himself has miraculously created an image of his countenance: the image he sent to King Abgar.[38] This and other similar legends provide the iconophiles with the certainty that the icons are part of the original apostolic tradition:[39] "Christ himself has entrusted his Catholic Church with the icons."[40]

After reading this dispute, one cannot help having mixed feelings, not only because its quality is not always very high or because of the bishop's massive Caesaropapism, but above all because we see here two positions poised in irreconcilable confrontation instead of understanding each other as two complementary viewpoints. Do not the iconophiles all too readily infer, from the

[34] Melioranskij, *George Cyprius,* XVI.

[35] Ibid., XIII.

[36] Ibid., XIX.

[37] Ibid., XV: The law would ban images, not of *Christ,* but only of *idols.*

[38] Ibid., XXIf. Gregory relies for this story on St. Ephrem. The different variants of the Abgar legends have been carefully collected by E. von Dobschütz, *Christusbilder. Untersuchungen zur christlichen Legende* (Leipzig, 1899).

[39] At any rate, George adds this qualification: Christ has given his icon, true; but he has not commanded worship of it, because in those days the danger of making the image into something divine was still too great. Melioranskij, *George Cyprius,* XXII.

[40] Ibid., XXIIIf.

fact of the Incarnation, the necessity of images depicting the One incarnated? And do not the iconoclasts all too quickly make the ban on images into a total rejection of any earthly manifestation of things divine? Throughout the history of the Church, the two tendencies, one toward the elimination of images, the other toward pervasive use of images, can be found at one time or other.[41] The extremes threatening both tendencies are, on the one hand, to put such a huge distance between image and original as to make any image appear preposterous or impossible, and on the other hand, to see such a closeness between original and image as to confound one with the other. The following description of some stages of image theology will show that there are among the defenders of icons shifts in emphasis as substantial as we witnessed them among the iconoclasts.

3. *The Icon as Grace-Filled Matter: John Damascene*

John Damascene (675–749 A.D.) is without doubt the most important theologian among the early defenders of icons. He was the first to present a true synthesis of icon theology. His influence is pervasive, even though it may be somewhat exaggerated to declare him the greatest of all theologians in the field of the icon.[42] Certain aspects he leaves undetermined, to be clarified only in the second stage of the icon controversy.

John wrote his "three discourses against those who reject images" around 730 A.D., in the very early period of the icon con-

---

[41] J. Gouillard has published a thorough study on these two currents: "Contemplation et imagerie sacrée dans le christianisme byzantin", in idem, *La vie religieuse à Byzance. Variorum Reprints* (London, 1981).

[42] So J. Nasrallah, *Saint Jean de Damas, son époque, sa vie, son oeuvre* (Harissa, 1950), 116; on John's icon theology: H. Menges, *Die Bilderlehre des Hl. Johannes von Damaskus* (Münster, 1938); T. Nikolaou, "Die Ikonenverehrung als Beispiel ostkirchlicher Theologie und Frömmigkeit nach Johannes von Damaskus", *Ostkirchliche Studien* 25 (1976):138–65; also our own contribution, "La sainteté de l'icône selon S. Jean Damascène", in *Studia Patristica*, E. A. Livingstone, ed., vol. 18 (Oxford and New York, 1982), 188–93.

troversy.[43] His topic, accordingly, focuses mainly on the accusation of idolatry, the central point of the debate at the time. Yet the Damascene went further: he attempted to lay a solid foundation for the veneration of images. Thus he first discusses the image, then its veneration.

One of his most important contributions is the clarification of the very concept of "image". "Image" can evidently mean quite different things. Generally we can say: "An image is a likeness expressing [*charaktêrizon*] an original, yet being distinct from it in certain respects."[44] Depending on the greater or lesser distance based on these "certain respects", the image, too, is more or less perfect. John lists five (or six) categories of images,[45] beginning with the most perfect: the consubstantial image, totally fulfilled only in the Son, the image of the Eternal Father. There follows then, on the scale of perfection, the archetypes of all things in God, that is, the everlasting counsel of God, containing all things in the form of archetypes. The third category consists of all visible things, insofar as they are images of the invisible realities and material depictions of them, so that through the material things we gain a certain inner idea of the immaterial realities. In this category, John includes sacred Scripture, which conforms to our earthly clumsiness in order to awaken in us the yearning for the invisible gifts. The manifestations of the Blessed Trinity in visible creation are listed here. The fourth kind of images is similar to the third: something present can be an image of something to come.

The fifth category follows, directly touching on our topic: the images of things past, whose memories we wish to preserve. They can be of two kinds: those drawn up through words in books, and those painted in images. To this category John assigns the icons. In his third discourse,[46] John mentions one other category, inserted

---

[43] With regard to the chronology, cf. the introduction by B. Kotter in vol. 3 of the critical edition of John Damascene's writings, *Contra imaginum calumniatores orationes tres* (Berlin and New York, 1975); our quotation is taken from vol. 94 of PG.

[44] Ibid., I, 9 (PG 94, 1240C).

[45] Ibid., I, 9–13 (1240C–1244A); with more detail in III, 18–23 (1337C–1344A).

[46] Ibid., III, 20 (1340D).

between the ideas in God (second kind) and the reflection of the spiritual things in the visible things (third kind): man as the image of God (Gen 1:26), an image, that is, created by God in imitation of himself.

"Image, therefore, is an analogous concept", and in the case of the icon, the analogy is a most remote one, for the bond of unity between icon and original is incomparably weaker than in all the other categories. In what does this bond consist?

Now, this is amazing: John does not say! He does not develop the analysis of his concept of the image any further. His main consideration is the idea of participation. Similarity to the original, which renders an image more or less perfect according to how close this similarity comes, is seen by John entirely from the perspective of participation. The smaller the participation of the image in the original, the smaller the similarity. The most perfect participation is realized in the eternal Son: he is "consubstantial with the Father". But how about the place of the least and lowest kind of image on this scale of graduated participation, the icon?

Again, an amazing fact: in his listing of different kinds of images, John omits one distinction that would become essential for the subsequent doctrine on images and is rather obvious: the difference between *natural and artificial image.*[47] Why this omission? Could the reason be that in the perspective of "participation" only natural images are being considered? Clearly, only a natural image on the level of its essence can participate in its original. Artificial images can only possess a relationship of *extrinsic* similarity between image and original. A portrait does not in essence participate in the person so depicted. The relationship is of a different kind. Did John Damascene define this difference adequately? Before we address this question, we shall turn to another aspect of iconology, an aspect often and correctly underlined nowadays: its positive attitude toward *matter.*

Against the accusation of the iconoclasts that the veneration of icons is all caught up in what is earthly and physical matter, John

---

[47] Cf. Menges, *Die Bilderlehre,* 42.

emphasizes, based on Christology, the positive role of matter. We have to quote this important text at some length:

> In olden days, God who was without body or physical form, was not depicted at all. But now, since God has appeared in the flesh and has interacted with man, I am able to depict the visible aspect of God. I do not worship matter, I only worship the Creator of matter, him who for my sake became matter himself, and took it upon himself to dwell in matter, and who by means of matter brought about my salvation. And I shall never cease to honor that matter through which my salvation was accomplished. But, of course, I do not honor it as if it were God—far from it! For how could something be God, after it received its being out of nonbeing? Though the body of God is also God, as through the substantial union it has turned immutably into the same substance as the one who anointed it, while also remaining that which it was by nature, namely, flesh animated by a rational and spiritual soul, with a definite beginning and not belonging to the realm of uncreated essences. All other matter, however, I simply honor and venerate, insofar as it was instrumental in my salvation, and for this reason is endowed with divine power and grace. The wood of the cross, full of gladness and blessedness—is it not indeed matter? The venerable, sacred mountain [Calvary], the Skull Place [Golgotha] —are they not matter? The life-bringing, life-giving Rock, the sacred tomb, font of my resurrection—are they not matter? The gold and silver used to make crosses, patens, and chalices—are they not matter? And is not, before everything else, the Lord's Body and Blood also matter? You ought to ban the cult and veneration surrounding all these things, or else, leave in force the tradition of venerating also images that are sanctified by the name of God and his friends, and thus are overshadowed by the grace of the divine Spirit. —Do not despise matter! It is not without honor. For nothing that comes from God is without honor.[48]

In Christ himself was matter sanctified: first the body of Christ, which through its union with the Logos became sacred, grace-

---

[48] Damascene, I, 16 (1245AC); translation, slightly adapted, taken from H. Hunger, *Byzantinische Geisteswelt* (Baden-Baden, 1958), 121f.

filled, "deified";[49] and then, beyond this, matter in a broader sense, as our text illustrates so succinctly. In another passage, John states: "I honor material things, not as though they were God, but inasmuch as they are replete with divine energy and grace."[50] — "Do not despise matter!" John touches here the critical spot of those iconoclastic tendencies for which the materiality of the icon becomes an insult to the divine original. "Through matter my salvation is accomplished." Matter does not lie in the farthest and lowest regions of relationship to God, as Neoplatonism holds; it is not farthest away from the spiritual realm and therefore utterly without salvific value. On the contrary: the entire economy of salvation has always employed material things too. Thus matter is not at all an obstacle on the way to God, but becomes by its participation in Christ's mystery the medium through which salvation is accomplished.

In this positive view of matter, however, John does not sufficiently elaborate that not every material thing is by itself already an instrument of salvation. John does not distinguish clearly enough between, for example, the body of Christ and other material realities (such as the cross, icons, etc.). The body of Christ seems to stand on the same level with the icon: both are matter, and God's power and grace work through both. John fails to elaborate sufficiently that there are differences in degrees, even in essence. For the body of Christ, by being one with the Person of the Logos, is "divine" in a sense entirely different from the way it applies to the icon, which relates to Christ mainly by depicting him. It is therefore no mere accident that John pays remarkably little attention to this aspect of the icon (the relation of similarity to the original). The following passage brings this out: "The material things as such have no claim to veneration. But if he whose likeness the icon depicts was full of grace, then this icon, too, participates in such grace according to the analogy of faith."[51]

Here John's understanding of the icon becomes especially clear:

---

[49] Damascene, I, 4; cf. Expos. fidei (PG 94, 1069A); cf. Jacobitas (PG 94, 1481C).
[50] Damascene, II, 14 (1300C).
[51] Ibid., I, 36 (1264B).

the sacred image is endowed with grace; in a certain sense it even has become a vessel of the spirit as was the one it depicts.[52] John focuses more on the grace offered by the icon than on any visual similarity. Two examples should illustrate this emphasis. John at one point compares the sacredness of the icon with the emperor's garment: in itself, it cannot claim special honors, but after the emperor has donned it, the honor due the emperor is also transferred to the garment.[53] Once again, the notion of participation prevails, not the relationship of similarity between original and likeness. This tendency also shows how John Damascene compares icons to relics. They have in common being bearers of grace and divine power. Here, too, the characteristic of the icon, the relationship of similarity, moves to the background; the icon appears foremost as a sacred vessel imparting grace. We shall see that the later great theologians of the image, Nicephorus and Theodore the Studite, put much greater emphasis on the *personal* relationship between the icon and the one depicted in it.

To be sure, a more *personalistic* view of the icon is not totally absent in John Damascene. He points out, for instance, that icons are sanctified by the *names* of the persons depicted there, names written on the icons.[54] Consequently, he says, the faithful who look at the icons behold the persons themselves of the ones so depicted. John then adds to the words of Jesus, "Blessed are your eyes that see" (Mt 13:16), his own, "We, too, yearn to see, as much as possible."[55] In one passage, John even asserts: "I have seen the human form of God, and my soul found salvation."[56]

The one thing a Western reader might find most peculiar in John Damascene's interpretation of icon veneration is his general *identification* of icon and original. He who sees the icon, sees Christ; Christ himself is present in his image: "Should someone

[52] Cf. ibid., I, 19 (1249C). According to the critical edition by Kotter, 95 and 50, note 92, this passage is not with certainty authentic; but it is entirely in line with John Damascene's other statements.

[53] Damascene, I, 36 (1264B).

[54] Ibid., I, 36 (1264B).

[55] Ibid., II, 20 (1308A).

[56] Ibid., I, 22 (1256A).

depict Christ the Crucified in an icon, and then is asked, 'Who is this?', he will answer, 'Christ our God, who for us has become man.' "[57] The icon theologians of the early ninth century tried to define more specifically the *type* of this identity, as we shall see below. Regardless of the differences in placing their emphasis, all proponents of icon veneration in the Eastern Church show this common trait: the conviction that in the icon we encounter Christ himself.[58]

We have covered only certain aspects of the Damascene's icon theology, those that seemed to us particularly typical to him. There would be much more to consider: such as the distinction between adoration (*latreia*), which only God can claim, and veneration (*proskynêsis*), which may also be offered to the saints or to holy objects; John was the first to employ this distinction systematically.[59] But this distinction played a rather unfortunate role in the discussion of images in the Western Church, as both terms were translated as *adoratio* (adoration),[60] causing countless misunderstandings.

It also goes to John's credit that he showed, with singular clarity, the limits of the emperor's power regarding the Faith.[61] He gained one more merit: thanks to his admirable knowledge of the Eastern tradition, he was able to collect an impressive anthology of patristic texts favoring images. Even though his influence, initially, might not have been too strong[62] — not least because of the Islamic occupation of Palestine — it nevertheless goes to his credit that the Eastern custom of venerating images received a

[57] Ibid., I, 67 (1281C).

[58] Cf. Schönborn, "La Sainteté de l'icône"; cf. also idem, "Art et contemplation. Les Icônes du Christ", in *Die Kunst und die Technik* (Freiburg, 1979), 11–20 (vol. 4 of the series, "Herausforderung und Besinnung").

[59] Occasionally, they are found already earlier, such as in Prokopius of Gaza, PG 87/1, 607–8.

[60] In the first translation of the conciliar decrees of 787 A.D.; cf. G. Haendler, *Epochen karolingischer Theologie. Eine Untersuchung über die Karolingischen Gutachten zum byzantinischen Bilderstreit* (Berlin, 1958), and Gero, "The Libri Carolini and the Image Controversy", *Greek Orthodox Theological Review* 13 (1973):7–34.

[61] Damascene, I, 21 (1252BC); III, 3 (1321A).

[62] Cf. the remarks by P. van den Ven, in *Byzantion* 25–27 (1955–1957):337f., and by J. Gouillard in *Istina* 1976, 31.

solid theological foundation. Others could thus build on this foundation as well as correct certain shortcomings present in his first attempt.

II. The Second Council of Nicea (787 A.D.)

The three theologians we have briefly presented here were dealing with an iconoclasm still undeveloped theologically. An entirely different situation had to be faced by those orthodox Church leaders who after 754 A.D. set out to defend the veneration of images. The theological work of Emperor Constantine V and of the iconoclastic synod of 754 A.D. had changed the situation radically. Iconoclasm now had robust christological arguments on its side. It is surprising how long it took for the orthodox to develop an image theology truly confronting these arguments. They had to wait until the Patriarch Nicephorus (806–829 A.D.) and Theodore the Studite (d. 826 A.D.) accomplished this theological feat. Yet these two authors wrote during the second period of iconoclasm, which began under Emperor Leo V (813–820 A.D.). What was going on among the orthodox during those sixty years in between?

During the long and harsh rule of Emperor Constantine V (741–775 A.D.), the iconophiles had little leisure for theological reflection. Persecution was oppressing them. The bishops were beholden to the emperor; thus all the more courageous was the fight of most monks. Many of them paid for their loyalty to the sacred images with exile, imprisonment, torture, and martyrdom. The contemporary documents attesting the zeal to the point of martyrdom present in this early Christian period are truly impressive.[63]

While in the Byzantine realm the voice of orthodox theology

---

[63] Cf. A. Tougard, "La persécution iconoclaste d'après la correspondance de saint Theéodore Studite", *Revue des questiones historiques* 50 (1891):80–118; B. Hermann, trans., *Des heiligen Abtes Theodor von Studion Martyrerbriefe aus der Ostkirche* (Mainz, 1931).

appeared silenced, in Palestine under Islamic occupation, the iconophile theologians were able to continue their work; synods of bishops condemned the Byzantine iconoclasm, and monks who had fled the Byzantine realm spurred the zeal of the defenders of images even further. The iconophile tracts of this period almost all originated in the Palestine area.[64] The arguments were mainly borrowed from John Damascene; nobody addressed the christological arguments of Emperor Constantine and the synod of 754 A.D. Even when under Emperor Leo IV (775–780 A.D.) the persecution of the iconophiles diminished and finally, after his death, ceased altogether, there were no Byzantine theologians to be found who might have confronted the biting christological dialectic of the iconoclasts. The veneration of images was indeed solemnly reinstated by the Council gathered in Nicea in 787 A.D., yet theologically the Council's efforts remained rather disappointing. The detailed refutation of the iconoclastic decrees of 754 A.D.,[65] authored most probably by the Patriarch Tarasius himself, at no time addressed that synod's christological arguments. Instead, the opponent receives an elaborate tongue-lashing. The *argumentum ad hominem* (personal attack) largely replaces any theological argument. We would do an injustice to the Council, however, if we would expect elaborate theological discussions there. A council is not an academy of theological scholars. A council's task is to profess and present the Faith; it falls to the theologians to interpret this profession and support it with arguments.

The true accomplishment of the Council of Nicea, therefore, consists in its document of faith, promulgated on October 13, 787, with the signature of all 310 attending bishops. The importance of this document far exceeds the value of the rather weak discussions preceding it at the Council, as it represents the most solemn and extensive declaration on the question of images ever issued by a

[64] We should mention the two texts by John of Jerusalem (PG 95, 309–44, and 96, 1348–62), the *Synodika* of Patriarch Theodore of Jerusalem (745–767 A.D.) contained in the acts of the Council of 787 A.D. (Mansi 12, 1135–1146), and the quite original Arabic treatise of Theodore Abû Qurra, German trans. in G. Graf, *Die arabischen Schriften des Theodor Abû Qurra* (Paderborn, 1910), 278–333.

[65] Mansi 13, 205–364.

council. In what follows, we shall quote the more important passages of this Council's definitions, and then comment on them briefly.

Christ, our God, has given us the light of his knowledge and liberated us from the darkness of idolatrous folly; he has betrothed himself to his Bride, the holy Catholic Church, which is without blemish or wrinkle (cf. Eph 5:27). He also promised to preserve her in this state. Regarding this he assured his disciples in these words: "I shall be with you always until the end of time" (Mt 28:20). This promise he proclaimed not only to them but also to us who by its force believe in his Name.

Some now despise this gift, incited by the trickeries of the Enemy [that is, Satan], and have deviated from the orthodox doctrine. They have contradicted the tradition of the Catholic Church and have fallen into error regarding the knowledge of truth.... For they dared to reject the godly embellishments [*eukosmia*] of our churches.... And more: they accuse the holy Church, the Bride of Christ; they do not make a distinction between the holy and the profane, and call the icons of our Lord and of the saints idols just as if they were the graven images of the satanic false gods. But the Lord God would not allow his people to be contaminated by this plague. For this reason, he has called us bishops together from everywhere through the holy zeal and the command of our devout emperors, Constantine and Irene, so that the sacred tradition of the Catholic Church be restored by our unanimous decree. As we now diligently examine and investigate and pursue the goal of truth alone, we add nothing, but preserve in purity everything that pertains to the Catholic Church. Thus we imitate the six Ecumenical Councils.... [Here the Creed of Nicea to Constantinople follows, as well as the condemnation of several heresies.] In short, we preserve all the Church's traditions, whether handed on to us in writing or orally, without disfiguring them through innovations.

One of these traditions is the painting of icons. As it is in harmony with the accounts of the gospel, it serves the purpose of strengthening our faith in the true and not imagined Incarnation of the Word of God, and of enriching us immensely. For these things that shed light one on the other [gospel and icon, word and image] evidently have the same meaning. We therefore walk a royal path as we follow the teaching of our holy Fathers, a teaching inspired by God, and the traditions of the Catholic Church, for we know that this tradition comes from the Holy Spirit, who dwells in the Church.

For these reasons, we now define with all diligence and precision that, in the same way as the venerable and life-giving cross, also the revered and holy icons be displayed, to the glory of God, in the churches, on sacred vessels and liturgical vestments, on walls and boards, in houses and at waysides; icons made of paint, mosaic stones, or any other suitable material; icons of our Lord and Savior Jesus Christ, the Blessed Virgin and Mother of God, the angels, and any of the saints.

The more often we look at them through means of images, the more we remind ourselves, as we see these likenesses, of the true and living originals whom we love, and we kiss and venerate their images; though not in that kind of worship reserved, as our faith says, only for what is of divine nature, but rather in the manner we employ in our veneration of the revered and life-giving cross, the holy gospels, and other sacred objects: by honoring them with incense and candles, according to the devout customs of our ancestors. "For the honor shown to an icon applies directly to its living model."[66] *He who venerates the icon, therefore, venerates in it the person [hypostasis] of the one so depicted.*[67]

Nobody should expect a detailed theological discussion in a conciliar definition. The text stands in the line of the definitions coming from the preceding councils. The credal decree of the Second Ecumenical Council (381 A.D.) is explicitly quoted. The text intends to present the Faith of the Church. This explains its specific emphasis.

The *argument from tradition* is mentioned first. The painting of icons is part of a larger context that the Church has received as tradition and feels called to keep alive and hand on. Such an argumentation, nowadays, would raise the suspicion of being a form of blind traditionalism. Yet something totally different is at

[66] Basilius, De Spiritu Sancto 18; *PG* 32, 149C.
[67] Mansi 13, 373D–380A.

stake here. The early Church lived with the strong awareness that the living tradition of the Church provides, as it were, the "environment", the "medium", through which the Holy Spirit works and dwells in the Church. Tradition, in this sense, is the living bond connecting all generations of believers with the historical origin of their Faith, and keeping this origin constantly present. The opponents of images, too, use tradition as an argument. They consider the veneration of images to be a corruption of the original, purely spiritual Christian Faith. But in so doing, they represent a different view of tradition and Church. For them, true tradition has been encrusted with later distortions. The iconoclasts, therefore, see themselves as the restorers of the original tradition. Yet such a regress to the unadulterated origins is possible for them only by rejecting the living tradition of which they themselves are a part: the tradition of an iconophile Church. With this, however, the living tradition loses its character of being a "medium", in which the truth is opened anew to each generation. It becomes, on the contrary, an obstacle that can be overcome only by critically going back to the things lying behind this tradition. The relation to the present and living tradition turns into one of suspicion. Wariness is in order. Since it is seen as corrupted in one respect, the question arises whether it might not be corrupted in other respects as well. The certainty as to what is original and what is not, as to what is genuine and what is corrupted, now has to be looked for in places other than living tradition. Living tradition as the medium that makes present what was in the beginning is being rejected, and so the certainty about the original state can be found only through one's own reconstruction of this original state. Yet is there anything more uncertain, more hypothetical than such reconstructions? They usually turn out to be projections of one's own wishes and ideas back to an ideal yet really fictitious beginning. The icon controversy illustrates, as a prime example, the problematic nature of all those "reforms" that set out to recover, by piercing through the presumed corruption of existing tradition, an original "purity". The eventual triumph of the iconophiles was also the triumph of a certain view of tradition: tradition as an organic and living unfolding of truth, always new, yet always faithful to the origins.

In addition to the arguments from tradition, the Council's definition also offers some arguments closer to the subject matter at hand. The accusation that the veneration of images is idolatry is rejected by means of two arguments, both of primarily christological nature: (1) Christ himself (and therefore nobody else, not even the emperor) has freed us from the darkness of idolatry; (2) it is not possible to compare the icon of Christ to idols.

The first argument is supported by the explanation that the icons have no other purpose than that of the gospels: to proclaim the liberating Incarnation of the Word of God. Word and image reinforce each other, just as man's eye and ear complete each other.[68] Behind this anthropological argument there appear the outlines of a christological principle. The Incarnation means that the Eternal Word has become audible in human words, but also visible in human form. What the gospel proclaims in words, the icon expresses in image. Having said this, the second argument also becomes convincing. There are obviously certain parallels between pagan myths and the Christian gospel.[69] In the same way, there are similarities between pagan idolatry and Christian icon cult. The difference lies in the respective subject matter. The gospel and the icon both refer to Christ. And the Council is able to invoke St. Paul (1 Cor 10:20) in calling the cult of idols a cult of demons.

Venerating images cannot be idolatry if it is performed in the right spirit. For this right spirit moves the hearts of those who pray in front of the icon to loving adoration of him who is depicted in the icon. Here, the Council quotes a statement by Basil, referred to over and over in explaining the meaning of the icon cult: "The honor paid to the image applies to its living original." Basil employs this statement in the context of his trinitarian doctrine. The fact that equal honor is offered to the emperor and his image serves as comparison to explain the consubstantiality

---

[68] Cf. G. Lange, *Die katechetische Funktion des Bildes in der griechischen Theologie des 6. bis 9. Jahrhunderts* (Würzburg, 1968).

[69] On this cf. our book, *Das Geheimnis der Menschwerdung* (Mainz, 1983).

of the Father and the Son.[70] Some drew from this the conclusion that the iconophiles were mistaken in quoting Basil's words.[71] But in truth this comparison is right on target.[72] The reason for this is found in the following sentence, probably the most important line in the Council's definition: "He who venerates the icon, venerates the person depicted in it." Venerating the icon means venerating the *person* so depicted. This statement sounds rather obvious. Yet in spite of its simple content, it contains the key to address the complicated christological dialectic of the iconoclasts. The Council merely readied this key. It still had to wait for the eminent theological work of a Nicephorus and a Theodore the Studite in order to open the door that would lead to an elaborate theology of the icon. Our next chapter will be dedicated to this. But first a few more comments on the definition offered by the Council of 787 A.D.

The Council puts the icons on the same level as the cross and other sacred objects. These together form one unity: the harmonious decoration (*eukosmia*) of God's house. Those who reject or even destroy the icons will soon abandon the reverence for the other sacred objects as well. On the other hand, the veneration (*proskynêsis*) of the icons is part of that reverence due in general to all sacred objects. The outward signs of such reverence are justified.

The Council's definition shows a certain restraint. Not one word is spoken about any sacred and grace-filled nature of the icon, nor is the necessity of icons used as an argument, the way the theologians of the iconophiles were wont to; only their usefulness is mentioned. The Council is content to point to the legitimacy of images. The painting of icons is presented as *one* of the Church's traditions. Thus inserting icons into the larger context of the

[70] Athanasius uses this comparison in the same sense; cf. above p. 12, note 29. Eusebius employs it to show the dissimilarity between Father and Son; cf. above p. 64, note 52.

[71] So F. X. Funk, "Ein angebliches Wort Basilius' des Grossen über die Bilderverehrung", in *Kirchengeschichtliche Abhandlungen und Untersuchungen*, vol. 2, 251–53; first published in *Tüb. Theol. Quartalschrift* 70 (1888):297f. Funk's opinion has been repeated frequently, for instance by W. Ellinger, *Die Stellung der alten Christen zu den Bildern in den ersten 4 Jahrhunderten* (Leipzig, 1930), 60.

[72] This is also pointed out by Nikolaou, "Die Ikonenverehrung", 161–63.

living, "written and unwritten" tradition of the Church, on the one hand, makes the entire question relative, and on the other, brings out the fact that iconoclasm implies more than the rejection of a merely inconsequential detail. Ultimately the icon dispute, too, involves the totality of the Christian Faith.

III. The Golden Age of Icon Theology

The iconophile period was not to last. Under Emperor Leo V, the Armenian (813–820 A.D.), the iconoclastic movement flared up once again. Only in 843 A.D. did the iconophile orthodoxy finally prevail. The iconoclastic council of 815 A.D., convened by Leo, could count on the support of John the Grammarian, without doubt one of the most cultured figures of his time.[73] The leading theologians of that period, however, in contrast to the year 754 A.D., are found in the camp of the iconophiles. Two personalities stand out: Nicephorus and Theodore the Studite. Their writings on the question of images are among the best that the ancient Church has produced on this topic.

1. *The Patriarch Nicephorus of Constantinople* (750–829 A.D.)[74]

St. Nicephorus was involved in the icon controversy very early. Still a layman, he had taken part in the Council of 787 A.D. as one of the emperor's representatives. Then as bishop he refused, just as his saintly predecessor Germanus, to submit to the religious and political ideas of the emperor, when the latter, in 813 A.D.,

[73] Jean Gouillard, "Fragments inédits d'un antirrhétique de Jean le Grammairien", *Revue des Etudes Byzantines* 24 (1966):171–81, classifies John as standing in the Evagrian–Origenistic line of thought, for which the final end of man consists in purely spiritual, nonvisual contemplation.

[74] The most comprehensive work on Nicephorus is P. J. Alexander, *The Patriarch Nicephorus of Constantinople: Ecclesiastical Policy and Image Worship in the Byzantine Empire* (Oxford, 1958).

set out to start the quarrel about images once again. Nicephorus, in 815 A.D., chose exile, again like Germanus, where he would remain until his death. The hardships of his exile did not keep him from writing untiringly against the iconoclasts. His elaborate counter-treatises focused on the most important patristic representatives used in support of the opposition: Eusebius, Epiphanius, Macarius, Magnes,[75] as well as the writings of Emperor Constantine[76] and the decrees of the council of 815 A.D.[77] We cannot here present Nicephorus' entire doctrine regarding images. Much of it is found already in his predecessors. We limit ourselves to his christological reflections, which for the first time attempt a serious reasoning against the arguments of Constantine V and his council (754 A.D.).

a. "To circumscribe" and "to paint" — clarifying the concepts

Eusebius of Caesarea had paradigmatically formulated the christological program of iconoclasm: an image of Christ is not possible because Christ's humanity is perfectly glorified and made divine. Eusebius spoke of a total transformation of the "form of a servant" into the "form of God" (cf. p. 58f.). After the Council of Chalcedon, after the proclamation of an *unmixed* unity of Christ's divine and human natures, such argumentation had become impossible. A new formulation had to be found, one that would fit within the post-Chalcedonian christological perimeters.

According to the unanimous testimony of Nicephorus and Theodore the Studite, the iconoclasts found this new formulation in the concept of *aperigrapsia,* that which *cannot be circumscribed.* "This concept", says Nicephorus, "they erected as a bastion, all but impenetrable, against the orthodox believers."[78] And Emperor

---

[75] "Contra Eusebium", in J. B. Pitra, ed., *Spicilegium Solesmense,* vol. 1 (Paris, 1852), 371–504; "Adversus Epiphanidem", vol. 4, 292–380; "De Magnete", vol. 1, 302–35.

[76] Apologeticus maior, and three Antirrhetical treatises, PG 100, 205–833.

[77] The unpublished *Elenchos,* of which P. J. Alexander (*Patriarch Nicephorus*) offers a detailed summary.

[78] PG 100, 209B.

Constantine, according to the same author, "invented this formula as an appropriate instrument of his impious schemes".[79] In fact, Constantine V, closely following certain passages of Eusebius, once wrote:

> You [iconophiles] say that in the icon you *circumscribe* Christ, the way he was before his suffering and Resurrection. Yet what will you say about Christ after his Resurrection? Then things are quite different: now the body of Christ has become incorruptible, as it has inherited immortality. Where does this leave the possibility of circumscribing it? How could something be circumscribed that visits the disciples through locked doors, and that is not confined by any barrier?[80]

Does this mean that Emperor Constantine proclaimed Christ's human nature to be beyond "circumscription"? He assumed this most certainly as regards Christ's glorified humanity. Whether he asserted this also regarding Christ's existence in the flesh is less clear, but certain indications point in this direction.[81] This would support the suspicion that considers the emperor's christology to be strongly influenced by Monophysitism. The authors of the conciliar decree of 754 A.D., in their attempt to straighten out the emperor's unorthodox pronouncements, meticulously avoid saying anywhere that Christ's humanity cannot be circumscribed. But they equally avoid saying the opposite.[82] The discourse on Christ's humanity as "not circumscribable", therefore, remains vague and ambiguous. All the more is it a handy slogan against the veneration of images.

Nicephorus deserves credit for having shown the imprecise application of this concept. His point of departure is the question whether the angels, who were certainly invisible, might be depicted in images. The iconoclasts deny it, since angels cannot be "circumscribed". Nicephorus, showing himself the well-versed logician, determines first that it is not at all the question here whether

---

[79] PG 100, 285B.

[80] PG 100, 437B.

[81] The statements here are not unequivocal; cf. PG 100, 332B, 297A, 301C.

[82] Cf. the (intentionally?) ambiguous statement in Mansi 13, 252A.

angels can be "circumscribed" (*perigraphontai*), but rather whether they can be "painted" (*graphontai*).[83] The "bastion" of the icono-clasts relies on a misunderstanding of words. To paint, to draw, is not the same as to circumscribe. The iconoclasts' play with words leads in the wrong direction. The fact that both things are described in Greek by the same word does not at all imply an identical meaning. Nicephorus then sets out to analyze both concepts. The original meaning of *graphê* is "to scrape, to engrave". From there, the two activities named by this term are derived: to write and to paint; the activity of the *logographos,* and of the *zôgraphos,* the "tracer of words", and the "tracer of life", the very expressive Greek words for "poet" and "painter".[84] But the word *perigraphê* has an entirely different meaning:

> Something can be "circumscribed" as to its place, its time, its beginning, or its understanding.... "Circumscribed" accord-ing to time and beginning are those things that had their origin in time. It is in this sense that we call the angels or the human soul "circumscribed".... "Circumscribed" according to under-standing are those things that are comprehended by the mind or by reason.... "Not circumscribed" are all those things that have nothing in common with the things just mentioned.[85]

This conceptual clarification is helpful. The question whether something can or may be painted is clearly distinct from the question whether, and how, something is "circumscribed". In a certain sense, all created things are "circumscribed", that is, contingent, restricted within the limits of a finite existence. This applies even to the entirely spiritual and invisible soul, which as such cannot be depicted.

b. The image as a relation of similarity

Nicephorus is now able to define the concept of the image more precisely and develop safeguards against its misinterpretations.

[83] PG 100, 345D.
[84] Cf. PG 100, 356AB.
[85] PG 100, 356B–357A; cf. Theodore the Studite PG 99, 396A.

The *graphê,* the painting, is characterized by its relative likeness to its original. But the painting is distinct from the reality so depicted, it is a different reality, and separate from it. Not so regarding the *perigraphê,* the status of being "circumscribed". This is a characteristic always inseparably tied to the one possessing it. Man, for instance, always exists in space and time; he is always characterized by his status of being "circumscribed". This quality has nothing to do with the relationship of similarity or of dissimilarity; nor does it possess its own form in the way a painting does; it is but a conceptual characterization of finite beings. It is, therefore, meaningless to assert (as do the iconoclasts) that painting someone means "circumscribing" him, even though, in reverse order, the status of being "circumscribed", that is, finite, is the prerequisite for the possibility of being depicted.[86] God alone, being totally "uncircumscribed", is the one that can in no way whatsoever be depicted.

The (conscious?) confusion of *graphê* with *perigraphê* on the part of the iconoclasts results from a mythical notion of the image, as Nicephorus convincingly demonstrates: the image, they say, must be an accurate definition of its original, and so must depict the original not simply in its external form but must altogether "circumscribe" it. The total reality of the one depicted would have to be "captured" in the image. True, it cannot be denied that certain customs of the iconophiles may suggest such a conception. To counteract this mythical identification of image and original, Nicephorus introduces the distinction between natural and artificial image, not yet employed by John Damascene. The icon is obviously an artificial image. It imitates nature, but is not of the same nature as its living model.[87] Nicephorus then defines the *artificial image:*

> It is a likeness of its living model, and through this likeness it expresses the entire visible form of the one it depicts; yet it remains in essence distinct from this model because it is of a

[86] PG 100, 257D–360B.
[87] PG 100, 225D, 405D–408A; cf. Theodore the Studite PG 99, 417AC; 500B–501B.

different matter. Or else: the [artificial] image is an imitation of
the original, as it is its representation; it is distinct from the
original because it is different in essence. . . . Of course, if it
were not distinct from the original in anything, then it would
not be an image but the original itself.[88]

John Damascene had already shown that the concept of the
image requires an element of difference with regard to the
original.[89] He had not mentioned, however, that this would
mean a difference *in essence*. Since he did not make the distinction
between artificial and natural image, he viewed the difference
mainly as a gradual ontological participation of the image in the
original. Nicephorus now is able to demonstrate much more
clearly that the icon, an artificial image, has to be distinguished
from its original by reason of its different essence. Nicephorus
finds the conceptual tools in the *Aristotelian categories;* the artificial
image, the icon, he assigns to the category of relations, of relational affinity:[90]

> The image belongs to the category of relation [*pros ti*] . . . for
> the image is always an image of an original. Nobody would call
> "image" anything not representing a relation. For image and
> original are always connected, . . . and even though an original
> may on occasion disappear, the relationship still endures. This,
> for example, may happen with a father and a son. Should the
> father go away, he nevertheless remains present due to the
> similarity, the recollection, or the shape of the son showing his
> likeness. Thus a relationship remains regardless of the passage of
> time.[91]

The image, then, is purely relational. Nicephorus no longer
explains the defining character of the artificial image with the idea
of ontological participation, as the Damascene did, but exclusively

[88] PG 100, 277A.

[89] PG 94, 1240C.

[90] This is shown in detail in the intensive study by Marie-José Baudinet, "La
relation iconique à Byzance au IXᵉ siècle d'après Nicéphore le Patriarche; un destin
de l'aristotelisme", *Les études philosophiques* 1 (1978):85–106.

[91] PG 100, 277D–280A; 364A; *Spicilegium Solesmense,* vol. 1, 444f., 413.

with the relational connection of similarity. It has been asserted time and again that the Eastern Church derives its concept of the image from Plato's doctrine of Idea and Phenomenon. Though this may be true to some extent for John Damascene, and certainly for the iconoclasts themselves, it does not apply to Nicephorus.[92] Due to his Aristotelian epistemological categories, Nicephorus succeeds in "de-mythologizing" the image, as it were; he assigns the image its proper place, without mystification, and so overcomes the exaggerated identification of image and original, which to such an extent had held captive the thinking of iconoclasts and iconophiles alike. Based on his Aristotelian realism, Nicephorus can determine more specifically the formal elements defining the icon:

> Similarity is a certain relation placed at the center between two ends or poles: between the likeness and the one to whom it is like. Both are united and connected by the [same] appearance, while both are different as to their nature. And even though both, image and model, are each *different* in nature, they nevertheless do not represent something altogether different, but both represent *one and the same* reality. For through the image, we gain the knowledge of what the model originally looked like, and in this depiction we can behold the *person* of the one so depicted.[93]

Thus Nicephorus, too, accepts a certain identity of image and model. But this is not an identity on the level of essence nor of being, only an identity as to form, appearance, and likeness. Image and original coincide insofar as they both represent the same person. Nicephorus for this reason refuses to consider allegories as icons proper, because they do not depict a visible model (such as allegories of the virtues):[94] "If you cannot see someone, you

---

[92] Cf. on this E. von Ivánka, *Hellenistisches und Christliches im frühbyzantinischen Geistesleben* (Vienna, 1948), 105–10; and *Plato Christianus,* (Einsiedeln, 1964). Regarding the Aristotelianism at the time of Nicephorus, cf. P. Lemerle, *Le premier humanisme byzantin* (Paris, 1971), 211f.

[93] PG 100, 280A.

[94] PG 100, 364AB.

cannot depict him either."[95] Nicephorus here goes back to the simple fact that was the starting point for Emperor Constantine V: every icon is the image of a person, depicting the visible form of a specific human being. The Second Council of Nicea had stated the same thing. Yet the opinions diverged when they had to consider the consequences of this simple statement of fact. Is it possible to depict the person of Christ just like any other human person? Or is his divine-human person beyond depiction? Nicephorus brought clarity to this question, which is, of course, the christological question.

c. The christological realism of St. Nicephorus

Since Eusebius, the main argument of the iconoclasts stated: the mystery of Christ transcends anything that could in any way be captured in an image. According to Eusebius, the glorified Christ is beyond all limits of our human, earthly existence in the flesh. Constantine V repeats the same thought by asserting that Christ's glorified body has become not only immortal but also impossible to be "circumscribed". Nicephorus feels compelled to restate, by way of reminder and against this argumentation, certain christological principles. Using gospel texts as his starting point, he shows that Christ's risen body did indeed still preserve the character of being "circumscribed". The very fact that the risen Lord enters through closed doors is proof for the still finite "circumscribed" mode of existence of his body, even though it is no longer subject to mortality.[96]

But Nicephorus identifies one more mistaken element in Constantine's conception. Constantine appears, not unlike Eusebius, to attribute any possibility of "circumscribing" Christ's body to the same condition that would produce corruptibility: the consequences of original sin. Nicephorus, in contrast, presents the reminder that one has to distinguish those qualities that define human nature in its original state from those that were added

[95] PG 100, 257D.
[96] PG 100, 437C, 440A.

afterward and "extrinsically", through man's disobedience: being "circumscribed" belongs to the former category, just as visibility, and bodily existence in general; mortality and death, on the other hand, belong to the latter category. The Lord, the Creator of man's nature, not of its death, became man in order to free man from death, not from his nature.[97] Here now appears the wider consequential nature of the icon controversy:

> The body had no need to become incorporeal, so that it would then become also incapable of being "circumscribed". For man was not created without a body, nor was the body later added on because of sin. . . . In Christ, then, human nature was renewed and preserved; and even though the body taken on by God became entirely divinized, was transformed and elevated, and received inexpressible glory and decor, so that now it is thoroughly spiritual and exalted above all earthly and material encumbrance, in spite of all this it still continues to be a body, regardless of his present condition, and therefore it remains a body that can be "circumscribed". For the quality of being "circumscribed" does not arrive in the body "from the outside" because of sin, as it is for mortality and the rest of human suffering, but resides in the body "intrinsically", being part of the body's very constitution, of its definition, and its essence.[98]

Constantine and the iconoclasts come perilously close to counting the quality of "circumscription", and thus of being a body as such, among the consequences of sin, which would make salvation not only a liberation from the corruption of sin but also from corporality itself. Nicephorus, with clear insight, recognized here the spiritual affinity to the kind of thinking that had already determined Eusebius' iconoclasm: Origenism, which considers corporality itself a consequence of sin. Opposing all "platonizing" contempt for the body, Nicephorus insists on the positive and inalienable specific reality of the body, which ultimately is rooted in the ontological principle of being a created reality. Each created thing has its own inalienable "essential permanence" (*logos*). The perma-

---

[97] PG 100, 440C–441B.
[98] PG 100, 444AB.

nence of all things in their essential constitution is guaranteed by the "divine Ideas", the way all things exist as archetypes in God. If any element pertaining to the "essential permanence" of a created reality is being changed, then we are no longer dealing with the same essence.[99] If this simple principle of creation theology is taken seriously, then those statements affirming the "total trans-formation" of Christ's humanity become rather questionable. Nicephorus relentlessly exposes the dangers of a metaphorical way of speaking that is as high-sounding as it is imprecise.

Armed with the entire arsenal of Aristotelian logic, Nicephorus attacks the formulation of Eusebius: "The form of the servant has been totally transformed into ineffable, inexpressible light, into light proper to the Word of God."[100] What kind of transforma-tion is here implied? Is it a transformation of properties, qualities, or quantities? If so, it would not be the "total" transformation asserted by Eusebius. Is it a transformation in substance? Substan-tial transformations imply becoming and disappearing. In this case, Christ's humanity would have disappeared. And into what kind of light has "the servant's form" been transformed? Is this light a substance existing in itself? If so, what substance? The angels (according to Gregory of Nazianzus) are but "secondary light" deriving from the "primary light", from God. This light, therefore, cannot be the light of the angels. Is it, then, of divine essence? If so, it could only be the essence of God himself. Christ's humanity, in this case, would then totally become absorbed in God's essence. Or is this light a quality that receives its being from somewhere else? In this case, it would inhere in another substance. No matter what this light might be after all, either substance or quality, this applies: if Christ's humanity is transformed into such a light, then Christ's body will lose its specific essential reality, its nature.[101]

Underlying these Scholastic disputes, which clearly show that even in Byzantine theology there exist tendencies akin to Scholas-

---

[99] *Spicilegium Solesmense,* vol. I, 425f.
[100] Ibid., 415f.
[101] Ibid., 416f.

ticism, we discern the seriousness of the subject matter itself: the orthodox view of creation and salvation. The kinship of iconoclasm with the theology of Eusebius becomes evident. Material things, the body, the entire world of temporal realities are being devalued. The somewhat vague idea of the "dark matter" being transformed into "ineffable light" only disguises this devaluation. Yet in the iconoclastic furor it is openly displayed. Nicephorus stands in the great patristic tradition of the Cappadocians and of St. Maximus Confessor, as he analyzes the "platonizing" view of making man divine—the "assimilation" of a lower reality into a higher reality, of which the lower reality is but a mere shadow—and confronts it with a "Christian Aristotelianism", or more precisely, with his "Chalcedonianism", which was formulated in the decrees of Chalcedon:

> So, then, they will reproach us, the natures in the mystery of Christ are not made new? Indeed, they are *made new but not transformed!* Transformation is one thing, being made new another. The former implies a disappearance and the cancellation of essential constituents [*logous*], by which a nature exists. The latter affects only a nature's mode of existence [*tropos*]. [102]

Nicephorus here invokes again the distinction between permanent essence (*logos*) and mode of existence (*tropos*), already employed by Maximus. It is not that a nature here requires transformation, rather that a mode of existence needs renewal. The divinization of man, the ultimate purpose of creation, cannot mean the disappearance of that same creation. The paradox here lies in this: in Christ, our human existence is to be made divine, while it does not cease to be "human flesh and blood". The icon, depicting Christ in his human likeness, serves as a final assurance, some kind of imprinted seal, of this belief.

---

[102] Ibid., 430; cf. 409 and 490f.

d. A defective Christology?

Nicephorus has defended, in the most resolute terms, the indispensable and specific intrinsic reality of Christ's human nature,[103] and thus of all created nature as such. Did he go too far in emphasizing the difference between divine and human nature, to the detriment of Christ's personal unity? He was occasionally accused of "Nestorian" tendencies, which would insufficiently pay attention to the unity of Christ's person.[104] Does this accusation apply? If so, to what extent does it influence Nicephorus' icon theology?

We have previously quoted a text (p. 212) in which Nicephorus clearly states that the icon shows the person of the one so depicted. In the case of an icon of Christ, is the person shown the divine-human person of the Eternal Word? Does the icon depict the Divine Person? Amazingly, this question appears of minor importance in Nicephorus' reflections. This is all the more surprising since Emperor Constantine V had put the very question as to the possibility of depicting a person at the center of his arguments against images, and Nicephorus had discussed and refuted the emperor's writings word for word. But let us listen to Nicephorus himself. In his first treatise against Emperor Constantine, he addresses the accusation that the painted icon separates the unity in Christ, since it depicts him only as man but cannot portray his divinity, and so is tearing apart the divinity and the humanity in Christ. Nicephorus gives this answer:

> [The icon] does not solely make present the visible form of Christ's humanity . . . but also the Logos himself, even though he is not (together with Christ's humanity) "circumscribed" and depicted as to his own inner nature, since he is invisible and totally one; but since, on the level of the person,[105] he is one and indivisible, therefore he [the Logos], too, is called to mind [through the icon].[106]

---

[103] Cf. PG 100, 272D, 273D.
[104] J. Meyendorff, *Le Christ dans la théologie byzantine* (Paris, 1968).
[105] In the Greek text, *kata* should be added.
[106] PG 100, 256AB.

Nobody can claim that this text completely satisfies our doubt mentioned above. What precisely does Nicephorus mean when he says that "the Logos" is also "made present" and "called to mind" in the icon? It certainly is true that the Logos, in his divine *nature,* remains beyond any possible "circumscription"; but should we not say at the same time that the Logos as Divine *Person* and through the Incarnation can now be "circumscribed" and has become tangible and visible? Is the *Person* of the one who is both God and man not at the same time capable and incapable of being "circumscribed"? It seems that this escapes Nicephorus.[107] True, he knows the concept of the "composite hypostasis" or person.[108] Yet nowhere does he employ it in connection with the image controversy. His entire effort aims at demonstrating that Christ's *humanity* can be "circumscribed", and therefore also depicted.[109] Whenever he speaks of the "imprinted individuality [*charaktêr*]" of Christ, he speaks of the *charaktêr* of Christ's body, of his human nature.[110] Yet *this* is manifestly *not* the problem voiced by Constantine V. The question rather is this: Is it possible to depict a person (icons can depict only *persons,* never abstract natures!), who is not merely a human person but the incarnate eternal Son himself? Nicephorus, by ultimately avoiding this question, leaves his answer to the iconoclasts' christological perplexity as a half-measure. The "Nestorianizing tendencies" of this great patriarch, however, always remain within the boundaries of orthodoxy. In his concern to safeguard the inseparable and permanent significance of Christ's humanity, he emphasized too one-sidedly the distinction between both natures in Christ. This, then, robbed him also of a clear recognition of the core and center of all icon theology: the mystery of the *person* of Christ as both God and man. It was left to St. Theodore the Studite, the most important and also the last of the great defenders of images, to complete the

---

[107] We found only one passage in which Nicephorus faces this question, without, however, looking for an answer; PG 100, 237C.

[108] For example, PG 100, 297CD, 309C, 341B, 420C; *Spicilegium Solesmense,* vol. I, 392, 398.

[109] For example, PG 100, 261A, 285A, 301D, 305A.

[110] Cf. PG 100, 313D–316A.

icon theology with a balanced and satisfying interpretation in this regard.

2. *The Abbot Theodore the Studite (759–826 A.D.)*

"The One who is invisible becomes visible":[111] this is the paradox of the Incarnation. St. Theodore, abbot of the Studios monastery in Constantinople, constructed his entire theology of the icon on this paradox. He is less a logician, less a system-builder, than Nicephorus. In exchange, his iconology is focused much more on the specific theological core: on the mystery of the person of Christ.[112] As we now embark on the last stage of our journey through the centuries of christological development, presenting the major elements of Theodore's icon theology, we will encounter once again, almost in the manner of a musical *coda,* the salient themes of our research.

a. *The icon: image of the person*

"The One who is invisible becomes visible": this means that the Eternal Word of the Father has appeared in visible form to our mortal eyes. We have, therefore, seen the *Person* of the Son of God, or in theological terms: the hypostasis of the Logos. Theodore the Studite constructed his entire icon theology under this perspective. *"The icon of someone does not depict his nature but his person"*, he states,[113] and he is the first to offer a theologically

---

[111] PG 99, 332A. Theodore's writings are quoted here according to Migne, PG 99, except for the 277 letters edited by J. Cozza-Luzi, in A. Mai, *Nova patrum bibliotheca,* vol. 8. More recently an English translation of his three *Antirrhêtikoi* is available: *St. Theodore the Studite, On the Holy Icons,* Catherine P. Roth, trans., (Crestwood, New York: St. Vladimir's Seminary Press, 1981). A lively description of Theodore's life and work is offered in Max von Sachsen, *Der heilige Theodor, Archimandrit von Studion* (Munich, 1929).

[112] Theodore does not want to use the "Aristotelian technology", even though he does not reject the simpler forms of logical conclusions; PG 99, 389A. He prefers simple faith over conclusions based on logical reasoning.

[113] PG 99, 405A.

balanced explanation for this simple observation that had been made time and again during the icon controversy.[114] Theodore gives this clarification:

> For how could a nature be depicted, unless it is concretely seen in a person? Peter, for example, is not portrayed in an icon insofar as he is a being endowed with reason, mortal, and having a mind and intelligence. For all this characterizes not only Peter but also Paul and John and everyone else belonging to the same species. Peter rather is portrayed according to those specific qualities he possesses in addition to the common definition as a human being, such as the curved nose, the curly hair, the pleasing complexion, the kindly eyes, and anything else in terms of specific properties of his appearance, by which he is distinguished from the other individuals of the [human] species.[115]

Every icon portrays a *person*. But how about the case where this person is divine, the eternal Son of God? Is Christ a person in the same sense as every other man? Is it possible to attribute to him an individual personhood comparable to all the other individuals of the human species? Theodore, in this context, quotes an objection raised by the iconoclasts, nowhere else documented but nevertheless appearing to be genuine. They say that Christ had indeed accepted the human nature into his own hypostasis, but this human nature was not particularized, or "characterized"; it did not represent this particular man but humanity in general.[116] Christ, in this view, would have assumed human nature in general, not its individual expression in a particular human being. For this reason, according to the iconoclastic argument, Christ's humanity cannot be "circumscribed". This argument offers Theodore an opportunity to define more precisely the relationship between icon and person: "What is general exists only in individuals; for example, humanity exists only in Peter, Paul, and the other individuals of the human species. If

---

[114] K. Holl has already pointed out that Theodore had a much better grasp of the christological problem than Nicephorus: "In this respect, Theodore the Studite is way ahead of him" (*Gesammelte Aufsätze zur Kirchengeschichte*, vol. 2, 369, note 2.

[115] PG 99, 405AB. This text distinctly echoes Gregory of Nyssa's "38th Letter".

[116] PG 99, 396C; a similar thought is found in John Philoponus, PG 94, 748f.

there do not exist any individuals, then humanity in general does not exist either."[117]

Theodore holds, in the full Aristotelian sense, that the general concept subsists only in the concrete individuals. Contrary to Platonism, he considers as really existing only the concrete individuals, while general concepts exist only in abstract and mental form. "What is general we grasp only with our reason and our mind; what is particular, however, we grasp with our eyes, as they see the things of the senses."[118]

The icon portrays only what is visible in a man, only what is particular in him, what distinguishes him as *this* man from all other men. From this there follows the application to the relationship between nature and person: "When I say, 'man', I refer to a general essence. Adding, 'this', I refer to the person, that is, the intrinsic existence of the one so referred to, and as it were, his 'circumscription', composed of specific properties through which he is distinct from the other individuals of the same nature."[119]

"Person", then, is defined by Theodore under two aspects: for one, it is an "intrinsic existence", and secondly, it is characterized by specific properties. Theodore, more clearly than Gregory of Nyssa, is aware of the difference but also the convergence of these two aspects: on the level of being, and on the level of knowing. On the level of being, a person has to be defined as a subsistence; on the level of knowing, we can reach a person only through particular "descriptive" properties.[120] Icon theology, of course, is mainly interested in the "knowable" aspect of a person. The ultimate ontological core of a person, its independent being, its subsistence, can obviously be known only indirectly, through a person's outward behavior, through his properties and specific qualities. The icon, indeed, mediates such knowledge, too. But beyond that, it should be pointed out that only the presupposition of the ultimate ontological core of a person can sustain and

[117] PG 99, 396D.

[118] PG 99, 397A.

[119] PG 99, 397B.

[120] This correlation is pointed out by H. J. Vogt in his detailed review of this book's French edition, in *Jahrbuch für Antike und Christentum* 20 (1977):195–98.

explain the visible expressions of this person. Theodore the Studite, of all the icon theologians, has doubtlessly shown this in the most lucid terms. This is his answer to the iconoclasts:

> If Christ, paradoxically, has taken on flesh in his own person, but if then, as you assert, this flesh is not "characterized" or expressing someone in specific terms, rather "man" generically, how could his flesh [his humanity] ever possess a subsistence in him? ... For Christ would not possess a human nature at all unless it dwells in him, in his particular person, in individual existence. If it were not so, the Incarnation would be a fictitious fantasy; Christ could not be touched nor portrayed with various colors: this would be nothing but the Manichaean viewpoint.[121]

If Christ had taken on the general human nature only, then he could not be recognized as man except on an intellectual and conceptual level.[122] Christ, of course, has assumed also the general human nature, but since this nature exists in fact exclusively in the particular individual, Christ is true man only if his humanity exists as this specific, individual manifestation.[123] In what, then, does Christ's individual humanity consist? What is its proper character? Theodore at this point repeats almost word for word the profound reflections of Maximus Confessor on the relationship between person and nature: "Christ, therefore, is truly one of us, though he is also God; for he is one of the three Divine Persons. As such he is distinct from the Father and the Holy Spirit by his property of being Son. He then, as man, is distinct from all other men by his personal [hypostatic] qualities. ... "[124]

The particular qualities, by which Jesus of Nazareth is distinct from all other human beings, are the "personal qualities". But which person are we considering here? This is the decisive point. The iconoclasts say that every icon depicts a person; but since Christ is a Divine Person, he cannot be depicted. Any such attempt would mean to assign to Christ a second person, entirely human,

[121] PG 99, 396D–397A.
[122] PG 99, 397A.
[123] PG 99, 397C.
[124] PG 99, 400A.

and portrayable. Theodore replies to this ingenious argument by briefly recalling the Church's doctrine of the "composite person" as developed in the wake of the Fifth Ecumenical Council (553 A.D.):

> Were we to assert that the flesh taken on by the Word possesses its own hypostasis, the argument [of the iconoclasts] would be valid. But we follow the Faith of the Church and profess that the Person of the Eternal Word became the person common to both natures, and that this same person provided the intrinsic existence to the particular human nature with all its properties by which it is distinct from all other human beings. Thus we are justified in proclaiming that the one and the same Person of the Eternal Word, as to its divine nature, cannot be "circum-scribed", yet as to its human nature, can certainly be "cir-cumscribed". The human nature of Christ does not exist beside the person of the Logos, in an individual, independent person; it rather obtains its existence in the person of the Logos (for there is no nature that would not subsist in a specific hypostasis), and in the person of the Logos can—as specific individual—be seen and "circumscribed".[125]

The abbot of Studion applies here to icon theology what the monk Maximus had already formulated, in similarly dense and precise terms, regarding the general relationship between person and nature in Christ. The Person of the Eternal Word itself, by taking on flesh, becomes the vehicle and source of a human existence and all its distinctive individuality. In other words, the very same properties that define Jesus as this specific man also render his divine person visible. The paradox of the Incarnation consists in the fact that the Divine Person of the Eternal Word can now be seen "circumscribed" in the individual, personal counte-nance of Jesus.

Emperor Constantine, therefore, was correct in saying that the icon of Christ "circumscribes" the Eternal Word of God; but then he was mistaken in rejecting the icon, for the Word became flesh and thus "circumscribed" himself, he became limited, "condensed" (following an expression favored by the Church Fathers), to such

[125] PG 99, 400CD.

an extent that he could express and communicate himself in a specific human individuality, and moreover, that this individual human existence would become *his very own existence*. This is the "scandal" connected with the Faith in God's Incarnation. This Faith professes that the Divine Person of the Eternal Son became visible in the human individuality of Jesus of Nazareth: "The person of Christ is 'circumscribed', not according to his divinity, which nobody has ever beheld, but according to his humanity, which has become visible as an individual human existence in the person [of the Son]."[126]

Theodore, different from Nicephorus, does not draw a strict line between *perigraphê* and *graphê,* between "circumscribing" and "painting". The iconoclasts were really not entirely wrong in recognizing a close connection between these two concepts. They were right in asserting that painting someone's picture amounts, in a certain sense, to "circumscribing" him. The decisive question was indeed the one asked by Constantine V: Can the *person* of Christ be portrayed? And he was also correct in determining the possibility of "circumscription" to be the prerequisite for a depiction in an image. Theodore the Studite, relying on his sound doctrine of Christ's "composite person", was able to expose more clearly than others the starting point of the iconoclastic theory: an insufficient, or rather, erroneous concept of "person".[127]

b. The icon—location of a personal presence

Nicephorus all but exaggerated the difference and dissimilarity between icon and original. In this he represents—within the field of common convictions among the iconophiles—the extreme opposite to the position of John Damascene, who did not make any distinction between natural and artificial images, but placed the

---

[126] PG 99, 401A. Theodore repeatedly states that the person of Christ is both "uncircumscribed" and "circumscribed" at the same time; PG 99, 332C, 332D–333A, 1216C. Here Theodore clearly goes farther than Nicephorus.

[127] Witness to this is also the correspondence with John the Grammarian, the leading thinker of the Second Iconoclasm and the Council of 815 A.D.; cf. Letter II, 168, PG 99, 1532BC.

icon, as a medium of grace, as close to its original as possible. Theodore the Studite occupies a middle ground between these two extremes. His clear doctrine regarding the person of Christ enables him to show, in balanced and convincing terms, in what sense we can speak of the presence in the icon of the person depicted there:

> The original model is not present in the icon according to its essence, otherwise we could call the icon "original" and the original we could call "icon". This would not make any sense, as both natures [that of the original and that of the icon] each have their own definition. Rather, the original is present in the icon based on likeness in relation to the person.[128]

Theodore goes so far as to declare that Christ and his icon have the same hypostasis: "In the icon of Christ there is no other hypostasis besides the person of Christ. It is rather the person of Christ himself, that is to say, his depiction [*charaktêr*], that through the form of his likeness in the icon is being expressed and venerated."[129]

The original is truly present in the icon, but this presence is entirely based on a relationship to a person. This alone constitutes the icon's dignity. With this, St. Theodore corrects a certain questionable tendency (which we found, in rudiments, in John Damascene) to consider the icon itself and as such, in its material, to be some kind of grace-filled vessel, "as if it contained a divine nature or power that would require our veneration" (the way the Council of Trent describes this tendency).[130] Theodore the Studite does not hesitate to present this correction forcefully, so by his pointing out that God is neither more nor less present in the icon than in any other piece of wood:

> The depicted body is present in the icon, not as to its nature, but only as regards a relation [*schesis*]. Much less is the Divinity, which cannot be "circumscribed" at all, present in the icon . . . : not more than he is present in the shadow cast by Christ's body.

[128] PG 99, 420D; cf. also 1588D–1589A; 1640D.
[129] PG 99, 1589D.
[130] DS 1823.

Where in any rational or brute creature, where in any animated or lifeless creation would the Divinity not be present? Of course, he is present to a greater or lesser degree, according to the analogy of the receiving nature. Should someone say that God is present in this manner also in the icon, it would not be false. The same, then, certainly applies to the symbol of the cross and the other sacred objects. But again, the icon cannot claim in its nature a union with the Divinity (not even the transfigured body of Christ can claim this), but only a relational participation, for all these things (icon, cross, and so on) participate in the grace and glory of God.[131]

In order to demonstrate that the sacred character of the icon remains entirely on the level of the relationship between image and original and does not consist in some sort of "inherited" sanctity of the icon as such, Theodore quotes a custom already mentioned by Leontius of Neapolis and by Patriarch Germanus: once an icon is worn and has lost its "imprint" (*charaktêr*), it will without hesitation be thrown into the fire "like any useless piece of wood".[132] If the icon as such were a "grace-filled" object, nobody would dare burn it. It would in itself be some kind of sacred relic. Different from John Damascene, who positions icons and relics on the same level, Theodore the Studite sees the sacredness of the icon entirely in its *charaktêr,* its portraying depiction. Theodore, to illustrate this form of presence, likes to use as comparison a seal and its imprint:

Let us consider, for example, a ring in which is engraved the image of the emperor. It does not matter whether this signet ring is pressed into wax, pitch, or clay, the seal remains unchanged in these different materials. The imprint, however, can remain always the same only if it does not unite with any of the different materials but stays in the signet ring, separated from the materials into which it is pressed. It is the same with the likeness of Christ. Even though it may be expressed in different materials, it nevertheless does not unite with the matter that

131 PG 99, 344BC.
132 PG 99, 464D.

bears its form, it rather remains in the person of Christ as his most intrinsic likeness.[133]

All this does not mean, though, that material things would somehow be worthless. Theodore emphasizes their proper value.[134] But he refuses to assign some kind of sacred character to material things, by which the icon would be raised onto the level of a sacrament. Material things as such receive in the sacramental mysteries a certain healing and sanctifying power. The bread, changed into the Eucharist, is really the Body of Christ; it is not his image. The baptismal water obtains its sanctifying power through the Holy Spirit. The wood of the icon, in contrast, does not turn in such a way into a vehicle of grace. True, the icon also sanctifies, yet not in the manner of a sacrament but rather through the spiritual relationship it fosters to the person depicted. This difference is once again clearly presented when Theodore explains in what sense one can say that the icon of Christ is Christ himself:

> If we consider both as to their nature, then Christ and his icon are essentially different one from the other. And yet, as to their name, both are the same. Based on the icon's nature, we call its visible reality not "Christ", not even "image of Christ", but "wood", "paint", "gold", "silver", or some other material employed. Yet based on the image of the person depicted, the icon is called "Christ" or "image of Christ"; "Christ" because of the identity in name, "image of Christ" because of the relationship [of the image to Christ].[135]

From this follows how important it is to label the icon correctly. The assurance in this regard lies in the fact that there is always the name of the depicted person inscribed on the icon. The name on the icon indicates that the icon would make possible a personal relationship to the one so named. The act of inscribing the name on the icon, as it was understood then, constitutes the consecration as such of the icon.[136] Consequently, St. Theodore insists that

[133] PG 99, 504D–505A.
[134] PG 99, 464AB.
[135] PG 99, 341BC; cf. 337C, 340A, 1184A, 1589CD; Mai, *Nova patrum bibliotheca*, 139.
[136] Cf. Mansi 13, 269D–272A.

on the icon not be written "image of Christ" but "Christ", since we really behold Christ himself, his person, in the icon;[137] which does not imply some kind of "hypostatic union" between Christ and his image, but is only based on the relationship of intention and similarity between the icon and the person of Christ, even in the case of a rather remote similarity, for example, when the artist's skill is wanting.[138]

c. Seeing with physical or spiritual eyes?

Does this last passage not illustrate how problematic this view of the icon really is? Not many pictures are of such artistic perfection as to lead to a personal relationship with the person depicted and not in fact rather hinder it. And even the most perfect images are still nothing but images and ultimately are in no way on a par with the original. Do not the iconoclasts in fact have a point when they so forcefully underline this disparity? Moreover, is the ultimate goal after all not the desire to overcome the world of mere images? Is the final aim not some purely spiritual contemplation beyond all images?

We have encountered these questions time and again as we journeyed through five centuries of Christology. In the history of ideas they are closely connected with *Origenism*. No wonder that these questions were frequently discussed in a monastery as large and important as the one St. Theodore governed as abbot. The contemplative life, the nature and expression of contemplation, are at the center of the spiritual teaching Theodore offered his disciples regularly.[139] *Where is the place of the icon in the contemplative life?* Is it but a concession to human weakness, granted to those who have not yet progressed far enough on the contemplative path?

Reading certain texts of St. Theodore's, especially those in

[137] PG 99, 1184C, 1296AB, 420D.

[138] PG 99, 421CD.

[139] Summarized in the *Magna Catechesis*, A. Papadopoulos-Kerameus, ed. (St. Petersburg, 1904), and the *Parva Catechesis*, Auvray, ed. (Paris, 1891).

which he speaks *"dionysiastikôs"*, [140] in the manner of Dionysius the Areopagite, we gain the impression that Theodore himself was of this opinion. For according to Dionysius, images serve no other purpose than to lead us as much as possible to spiritual contemplation.[141] Theodore, too, speaks in this vein: "What could be more useful, what could be more uplifting than an image? It is indeed a prefiguration of the final contemplation and can be compared to the light of the moon in relation to the light of the sun."[142]

The image here appears as the shadow of a higher, indeed of the true, reality. The image points beyond itself to that reality of which it is but a pale shadow. Adoration in spirit and in truth requires a certain ascent beyond the material realm, "so that the spirit can soar up to God".[143] Theodore also points out that it is not enough to gaze at the icons with only our physical eyes. In this way, we will only see the depicted person's external features, but not contemplate the person himself, as person. Furthermore, icons are not always at our disposal. All this demands "that we venerate Christ also in a purely spiritual way, without the icons".[144]

Do not considerations of this kind considerably limit the importance of icons? Passages such as this one are the main reason why the icon theology of the Studite has time and again been declared to be Platonic.[145] Those who attribute to the image only an "anagogical" value (as guide to a higher reality) devalue the world of images in favor of some "true reality" beyond all images. The image here is then seen as an *essentially* imperfect reality.[146] To rely on an image, therefore, becomes a misguided attitude.

It would be a thorough misunderstanding to include Theodore the Studite in this current of thought. The icon, in his view, has indeed and undoubtedly an "anagogical" function. But the spirit-

[140] PG 99, 1220B.
[141] Cf. De Eccles. Hierarchia I, 2; PG 3, 373B.
[142] PG 99, 1220A.
[143] PG 99, 344D.
[144] PG 99, 1288C.
[145] Cf. Meyendorff, *Le Christ*, 262.
[146] Cf. von Ivánka, *Hellenistisches und Christliches*, 108.

ual contemplation to which it leads us has no other object than the icon's: the incarnate Word. In *this,* Theodore clearly moves away from the Platonic conception of the image; *here, too, lies the decisive point of the entire controversy with the iconoclasts, from Eusebius to Constantine V:*

> Should somebody say, "Since I ought to venerate [Christ] in spirit, it is pointless to venerate him in his icon", he should know that with this he also abandons the spiritual veneration of Christ. You see, if he, in his spiritual contemplation, does not behold Christ in human form at the right hand of the Father, then he does not venerate him at all. On the contrary, he denies that the Word has become flesh. But Christ's icon is a reliable testimony to the fact that the Eternal Word has become one like us.[147]

It is not enough merely to rely on images. In themselves, images refer to a reality beyond themselves. Yet here the concept of looking at the image of Christ is essentially different from the Platonic concept. The visible image does not refer to a purely spiritual reality but rather to the risen Lord who is glorified in his body and exalted "at the right hand of the Father". The icon is imperfect not because it is part of the visible and material realm, for Christ himself is part of it even in his glorified body. The icon is imperfect because it is only an image of Christ. Yet we deeply desire to say with the apostles, "We have seen the Lord" (Jn 20:25). We desire to see him no longer only in his image but in himself, *in persona.* At issue here is neither a total concentration on the icon, nor an attempt to gain a completely spiritual contemplation without images. The icon veneration is at the same time visual and spiritual; *in* the visible likeness of Christ we venerate his mystery spiritually. Only in the next world shall we behold Christ in himself.[148] Christ's Incarnation is proof that the final fulfillment of the Christian contemplation cannot be a purely spiritual beholding: "If such were sufficient in itself, then there was no need for the Eternal Word to come to us in any other than purely spiritual

[147] PG 99, 1288CD.
[148] Cf. PG 99, 1288D.

form."[149] But Christ has appeared "in the flesh" (cf. 1 Tim 3:16). His Incarnation is not merely a stage that eventually would be obsolete. Christian contemplation, therefore, cannot disregard the path God himself has chosen when he came to us:

> The painted image is for us a sacred light, a salvific monument, as it holds up before us Christ in his birth, his baptism, his miracles, on the cross, in the tomb, in his Resurrection and Ascension. In all this we are not being deceived as though these events would not have happened. For what our eyes see supports our spiritual contemplation, so that through both experiences our faith in the mystery of salvation is strengthened.[150]

Here we encounter the existential *"Sitz im Leben"* (situation in life) of the veneration of icons. The image is not a concession to the "weak". It is rooted in man's nature, which the Eternal Word has taken on forever by becoming man himself. Consequently, contemplation does not exclude visual beholding. Indeed, the saintly abbot of Studion does not hesitate to instruct his monks not to neglect the power of imagination:

> Imagination is one of the five powers of the soul. It is a kind of image, as both are depictions. The image, therefore, that resembles the imagination, cannot be useless. . . . If imagination were useless, it would be an utterly futile part of human nature! But then the other powers of the soul would also be useless: the senses, recollection, intellect, and reason. Thus a reasoned and sober consideration of the human nature shows how nonsensical it is to despise the image and imagination.[151]

Imagination is not something negative, it is a natural potential. On the way to contemplation there is no need to eliminate it (as the Evagrian tradition teaches), it only ought to be purified, just like all the other powers of the soul. But, of course, the imagination is not purified by never engaging in it, but by focusing it more and more on pure and sacred matters. Here we should

[149] PG 99, 336D.
[150] PG 99, 456BC.
[151] PG 99, 1220BD.

recall the monastic tradition and experience of constantly having your mind on God as a way of purification. Theodore, in his instructions, reserved an important place for the mind's dwelling on God.[152] And the icon plays an essential part in this. The frequent gazing on sacred images purifies the imagination in the same way as the frequent listening to the word of God. As many writers before him, Theodore loves to draw the parallel between sight and hearing:

> Imprint Christ . . . onto your heart, where he [already] dwells; whether you read a book about him, or behold him in an image, may he inspire your thoughts, as you come to know him twofold through the twofold experience of your senses. Thus you will see with your eyes what you have learned through the words you have heard. He who in this way hears and sees will fill his entire being with the praise of God.[153]

There are not two categories of Christians in the Church, the mere "primitive" and simple Christians who cannot yet do without images because they are still too much "in the flesh", and the more "perfect" and spiritual Christians who no longer need such crutches. Theodore forcefully criticizes this "thoughtless division into two dissimilar groups",[154] a division out of place in the one priestly and kingly people of God. In answer to a certain bishop— quoted anonymously—[155]who would accept icons for "the primitive people" but denies such a need for himself, Theodore retorts: "No matter how perfect he may be, no matter that he is clothed with a bishop's dignity, he nevertheless still needs the book of the gospels as well as its visual presentations. For both are equally venerable."[156]

This distinction between "primitive" and "enlightened" Chris-

[152] Cf. for instance the 10th "Brief Catechism" on remembering God.

[153] PG 99, 1213CD; on the correlation between hearing and sight cf. also 344C, 349A, 392A–D, 1217C.

[154] PG 99, 1537C.

[155] Our gratitude to Gero for pointing out to us that this was Hypatius of Ephesus; cf. *Byzantinische Zeitschrift* 72 (1979):89; cf. also J. Gouillard, "Hypathios d'Ephèse", *Revue des Etudes Byzantines* 19 (1961):63–75.

[156] PG 99, 1537D.

tians is a constant threat to the Christian Faith. The claim on the part of the iconoclasts that "now light has shone for the Christians who were immersed in the darkness of ignorance",[157] would only foster such a division. Theodore the Studite confronts this claim with the attitude of humility "that imitates God".[158] Only the humility of God, who for his own creatures has taken on the form of a slave, is able to overcome such divisions. Theodore the Studite was convinced that iconoclasm ultimately is based on a rejection of this humility of God.

d. The icon—the seal of God's self-humiliation

"To represent Christ through the use of matter and things amounts to abasing and diminishing him."[159] The iconoclasts were afraid that an overly material and "unrefined" approach to the mystery of Christ would only detract from it. One should not immediately deny that this concern was inspired by religious zeal and ethical sincerity, as happened in the heat of the controversy on the part of the iconophiles. The iconoclastic movement, active throughout the patristic era, has certainly contributed to the repeated cleansing of the icon cult from certain excesses. Above all, it has forced the defenders of the icons to clarify and specify their theological foundations. The iconoclastic phenomenon is a constant reminder that between the transcendent mystery on the one side and our means of expressing it on the other, there lies an obvious deep gap. He who approaches the living God will unfailingly hear the admonition, "Take off your shoes, for you are stepping on sacred ground" (Ex 3:15); and with Peter he will say, "Lord, leave me, for I am a sinful man" (Lk 5:8). This strong sense for God's transcendence on the part of the iconoclasts leaves a lasting impression. Yet it has to be stated that, in addition to this transcendence so zealously guarded by the iconoclasts, there is also another dimension. Arius had already invoked this transcen-

[157] PG 99, 1172C.
[158] PG 99, 1240D.
[159] PG 99, 336B.

dence when he refused to acknowledge Christ as the consubstantial Son of God. The Church, time and again, has proclaimed a more majestic conception of God's greatness: the greatness of God who makes himself lowly even to the point of taking on the state of a slave to be like one of his own creatures. How could it then be an infringement of God's dignity to also depict the Incarnate God in an image?

> What you think to be improper and coarse is on the contrary godly and sublime, if you keep in mind the immensity of the mystery. For is it not an honor for the Almighty to humble himself, in the same way as the humble would be ashamed to be exalted? Thus it is with Christ: he does not abandon the exalted reality of his divinity, which is immaterial and cannot be circumscribed; and yet it is his glory to abase himself in such a noble manner down to our own level that now in his body he can be circumscribed. He has become matter, that is: flesh, he who sustains everything that exists; and he is not ashamed to have become what he has taken on (namely, flesh), and to be called such.[160]

Christ himself bridges the gap between his transcendence and our lowly condition. His *kenosis* reveals a greatness much more exalted than any idea we may have about greatness. Theodore at one point remarks:

> How could his self-abasement be the result of a free decision, if it were something despicable? Anything done voluntarily is also honorable, it does not carry with it the disgrace of things forced on us.[161]

> If, then, Christ has become lowly for our sake, how could the signs of lowliness not be visible, such as color, tangible form, a body? By means of all this and in all of this he now can be "circumscribed". Those who do not accept this, really destroy the salvific plan of the Eternal Word.[162]

---

[160] PG 99, 336C.
[161] PG 99, 1212C; cf. 405C.
[162] Mai, *Nova patrum bibliotheca,* 35f.

The icon draws our gaze to the countenance of him who, though being God, has nevertheless taken on the properties of an individual human existence. The icon of Christ testifies that we are privileged to approach our Savior without fear.[163] By contemplating the icon of the Savior, we are pervaded by the purifying and sanctifying mystery of the Incarnation. For this reason is the icon *"the most visible testimony to God's salvific plan"*.[164]

[163] PG 99, 352B.
[164] PG 99, 337A.

CONCLUSION

We now conclude our investigation into the theological foundations of the iconographic arts. The moment has come to consider the results and ponder further implications.

Our journey through the great stages of the theology of the first seven ecumenical councils, from the First to the Second Council of Nicea, confirmed in us the conviction already expressed by St. Theodore the Studite: those who in principle reject the icon, ultimately also reject the mystery of the Incarnation.[1] This result may well be most surprising to the modern reader. The icon controversy was primarily not a dispute about aesthetic ideas but about theological and christological fundamentals. This fact may also explain, at least in part, why the entire literature of that time (for or against images) does not contain any discussion about questions of aesthetic or artistic theories.[2] In our own day, one would very much expect instead discussions of those topics than the endless theological debates of the Byzantine icon controversy. Art as such was not a topic of discussion then. The interest focused on the limits of the use of art. The Byzantine iconoclasts tried to relegate art to the secular field; art in the religious sphere was to be only decorative, at most narrative, but not sacred as such.[3] Iconoclasm pursued some kind of secularization of the arts, which were considered too pagan[4] to be successfully "Christianized". The activity of the artist, too, seemed to be too worldly to be included in the domain of the sacred.

[1] Cf. PG 99, 472A–473A.

[2] Cf. G. Mathew, *Byzantine Aesthetics* (London, 1963).

[3] Cf. A. Grabar, *L'iconoclasme byzantin* (Paris, 1957), 143–80; Brown, "A Dark-Age Crisis: Aspects of the Iconoclastic Controversy", *The English Historical Review* 88 (1973): 1–34, here, 9.

[4] Cf. Mansi 13, 277CD.

If one single result of our investigation stands out, it is the fact that both parties tried to justify their positions with a specific concept of the mystery that is Christ. As we conclude our research, we dare to assert that there exists an intimate connection between the whole concept of the arts and the concept of the mystery of Christ as God and man. The Incarnation not only transformed our knowledge of God, it also changed man's view of the world, of himself, and of his activity in the world. The work of the artist, too, was drawn into the spell of this mystery.[5] If Christ appeared on earth in order to renew man in his total being, to form man after his own image, then we must also say that the artist's eyes, his sensitivity, and his creative powers, are included in this re-creation as well. Evaluating the icon controversy from this viewpoint, it would appear that the attempt to relegate the arts only to the secular field was a profound crisis of the entire concept of the world and man and their incarnational dimension. The reverse is also true: the affirmation of the intimate connection between art and religious ritual, between image and faith, turns out to be an affirmation of the mystery of the Incarnation. For both, art and ritual, have in common their flowing from an encounter between heaven and earth, between divine and human realities, and living out this encounter ever anew. Art and ritual are both expressions of the infinite contained in the seemingly irrelevant gestures and creations of man. This may have always been the case. All religions prompted the arts to flourish, and this fact is the most eloquent refutation of Sigmund Freud's assertion that religion is mankind's neurosis.

That which all religions perceive vaguely, which they express obliquely or clearly, finds its unexpected fulfillment in a *human face*. The face, the eyes, the voice, the countenance of a man, the One who is God and man, has become God's own Word, his personal gesture, his self-expression—this we believe without a full understanding.

[5] This applies to all the arts, with the surprising and regrettable exception of the dramatic arts, which, for the most part, until modern times encountered rejection from the Church; cf. on this, H. U. von Balthasar, *Theodramatik, Prolegomena* vol. 1 (San Francisco: Ignatius Press, 1989).

Art in the early Church, as we have seen, drew its life from the constant meditation on the mystery of the God-man. The immense flourishing of Byzantine art following the end of the icon controversy (843 A.D.) constitutes a fusion of artistic excellence with religious articulation rather unique in the history of the arts. The iconographic art of the Eastern Church, even in its painting technique, in its formal and structural elements, leads us to behold, in an image, what is divine in man and what is human in God.[6]

It would be tempting to examine other areas and artistic styles to find out whether and in what sense there might be found a similar correlation between artistic invention and theological conviction. For example, is the growing alienation between the Church and the arts, observable in the West since the Renaissance, in any way connected with the concurrent "decline in awareness of the incarnational mystery"?[7] Is the renewed, and often quite radical iconoclasm of the Reformation perchance connected with a shift in emphasis regarding the concept of the mystery of Christ?[8] Research should also be undertaken to find out whether the exuberant creative explosion of the Baroque era might not have been an attempt to arrive again and afresh at an "incarnational" synthesis, in which all possible artistic expressions were welcomed in the heart of the Church and her rituals, in which indeed all the beauty of the earth appears to be akin to the beauty of heaven.[9]

What about our own time? The relationship between the Church and the arts has hardly ever been so tense—or worse, so nonexistent—as nowadays. To sort out who is to blame and to assign fault proportionally to the Church or to the arts would be pointless. What is needed is a new way of seeing and hearing, a

---

[6] Cf. our article, "Art et contemplation. Les Icônes du Christ", in *Die Kunst und die Technik,* vol. 4 of Herausforderung und Besinnung (Freiburg, 1979), 11–20.

[7] This is the opinion strongly defended by M. J. Le Guillou, *Das Mysterium des Vaters* (Einsiedeln, 1974).

[8] Abundant material can be found in M. Stirm, *Die Bilderfrage in der Reformation,* vol. 45 of Quellen und Forschungen zur Reformationsgeschichte (Gütersloh, 1977).

[9] Some references are contained in H. Rahner, "Theologie des Barocken", in his *Abendland. Reden und Aufsätze* (Freiburg, 1964), 236–50.

new sensitivity to the mystery. It is not by way of ingratiating herself or by trying to be "modern" at any cost that the Church can once again become a space for the arts, but rather by cultivating an awareness of the mystery of the One who is both God and man. A Church that in her liturgy, in her very life, draws vitality from the sense of awe in facing the mystery, will provide breathing space for any art whose primary purpose is not a breathless pursuit of outward success.[10] The fascination with icons in our own days is a telling sign. In this we witness something more than mere nostalgia. Here we see a yearning for that pure and innocent beauty reflected in the icons. We do not imply, of course, that a revival of the ancient iconographic art would be *the* way toward the renewal of sacred art,[11] even though it can be, and frequently already is, *one* of the ways. Many contemporary artists, endowed with a profound sense for the mystery of the ineffable light, do not presume to depict directly the likeness of the Savior, and yet their creations are often touching testimonies for the mystery of the One who is God and man. This awe, this reverence could well be a necessary purification after centuries of a Christian art that may have forgotten how to tremble when confronted with the grandeur of its subject. Then, too, at no time in history has man's countenance been disfigured and degraded to such an extent as during the present century. The artists' reserve testifies to this as well.

A testimony of a special and striking character is also the face that appeared on the scene at the threshold of this century and that presents to us, at a time when images abound and art is rare, in unexpected directness the disfigured, martyred, and yet ineffably sublime countenance of the Crucified. When, in 1898 A.D., Secondo Pia photographed for the first time the Shroud of Turin, hardly anybody in the scientific world believed any longer in the authenticity of this relic. Yet when Pia developed his photographic plates, he became the first man who witnessed in the

---

[10] Cf. the interview with Bishop Dr. E. Kapellari on the relation between Church and culture, in *Herder-Korrespondenz* issue I (1983): 13–18.

[11] So L. Ouspensky, *Théologie de l'Icône dans l'Eglise Orthodoxe* (Paris, 1980).

Illustration 12

Illustration number 12: Photographic negative of the Shroud of Turin (detail).

Only the photographic technique has revealed that the faint shadows, revered for centuries as the imprints of Jesus' dead body, are in reality a negative image of a crucified man, an image that is mysterious, extremely precise, and still inexplicable even today. On the photographic negative, therefore, there appear the fine (positive) features of this man, who shows all the signs of torture reported in the gospels as having been inflicted on Jesus. The last extensive scientific investigation (1978) yielded many surprising new insights. None of these disprove the Shroud's authenticity, yet how it might have originated still remains a mystery. The Shroud—"an image of Christ not made by human hands"?

(See page 243.)

CONCLUSION   243

photographic negative the appearance of this unique, mysterious
face (see illustration no. 12), thus demonstrating that the image on
the Shroud was a precise negative imprint of this face. The
progressively ever more exact tests performed since then (up to
the most comprehensive examination in 1978)[12] were not able to
solve the Shroud's mystery. They only ruled out conclusively that
we might be dealing with a forgery. Not one piece of evidence
excludes the possibility that the man of the Shroud is indeed Jesus;
many clues support it. Nobody up till now was able to offer an
explanation as to how the image came about. Could it be meant as
a sign for us, that precisely in our time we are offered this image,
the countenance of a man crucified and tortured to death, and yet
a countenance conveying even in death his incorruptible dignity?
That we behold this unexplained image of a dead man, an image
perhaps created by the fact that in this man life defeated death,
that here the Rising One wanted to bequeath to us a token of his
victory over death,[13] the imprint of his face, the Face of the
incarnate God?

[12] An initial report on these broad research projects of 1978 is given by K. E.
Stevenson and G. R. Habermas, *Verdict on the Shroud* (Ann Arbor, Mich., 1981); in
French: *La Vérité sur le Suaire de Turin* (Paris, 1981).

[13] Cf. chap. 11 in the report *Verdict* mentioned in the preceding footnote, note 12.

INDEX

(Page numbers in italics refer to illustrations.)